AN
AMERICAN
IN OZ

AN AMERICAN IN OZ

SARA JAMES

ALLEN&UNWIN
SYDNEY·MELBOURNE·AUCKLAND·LONDON

The extract on page 33, from *Edward the Emu* by Sheena Knowles and Rob Clement, is reproduced with permission of HarperCollins Australia.

First published in 2014
Copyright © Sara James 2014

Allen & Unwin
83 Alexander Street
Crows Nest NSW 2065
Australia
Phone: (61 2) 8425 0100
Email: info@allenandunwin.com
Web: www.allenandunwin.com

Cataloguing-in-Publication details are available
from the National Library of Australia
www.trove.nla.gov.au

ISBN 978 1 74331 530 9

Set in 12/16 pt Bembo by Post Pre-press Group, Australia
Printed and bound in Australia by Griffin Press

10 9 8 7 6 5 4 3 2 1

MIX
Paper from
responsible sources
FSC® C009448
www.fsc.org

The paper in this book is FSC® certified.
FSC® promotes environmentally responsible,
socially beneficial and economically viable
management of the world's forests.

To my parents, Anne and Rob
And my sisters, Elizabeth and Susan

Home is the compass-star in the nearest lowest corner;
The scale is the distance a voice travels from room to room,
The distance a word moves from page to heart;
It shows a memory, a match struck in the kitchen at midnight,
Memory, a green fern opening on the windowsill.

John Holmes, *Map of My Country*, Part XII

CONTENTS

PROLOGUE

It is human instinct to give things a name. If we label the people we love, the things we fear or hold dear, and the events that define us, we shape our own small story. Syllables and symbols are tools to till a patch of order, bordered by the unknown and unknowable.

Back when maps were littered with dragons, continents had ambiguous edges and uncharted interiors, and the mysterious land down under was labelled *Terra Australis Incognita,* we knew how much we did not know. In these modern times, we sometimes forget.

But the fact is, only in retrospect was a sweltering summer afternoon in Victoria, Australia, called Black Saturday. The same way a sunny Tuesday in America would become 9/11. In each event, there was only surprise. Incomprehension. Dread. Then, stumbling forward through fear, towards a flickering hope. It was later we recognised those days marked doorways from Before to After.

But if Black Saturday and 9/11 bring to mind twin days of terror, my life has included many others to balance the ledger. A few Red Letter days, but most were days without capitals. Small days, marked by wonder or delight. Days that made me laugh. Or weep. Or shake my head.

The human impulse to label propels us to catalogue and cross-reference. To record not simply what happened, and who was there, but how we felt. What it signified. Or perhaps that's my perspective because I'm a journalist, and jotting things down is both instinct and profession. Like a prospector with a sieve, a reporter pans a river of information for the glint of a vivid detail, the sparkle of a captivating character, the mother lode of a 24-carat, spellbinding yarn. Writing stories is a way to brush aside sand and sediment, sift for nuggets of meaning. That's true when reporting the news and when exploring the *terra incognita* of a life.

I once lived in a wonderland called New York. Then I moved to an enchanted land Down Under, to become an American, in Oz.

Neither world is perfect. They are opposites, in many ways. But each is unique. Unforgettable. Extreme. That is why I love them both.

Although the day of 7 February 2009 would prove an exception.

1

THE FIRE KITE

The summer sky should have been blue. Or aqua, perhaps. Even grey would be acceptable, though impossible, because it would suggest rain. There had been none. But under no circumstances should the afternoon sky be a ruddy orange-brown, with gashes of purple, like an angry bruise.

The wind was even more ominous than the sky. Stepping outside felt like opening the lid of a kiln. Eyes squinted against the exfoliating blast, Andrew and I surveyed the paddocks behind his parents' farmhouse in Muckleford, Victoria. Sheep clustered, helpless. Everything that could flee had fled. Then I saw a lone dark bird high in the sky. I wondered if it was a kite. The black kite is a common bird of prey, but it has a curious distinction. Attraction to fire. The raptor's penchant for swooping down to capture lizards and other creatures escaping the flames of a bushfire had earned it the nickname The Fire Kite, or Firehawk. I'd read that indigenous Australians believed the bird could pick up a burning twig, then drop it again, to spread a blaze and continue hunting. The bird soared out of view.

My husband was dressed in white. Fine bits of red dust clung to his shirt. He rocked back and forth, left foot, right, shaking his head in vexation. I thought of a new word I'd

3

learned. This must be what Aussies meant when they called someone 'toey'.

'I can't believe they cancelled the cricket.'

'But it's 46 degrees!' I did the conversion in my head. 'That's 115 degrees Fahrenheit!'

'That's just summer.'

Not in New York, it wasn't.

'They're saying it's the worst day ever.'

Andrew snorted. 'That's what they always say.'

I turned towards the triple-gabled brick home behind us, the windows on the upstairs veranda shuttered against the heat. 'How can you breathe? I'm going inside to check on the girls.'

But Andrew didn't move. Suddenly, he brightened. 'Tell you what. You stay here with Nana and Pa, and I'll drive home. I'll set up for tonight.'

A wave of anxiety washed over me. 'But we . . .'

He waved a hand. 'Look, I know you're worried about how close our house is to the Wombat, but I'm not. Besides, I can move quickly, if there's any danger.'

I shook my head, unconvinced, but now that Andrew had a plan, he displayed the insistence of a front-end loader and scooped all objections out of his path.

'I'm telling you, these warnings—just a beat-up. Nine times out of ten, it's a total bust. You'll see. In a few hours, you and the girls will just drive home, and I'll have everything ready. Think of it this way. I'll do all the work!'

With a squeal of tyres and a wave, he was gone.

News organisations had predicted this would be a day of extreme fire danger, a potentially catastrophic day. Cameron Stewart, star reporter for *The Australian* and an old friend we'd invited to the house-warming, had called to make sure I understood how hot and dire the prediction was. But there had been many Total Fire Ban days that summer and nothing much had happened. I'd willingly adopted Andrew's 'She'll be right, mate' attitude. We lived next to the Wombat State Forest, so we would not Stay and Defend; but we would Depart and Return, in time to host an evening party.

Suddenly, that choice seemed foolish. As did Andrew's decision to return early, in the midst of the danger, to our house in the hills surrounded by thousands of hectares of eucalypts. The feel of the day was very different from reading the statistics, hearing the warnings. I was alarmed we had retreated, not to Melbourne, but further into the bushfire zone. I reminded myself I was an American, from the East Coast. I had no experience with bushfires, and was probably over-reacting.

Inside, it was surprisingly cool. The house had been built in the nineteenth century, with walls a double thickness of brick. It had stood for more than 160 years, impervious.

'Hi, Mum!' Sophie looked up from the chair in the lounge, where she was curled up with a Nancy Drew mystery.

'Hi, love. Which one are you reading?'

'*The Mystery of the 99 Steps.*'

I turned to Jacqui who was seated at the kitchen table, demolishing a piece of Nana's shortbread. I brushed the crumbs from her cheek as she dug a pinky into the jam thumbprint in the centre of the biscuit. I tried to relax.

Until that phone call.

Until that bulletin.

'*We interrupt this program to bring you a special bulletin from ABC Radio. The CFA has issued a watch and act bulletin for the following communities . . .*'

'Mount Disappointment!' Nana gasped. 'That's Annie!'

'*If you have not left, the CFA advises it is now too late,*' the announcer intoned. '*Prepare to enact your fire plan.*'

Sophie looked up from her book, with a child's barometer for a sudden change in pressure. 'Will Aunty Annie be okay?'

No one spoke. The only sound was the howling wind.

And that was when it hit me. I had been naïve. Woefully

ignorant of Australia, especially the countryside. My vision of life here had included cute kangaroos, cuddly koalas and a quirky, loveable cast plucked from movies like *Muriel's Wedding*, *Strictly Ballroom* or *The Castle*. I had imagined delving into Australian culture, learning about everything from Donald Bradman to the Dreamtime stories of the indigenous Australians.

The trade-off for leaving the bright lights of the big city would be the charm and relaxation of a bucolic life. Living in an Antipodean version of a Miss Marple village, nestled in a prosperous, amiable country where everyone spoke with an appealing accent. This was a kinder, gentler place. No crowds. No terrorism. No worries.

I had pictured a postcard, not a country.

I had been an idiot.

Australia wasn't a cliché. The place was complicated. Brawny, raw and unpredictable. And dangerous. Sometimes very dangerous.

But it was too late for reflections. I was stuck in the middle of country Victoria, 130 kilometres northwest of Melbourne, with our two little girls and my in-laws. The radio broadcast told us hurricane-force winds were sending fires hop-scotching across the countryside. And Andrew's aunt was among those trapped in the middle of an inferno. As for my husband, I felt sure he was hell-bent on a rescue mission. He had dropped off the grid.

Life in Australia had turned out nothing like I expected—not from the very first.

2

JOE BLAKE

There are some fundamental problems with reporting from a closet.

I covered the microphone with one hand to muffle the rustling noise as I pushed aside a hanger which had fallen on my head. Then I cleared my throat and resumed recording: 'Sorry, New York, let's take that one more time. This is Track Seventeen, Take Two, coming to you in three, two . . .'

Blast.

I fumbled to hit stop on the digital audio tape (DAT) recorder balanced on my knee, temporarily blinded by a sheet of sweat. On a blazing January afternoon, hunkered in a de facto yurt roughly the temperature of a sauna, I was a human Niagara Falls.

I contemplated grabbing a beach towel to dry my face, but knew that if I stood up, the jury-rigged recording studio—fashioned from a doona suspended by skirt hangers—would collapse. How was I going to re-create the pitch-perfect sounds of NBC Studio's recording booth at Rockefeller Plaza in New York City at my home on a dirt road next to the Wombat State Forest in country Victoria?

I'd been in a number of tricky spots during my reporting career, including several far more perilous, but for sheer discomfort, this had to make the top five: more claustrophobic than that tent in Southern Sudan, if slightly cleaner than the bombed out hotel in Mogadishu. I felt a sudden surge of solidarity for the burqa-clad Afghan women I'd met while reporting on the Taliban. They weren't just oppressed, they were roasting alive.

These days I often had frequent flashbacks to my old life as a globe-trotting network correspondent based in New York, a launch and landing pad for fifteen years as my career had rocketed along. When not on the road, I had been a regular substitute on NBC's *Today Show* news desk. That fortunate life had included chatting in the green room with stars like Oprah Winfrey, Pierce Brosnan, Renee Zellweger and Sandra Bullock, or conducting interviews with the likes of Hillary Clinton, Mitt Romney and Al Gore. Nights sparkled with black-tie dinners and red-carpet events where Bono, Nicole Kidman, Penelope Cruz, Bill Clinton, Jack Welch and Rupert Murdoch would be among those in attendance.

But that had been life before Oz.

Here on a new continent was a new life, full of uncertainty, but also opportunity. Instead of living in an apartment on the eighteenth floor of a skyscraper, with a 'peekaboo' view of Central Park, our ranch house on a ridge overlooked 10,000 hectares of pristine national forest in the Macedon Ranges, northwest of Melbourne. It was a beautiful setting, if so foreign I sometimes felt like I'd travelled to the other side of a rainbow, only to watch what had appeared clear and distinct dissolve into mist. It was impossible to guess the shape, fold or direction of life to come. Thankfully, I had a soft spot for adventure.

But none of this reminiscing was doing anything to finish the job at hand. I was halfway through recording the narration for my final reporting assignment for *Dateline NBC*, an American network television magazine show similar to Australia's *60 Minutes*. I'd recently travelled to Monaco to update a documentary about billionaire banker Edmond Safra, who had died in a mysterious fire at his luxury apartment in Monte Carlo in 1999. His private nurse Ted Maher, a former American Green Beret, had been convicted of setting the blaze in what the prosecution portrayed as a botched scheme to play the hero. What had prompted the update was that in October 2007, just a few months before we moved to Australia, Maher had been released from prison. NBC urgently needed my new audio tracks—the recorded narration of the revised script.

This was typically a simple assignment. Step into the Studio Bank elevator at 30 Rockefeller Plaza, press '5' and walk to the audio booth. But I was approximately 16,659 kilometres from the building affectionately known as 30 Rock. And while I had portable recording equipment, I could not find a soundproof room in our virtually empty new house. We had lived here for exactly two weeks, had pulled up old carpets, knocked down a fireplace, demolished with gusto. Not only was there no recording booth, there was no furniture. We lived in a large, zigzagging echo chamber.

The only possible option had been the closet in my bedroom. It was the quietest room in the house. But not quiet enough.

Audio engineers are an exacting breed. Cameramen—and most are still men—not only get kudos for stunning video, but also enjoy the fringe benefit that a camera is a well-known magnet for gorgeous women. But when it comes to sound, only the cognoscenti are truly appreciative. Lamentably, most of us only notice mistakes: sibilant 's's', the whine of a jet engine, a blast from a leaf-blower, even the subtle background hum of a refrigerator. Rare is the compliment for a job well done. Audio engineers are paid to be picky. And American network types are as picky as they come.

My first attempts to record the script—using every pillow in the house for soundproofing—were a flop.

'Too boomy! Wahddya do, record in a closet or something?' It seemed a question best left unanswered.

'Sorry, we just moved.'

An impatient snort. Reporters recorded in war zones. I was only in Australia.

'No dice, Sara. It sounds hollow. And you're popping your "p's". Back off the mike. We need these tracks now, okay?'

Over my years as a reporter, I'd learned time and again that when you had absolutely no idea how you were going to accomplish something—whether it was to get into a country illegally, bypass an inconvenient police barricade, woo a recalcitrant celebrity or shepherd gear worth hundreds of thousands of dollars through a third-world airport without being bankrupted by bribes—the trick was to display confidence. Never, ever panic.

'Look,' I responded, even allowing my voice to betray some annoyance, 'this is a quick fix. Grab a latte from Starbucks, and I'll have the tracks to you in twenty.'

I hung up. Okay, now I could panic.

Desperation aided memory. After a frantic rummage through boxes, I hauled out a merino blanket and a doona, and set to work. First I clipped the doona to the hangers to fashion my own circus big top. Then I crawled underneath with the blanket, and created a human tepee, my head serving as the tent pole. Suffocation was a problem, but not the only one. I was juggling a microphone, DAT recorder, script and torch, because the blanket inconveniently extinguished natural light, along with ambient sound. I kept dropping things. Then there was the fact that to prevent the blanket from grazing the super-sensitive mike, my elbows were extended in an unflattering approximation of the Chicken Dance.

If they could see me now, those old pals of mine . . .

Well, Sweet Charity, they could not. I took a deep breath, wished I wasn't entombed quite so near my old running shoes, and ducked back under the blanket.

'Three, two, one. Billionaire banker Edmond Safra remained holed up in the bunker of his luxury apartment. But what had been designed as a safehouse—was about to become a death trap. What Edmond Safra didn't kn—'

WHAM. WHAM. WHAM.

From somewhere outside the closet came a heavy, thudding sound, which melded into the Safra story in an eerie way—a terrified elderly man, cowering in a small room, fearing those outside were trying to kill him, not save him.

I paused briefly, but wasn't going to quit unless interrupted by nuclear war, raging fire or killer bees.

'Sorry, New York. This will be Safra Track Seventeen, Take Four. Coming to you in three, two, one: Billionaire banker Edmond Safra remained . . .'

WHAM! WHAM!

There it was again! It sounded like a shovel.

But why would someone—why would Andrew!—be using a shovel? When he was supposed to be going out for a motorcycle ride?!

I dropped the mike and leapt to my feet, trying not to trip as I disentangled from the blanket. Dashing outside I saw my husband, dressed like a Power Ranger, standing halfway between the house and his shed, a shovel poised like a cricket bat.

'G'day,' he offered cautiously. 'Finish your script?'

Such a casual, pointless bluff. It could only mean one thing.

'Andrew, what's going on?'

'Keep your shirt on. Just a Joe Blake.'

Usually, I liked Australian rhyming slang. Andrew and I had used it as our private code in New York. He'd nudge me to have a 'Captain Cook', and I would take a look. If he said he was on his Pat Malone, I could count on him being alone. Most Americans had no idea that 'What's the John Dory?' meant 'What's the story?' and would have been appalled that the expression for making an abrupt departure rhymed with the name of an Australian prime minister who had disappeared, and was presumed to have drowned. But just because I understood that Joe Blake meant snake didn't mean I was happy about it.

'I thought you said they don't come close to the house!'

Andrew spoke in a calm tone I usually associated with yoga instructors. 'It's not close to the house. It's in the shed.'

'As in, *near the girls' bikes, in that shed? And what kind of snake?*'

My husband shot me a look which indicated he fully recognised his peril, trapped between a deadly reptile on one side and a sweaty, deadline-stricken, dangerously unhinged American wife on the other.

'Black.'

Phylum Chordata, class Reptilia, order Squamata, suborder Serpentes, the Red-bellied Black (*Pseudechis porphyriacus*) is a species of elapid snake. Its venom causes a blood-clotting disorder, muscle and nerve damage. Among the less deadly of Australian snakes, which possess venom of the 'Supersize Me' variety, its bite is definitely poisonous enough to kill a child. I know this because I have children. And because I am phobic about snakes.

Of course, snakes are also protected species in Australia, and I usually adopt a 'live and let live' philosophy. But there are rules. Deadly snakes are not allowed in our house, or in our garden. And certainly not in the shed near the girls' bicycles. This was a big enough hazard for six-year-old Sophie. She had grown up in Manhattan, where most reptiles resided in zoos. But the thought of three-year-old Jacqui opening the shed door was nothing short of terrifying. Just a few days before, she'd picked up a black spider and carried it to me in her chubby hand. Luckily, it hadn't been one of the redbacks we'd discovered in a dusty corner. Thank goodness the girls were in town with Andrew's parents, Nana and Pa, who had taken them out for ice-cream.

I continued my interrogation. 'You used the present tense. Is the snake still alive?'

'Well, I nicked him, but unfortunately he's gone and hidden behind that corner pillar. See?' He gestured.

On a dial ranging from 'Cautious' to 'Cowardly', snakes prompt me to redline on the latter. It took a while before I was close enough to admire Joe Blake's clever hiding spot in the corrugated-iron shed. It had slid into a floor-to-ceiling crack between one of the shed's four metal uprights and the exterior wall. It had a good view of Andrew's cherished Guardsman blue, '64½ Mustang convertible, the bikes and us.

'It looks like it might stay there awhile,' my husband said. Andrew's flushed face indicated that wearing full motorcycle gear on a 40-degree day made huddling under a wool blanket seem positively chilly by comparison.

'Do you want a chair or something? Maybe a cold drink?'

'Thanks.'

Which was how I wound up serving afternoon tea, on a polished ebony tray decorated with blue irises, to my husband as he kept vigil by a snake.

It seemed there was a reason they called this place Oz.

Revived by the fortifying combination of tea, Tim Tams and adrenalin, I powered through the rest of the narration. Then I used my computer to upload the audio tracks, and dialled the edit suite in New York. After a sound check, the audio grudgingly replied, 'Thanks, Sara. It'll do.'

At least it was done. At the moment, figuring out how to report from Australia was last on the list of my priorities.

I headed back outside, to find Andrew standing next to a two-metre, headless snake.

'He stuck it out.'

Glossy in life, the snake's scales had already lost their lustre. It had turned a greyish-black. Without its sinuous muscularity, the snake seemed even uglier and more repellent in death, its red belly a dingy pink pinstripe.

'I actually feel bad,' Andrew said. 'They aren't aggressive. He was trying to get away.'

I nodded, but any tears I might have shed would have been of the crocodile variety. 'Why was it in the shed? Aren't they supposed to be shy?'

'Probably looking for water. With the drought, snakes have moved in closer.'

Just then, a grey Falcon sedan pulled into our driveway, enveloped in a cloud of dust. As I unbuckled Jacqui from her car seat, Andrew's parents headed over for a look, Sophie leading the charge.

'Wow! That's amazing! A real snake! Dad, that is awesome!'

Sophie still sounded like a New Yorker, but the speed with which she was morphing from city mouse to country mouse, from Eloise of the Plaza into Sybylla Melvyn of *My Brilliant Career* was a little unnerving. Less than 48 hours after our arrival, she'd disappeared into the henhouse to clip the wings of Nana and Pa's chooks, and she was very keen to test drive Pa's four-wheeler. I suppose I shouldn't have been surprised. Andrew's father, Bert Butcher, was a hay merchant, while his mother Bev kept the farm humming. Andrew and his brother and sisters were the latest in a long line of Butchers to be raised in rural Victoria. The country was in Sophie's DNA.

Sophie shot me a quizzical look.

'Mum, why don't you come any closer? It can't bite. Besides, you did that snake story with the Crocodile Hunter!'

'That was different.'

'Why?'

'I didn't live in Australia back then. Besides, those snakes weren't at my house.'

Back in 1997, *Dateline NBC* had sent me to profile a budding wildlife star by the name of Steve Irwin. Thanks to his hit show on the Discovery Channel, Steve was then far more famous in the US than Australia. We chased wily crocodiles in Far North Queensland, and tracked the notorious Fierce Snake (Inland Taipan, *Oxyuranus microlepidotus*, et cetera, et cetera). We had selected the Taipan because its venom was roughly as powerful as Kryptonite. But it turned out that many Australian creatures were so extravagantly lethal that hyperbole was unnecessary, if tempting. Much of the country's wildlife seemed to be vying for top honours in the Deadliest in the World Competition.

But the trip with Steve and his outgoing American wife Terri had also been the ultimate camping trip—a chance to see the rare beauty of Outback Oz, with a dynamic pair who knew it well.

On the first day of the shoot, at the family's Australia Zoo, not far from Brisbane, we accompanied Steve on a 'house call'. A fearful gardener living nearby had discovered a brown snake lurking under the grevilleas. Rather than try her luck with a hoe, she begged Steve to come catch the deadly snake.

'Crikey, that's more dangerous for you than the snake!' he told us. 'It's how most people get bitten. Better to call in an expert.'

But I didn't know any snake catchers in Victoria. And hard as it was to believe, the daring and irrepressible Steve Irwin had died from a stingray injury just the year before. I wondered how Terri and the children were faring. She and Steve had been a devoted couple, and their thrilling, unconventional life had been one of a number of lures to these southern shores.

It was late afternoon, and I looked up to see a flock of sulphur-crested cockatoos overhead. From the black and white of a Gotham winter, we'd been flung into the burnt orange and grey-green of summer in Oz. We'd arrived courtesy of a long-haul 747 rather than a twister, but sometimes I felt as bewildered as Dorothy. No comforting taxi horns or sirens to lull me to sleep. No cops on their megaphones, shouting at drivers stuck in the middle of an intersection, 'Hey you! Yeah, YOU! Don't block the box!' Instead, only silence. It could be terrifying.

But it was undeniably beautiful. I looked out across our front yard, at rolling hills, the lush forest. The sun was setting and making a proper show of it. Rose gold and copper, it was a molten display. After fifteen years spent living and working in the canyons of Manhattan, it was startling to see how vast a sky could be. I was glad that in moving halfway around the world, we had opted for the full Australian experience.

There was a sudden screech, as the flock of cockatoos dove in formation to alight on our front lawn.

'Look, Sophie and Jacqui,' I said, pleased by the diversion. 'Check out how much they like our bird feeder.'

A half dozen cockies had shoved their way onto a large bird-bath we had filled with seeds, bullying aside crimson rosellas, grass parrots and magpies.

Andrew's mother looked concerned. 'Are you sure you want to feed them, Sara?' Nana asked. 'Cockies are mongrel things.'

To me, the sulphur-crested cockatoos were the feathered equivalent of turban-wearing divas from the 1920s. Drop-dead gorgeous. They shared another feature with many silent movie stars of old—they might have ravishing looks, but their voices were shocking.

'But they have so much personality!'

The cockies eyed us insolently as they ate. If they had been smoking cigarettes in long ebony holders, they would have blown the smoke in my face.

'Maybe put the feeder further from the house,' Nana continued. 'They can be destructive.'

I nodded, but what was the point of feeding our parrots if you couldn't watch them? We were treated to a colourful spectacle every day, a rainbow spangle of plumage. Moving the feeder wasn't on my 'To Do' list, but plenty of other things were.

Andrew had just taken a new job as International Media Advisor for Telstra, which would involve a great deal of travel. My first job would be to keep the home fires burning. After many years of working full time for NBC, this was a new and uncertain role and it was difficult to know quite where to start. The house was a wreck. Our life was in boxes. Sophie started school in a week, and soon Jacqui would have kinder. There were doctors to call, appointments to book, all manner of logistics to sort out. I barely knew where the grocery store was. Our life had more than its share of complications.

I loved my career, but I was a mum, and I had made a decision. Full-time journalism would need to wait. I had left behind the red lipstick, the red carpet, the red tally light on the camera. I hoped it might prove true that I'd simply pushed the 'pause' button on reporting, and could press 'resume' when the time was right. But I knew there were no guarantees. I suppressed the tremor of anxiety caused by leaving my career the same way I dealt with the geographical distance from family and friends in America. I tried not to think about it.

Instead, I would focus on getting our family settled, and exploring a fascinating new land. I would be a journalist with a small 'j'—take time to investigate and contemplate the world around me. Examine the road less travelled. Which just happened to be one that led to our front door.

I had officially moved from the fast track, to a dirt track. And it was all because of an unlikely intersection on a wintry evening, in 1994.

3

MOUNTAIN LAUREL

If I had stayed home that February night and read a book as I'd intended, I never would have moved to Australia. Never would have met my Australian husband, never had our two daughters. It still stuns me, how a chance encounter can alter the trajectory of a life.

Instead of curling up near the fire in my apartment, I had reluctantly agreed to accompany a girlfriend to a gathering of journalists in mid-town Manhattan, just a couple of blocks from the NBC Studios. It was an enormous event, thousands of people jostling in a cavernous ballroom. In the midst of all that bustle and babble, I collided with a lanky, dark-haired reporter from the Melbourne *Herald Sun*. I couldn't quite catch Andrew's surname for the accent, but instantly warmed to his smile and self-deprecating humour. He was the kind of reporter who asked questions, rather than recounting all he had seen and done.

I can picture him later that night, on the corner of 53rd and 6th Avenue, laughing that his hands were freezing because his Australian gloves were too thin, both of us stamping our feet from the cold. Noticing he had long eyelashes. We swapped business cards, there was a mention of lunch. But I never expected to hear from him. I headed out of town on assignment the next day.

Yet, despite the fact that I was often on the road, despite the fact that Andrew soon moved to Tokyo to be the News Limited reporter there, despite the challenges, or perhaps in part because of them, we found time to be together, in the moments in between.

We were both cagey about the future. There was the distance. I was older. There were our families—we each came from a close-knit tribe. Someone would need to move.

Andrew's career was going well, and he was smitten by Japan. I had fallen for New York. After years in local news, I revelled in the breadth and depth of network news. I filled in on the *Today Show*—sometimes for co-host Katie Couric, often for newsreader Ann Curry. I anchored other network broadcasts, too.

But the job I loved most was that of correspondent. The title was a nod to the old days, when an overseas reporter corresponded from an international dateline. From Sarajevo to Somalia, Littleton to London, Port-au-Prince to Peshawar, Harbin to Honolulu, even down to the wreck of the *Titanic*, NBC sent me here, there, everywhere. I covered the headlines: 9/11, the Taliban, the Stolen Generation, the Bosnian war crimes tribunal, the Oklahoma City bombing, slavery in Sudan.

I witnessed the horrific, but also the heroic. I'm sure the uncut rush of raw experience was part of what hooked me, but I also felt a compulsion to claw fact and meaning from uncertainty and ambiguity. I never tired of the towering spectacle of a roadshow that was the messy, unfolding present.

But in the background, in spite of everything, love, a tenacious vine, had taken hold. Ultimately, the impossibility of being together was only exceeded by the impossibility of living apart.

Andrew moved to New York in 1998. We married later that year. He took a job as spokesman for media mogul Rupert Murdoch, which added more glittering opportunities to our New York life. There were A-list movie premieres, strolling down the red carpet past paparazzi out in force to capture the latest pictures of Angelina and Brad. There were fancy charity balls and swellegant dinners with Wall Street moguls and their bejewelled wives. Tickets to Broadway shows, or to watch the Yankees play. It was the starkest of contrasts to life on the road. It was giddy, frothy and superficial. It was a great deal of fun.

But the most captivating opportunity came in March 2001. We had a daughter, Sophie, and I discovered that the allure of the road had met a fearsome competitor in our bewitching child. I made less frequent trips, found opportunities to work from home. NBC was a ground-breaking employer for working women. I had freedom, flexibility, a fulfilling career. In 2004, we had a second daughter, Jacqueline, who proved to be special in her own right. The weathervane was turning, and pointing south.

I knocked on the office door of the Executive Producer of NBC's *Dateline NBC*. EPs are busy people, so I resolved to be Twitter-quick.

'I'm touching base to let you know I am moving.'

David Corvo nodded. 'Off to the suburbs. Greenwich? Scarsdale? Jersey?'

I cleared my throat. 'Actually, we're moving to Australia.'

My boss sat forward. 'Doesn't Andrew have that big job with Murdoch? Why does he want to leave New York?'

It was a reasonable question.

'I think it's an Aussie thing. It's like they come with a timer, and it suddenly went ding,' I said lightly. There was more to our move, but there was no need to go into great detail.

Corvo chuckled. 'Well, congratulations. I was there for the Sydney Olympics. Spent time on a yacht in that harbour. Beautiful part of the world. We'll miss you. But it's a great life for the family, I'm sure.'

We went on to discuss a few potential stories Down Under, but as I'd expected, there was no obvious full-time role for a *Dateline NBC* correspondent in Australia. This was in part because *Dateline* had begun to focus almost exclusively on the true-crime genre. There weren't likely to be many sensational murders in Australia perpetrated by ne'er-do-well Yanks. I also talked to colleagues at the *Today Show*, *Nightly News* and on the executive floor. They expressed similar caution. The *NBC* hub for international coverage was London, which deployed network crews around the world, as events dictated. I should keep in touch, by all means. But Australia wasn't exactly a hotspot.

In preparing for our move, I'd read any number of books, including humorist Bill Bryson's *Down Under*. Bryson, whose appreciation of the country was abundantly clear, scratched his head at the scanty American news coverage of Australia. His examination of the *New York Times* index for 1997 indicated Australia had made the papers only twenty times. As he pointed out, that compared to 120 articles on Peru, 150 on Albania, more than 300 stories on each of the Koreas and 500 reports on matters pertaining to Israel.

What did he surmise was the reason for such woeful under-reporting on all things Australian? 'Above all, Australia doesn't misbehave. It is stable and peaceful and good. It doesn't have coups, recklessly overfish, arm disagreeable despots, grow coca in provocative quantities, or throw its weight around in a brash and unseemly manner.'

Translation: Australia was a safe and delightful place to live. This made it a difficult posting for a foreign correspondent. Australia was simply too nice.

By 2007, Bryson's book was already a decade old, but the situation hadn't changed much. If anything, Australia had only become an even better place to live. The 'lucky country' was rolling in revenue from a mining boom, as the rest of the world hit the skids. What Australians referred to somewhat trendily as 'the GFC' or Global Financial Crisis, Americans and Europeans gloomily recognised as a recession. What with financial instability at home, and warfare and chaos in various corners of the globe, events in Australia rarely made news in the US. When they did, the item was apt to concern the environment, climate change or the country's wildlife.

During that self-guided NBC tour, there were conversations about whether I'd be interested in a full-time foreign correspondent role, based in Australia, covering the Pacific Rim and beyond. But unlike my role at the magazine show, which although busy was orderly and scheduled, life as a foreign correspondent was far less predictable. I knew what it was like to have the phone ring at three in the morning, to be sent wherever, and to stay there for as long as required. I had lived that life, even loved it. But it was a poor fit for current circumstances.

Our children were six and three. The girls and I would be living in a new country. Andrew would travel for his work. If I maintained my high-powered career, I felt sure it would put too great a strain on our family. Every mother I knew experienced similar challenges, struggled to navigate competing demands: whether to work, if she was lucky enough that it could be considered a choice; how much to work, and in how demanding a role; when to step in, and step up, whether to step back. It was a complicated dance, involving an intricate series of moves, and the dance kept evolving. But it was ultimately a choice for each pair of partners. And our family had more than its share of demands. Leaving a profitable career I enjoyed, in addition to saying goodbye to close friends and family, was disconcerting. But Andrew had moved for me, and everything had worked out. And I was willing to move for him.

Some friends and colleagues were incredulous. 'Are you crazy? Why?! What will you do? Where will you live? What about their doctors? *What are you thinking?*'

The astonishment that greeted our decision accompanied paradoxically enthusiastic—if hazy—praise for Australia. It was exotic. The accent was fetching, and the continent exuded a sunny, healthy energy. *Crocodile Dundee* had become an American classic; even those who had never seen it knew key lines. It somehow served to give our choice context and validity. Never mind that Andrew didn't live in the Outback and didn't carry a gigantic knife. He was from some place in the middle of nowhere called Muckleford, he had been known to ride a motorcycle while wearing a leather jacket, and how about that time he had shot a feral pig at Rupert Murdoch's California estate? Combined with his g'day mate accent and the fact that he wore R.M. Williams boots with a business suit, Andrew was unmistakably Australian, and that had a certain cachet.

It was simply that Australia was very, very far away. You couldn't fly there in a few hours, like London or Paris. It was perfectly fine to be from Australia—actually, it was pretty cool— and acceptable to return if you were an Australian, like Andrew. But for an American in television news, New York was the pinnacle. Moving to Oz was like electing to leap into a black hole, or the Bermuda Triangle. I would disappear.

I bridled. Hadn't anyone heard of Qantas?

I also detected more than a whiff of what I'd come to consider New Yorkeritis. New York is a hurly-burly conglomeration of five proud and distinctive boroughs, or neighbourhoods, each with its own storied history and claim to fame. But for certain New Yorkers, adoration of their hometown goes so far as to exclude anyone who lives outside Manhattan. As for the indistinct land mass beyond the George Washington Bridge—well, that issue had already been addressed by Saul Steinberg's classic *New Yorker* cartoon, *View of the World from 9th Avenue*. As any denizen of the city knew, the amusing pseudo-map depicted a detailed few blocks of the city next to the Hudson River, with the rest of the US represented as a tiny boulder-strewn, barely labelled square between New Jersey and the Pacific Ocean, and a few casually drawn lumps representing the world beyond.

For this breed of New Yorker, the tiny apartment and mammoth expense of living in Manhattan were worth every junk bond you paid for them. The real question was whether to live above or below 14th Street. To choose the Upper East Side, or the Upper West; to opt for a loft in TriBeCa or SoHo; or to select digs in The Village, Chelsea or Harlem. Temporary insanity or raising children were the only possible explanations for doing the unthinkable—becoming a B&T—some poor clod who had to cross a bridge or go through a tunnel to get to Manhattan. There were plenty of Manhattanites who reckoned life as a B&T was a fate worse than death.

As with any edict, there were inconsistencies. Brooklyn got a bye on B&T shame. Sure, it was one of the outer boroughs, but it had once been an independent city—even had a baseball team!—and many trendy artists and families were living there now. And The Hamptons were filed under the summer escape clause.

California received a different kind of exemption. New Yorkers liked to visit the West Coast and, truth be told, often envied their tanned, toned and famous LA brethren. But the NY/LA axis could be as dismissive of 'flyover people'—those who lived between the two coasts—as of B&Ts.

I had no such illusions. I was originally from Virginia, with a mum from Connecticut and a dad from Alabama. I passionately defended the south in the north, and vice versa. But there were plenty of New Yorkers—born, bred or transplanted—for whom our move to Oz was a genuine mystery, a puzzler to end all puzzlers. It was unthinkable to move ten miles from the city, much less 10,000.

'This is what comes of falling for the Man from Snowy River,' one wit sighed.

I tried to ignore the naysayers, and one ingredient leavening any trepidation or uncertainty was my enthusiasm at the prospect of a family adventure. I had carried on a flirtation with Australia for as long as I'd known Andrew. The spare, often fragile beauty of the place beguiled me, and I adored Andrew's family and friends. Although I had travelled widely, I had never lived overseas. I was keen to discover my own Australia, not the one on loan from my husband, nor the one divined from newspaper and magazine articles, books or movies. I wanted to find my own friends, discover my own cherished places and form opinions that were not revisions of borrowed judgments and assessments.

The only wrinkle was the F word. Forever. I was interested in a committed relationship with Australia but was American, born and bred. If we moved to Oz, I might one day want to come home. I had witnessed first-hand what could happen. In the same way that possession is nine-tenths of the law, living in a country engenders inertia and inevitability. Andrew had already lived in the States for a decade, and it was easy to see how ten years could stretch to twenty. There would never be a perfect time for us to make such a big move, but this seemed a perfectly good time. The girls were young, but not infants. Andrew had significant career opportunities in his home country. Everyone raved about Australia and its wonderful lifestyle. And it was Andrew's turn.

Andrew suggested I take a reconnaissance trip to Australia to investigate potential schools and neighbourhoods. My good friend Lisa, a former roommate from our days in local news in Richmond, Virginia, leapt at this chance for a girls' trip. Among her many talents, Lisa is canny at real estate and renovating houses.

From the quality of the Qantas service to the smoothness of Bundaberg rum and Penfolds wine, Lisa was impressed. In Sydney, we snapped photos at the Opera House, shucked local oysters, shopped at The Rocks and checked out the Bondi to Bronte cliff walk. In Melbourne, we wandered through the Botanic Gardens and Victoria Market, strolled by the Yarra and Federation Square, checked out the Eureka Tower and Flinders Lane. Then we collapsed at the gingerbread Victorian home in Brunswick that belonged to my sister-in-law, Christine.

But Chris woke us in the morning with chilling news. There had been a mass shooting at Virginia Tech University, in Blacksburg. Thirty-three people were dead, including the gunman, and twenty-three had been injured. While we breathed sighs of relief to learn no one we knew had been hurt, in the hours and days that followed, our accents acted as a lightning rod, especially since we had close ties to Virginia. We were asked repeatedly about the lack of gun control in the US, and reminded of the strict laws enacted in Australia after the massacre at Port Arthur in Tasmania. Why didn't America do the same?

I had covered the school shooting at Columbine High School, and the horrific carnage, and age of the victims, had affected me deeply. I was appalled by the prevalence of guns at home, and the easy access to assault weapons, and was in favour of stricter gun regulation myself. I said so. Nevertheless, it was unsettling to have our country considered 'extremist' by some of those we encountered. And it suddenly struck me that as an American in Oz, I would be called upon to answer not simply for myself, but to be an unofficial representative of my country—just as in New York, Andrew had often served as our unofficial representative of Australia. It was part and parcel of living overseas, even if I was only a jury of one. It was becoming apparent that this move would teach me about myself, and about America, as well as offering a learning curve on Australia.

For the first several days of our Melbourne visit, I looked into schools, and left Lisa to sightsee. Then it was time to scour neighbourhoods, in search of the perfect home. We were both bullish.

'Melbourne is a beautiful city,' Lisa reflected, as we sat sipping coffee at Brunetti's to fortify ourselves for the mission. 'With four million people here, there are bound to be lots of options. And if it's like back home right now, you'll probably find a bargain.'

By the afternoon, bleary-eyed and confused, we were overwhelmed, shaking our heads both at the prices, and at the vastness that was Melbourne. Manhattan was like a trim yacht. Unable to spread, it vaulted skyward, with virtually every square metre utilised. The imperatives of geography and population created a walker's paradise, one with plentiful mass transportation for days of inclement weather.

Melbourne seemed the opposite: sprawling and idiosyncratic, low-rise but high density. Each neighbourhood had its own character and charm, but for a pair of novices, it was hard to appreciate the distinctions, difficult to get a feel for each place as we darted here and there. A realtor cheerfully drove us through Surrey Hills, which seemed flat; bustling Richmond, which bore no resemblance to the city in which I'd worked and grown up; and Glen Something or other, without a glen in sight. The more we studied the high streets and highways, the tramlines and trains, the more confused we both became.

'I'm not sure I can tell Malvern from Hawthorn, Toorak from Timbuktu. Where does Kew begin, and does it actually end?' I grumbled. 'Can you tell the difference between St Kilda and West St Kilda? Does it actually matter? And what's an Elsternwick?'

'It's probably right next door to the Witches of Eastwick.'

'Have you had a look at the *Melway*?' I pointed at the thick book of maps. 'This city goes on forever. How am I supposed to choose?'

'I liked Albert Park,' Lisa offered, 'where those friends of Andrew's live.'

'Me too. But did you see the prices? Apparently no one here has heard about the recession. According to Rita Realtor, that tiny one that listed at 1.5 million went under the hammer for two! I've got sticker shock. I can live in a small, expensive place without a yard in Manhattan and save the airfare. Why would I leave New York?'

'I'm probably the wrong person to ask,' Lisa replied.

Melbourne real estate was on fire, and my daydream of purchasing a spacious house on a quarter-acre block was up in smoke. I called Andrew, who was unconcerned.

'I'll be over in a month, and can look then. In the meantime, when you and Lisa go see my parents, why don't you check out Mount Macedon on your way.'

✳

The Butcher family was not only close-knit but also geographically compact. Chris's house in Melbourne was an hour and a half from the family farm, while Andrew's brother Trevor, his wife Helen, and their three young children lived just down the road. Andrew's younger sister Katie lived on another farm with her husband Andy and their daughter, about thirty minutes from Nana and Pa. The family got together frequently, and I was already looking forward to seeing everyone and introducing Lisa to one of Nana's delicious roast dinners.

Chris had driven almost exactly halfway from Melbourne to Muckleford when she turned off the Calder Freeway and headed up a low, manicured mountain, past stately brick homes with curlicue wrought-iron gates and large, well-tended gardens. Someone with a steady arm and a chainsaw had carved names into the boxwood hedges. Sprinkled through the eucalypts, all of which looked identical to me, were a glittering array of deciduous trees I instantly recognised. On Honour Avenue in Macedon, the oaks and maples had put on an autumnal shimmer of russet and gold.

To my delight, these homes came with grassy lawns; there was space between each house and the one next door. The effect was picturesque. We continued up the mountain and pulled to a stop opposite a rustic, appealing general store, which also housed a post office and café, called the Mount Macedon Trading Post. As Lisa ducked down a lane to check out an art gallery, Chris and I sat on the front veranda with a local real estate agent. I was growing more excited by the minute. 'How long would it take for Andrew to drive to work in the CBD?'

'Forty-five minutes,' he replied.

'That's off-peak, Sar,' Chrissie cautioned.

I instantly dismissed her amendment. Forty-five minutes! That was like taking the train into New York from Greenwich, Connecticut or Montclair, New Jersey. It looked like I might just need to become a B &T, Melbourne style.

I was starting to envision my new life, and it was a rosy one indeed. Instead of living in a large, cosmopolitan city, we would live in a quaint country village. The girls would love it. So would Andrew. As for me, it might be a dramatic change, even an extreme one. But I had always liked the extreme.

Lisa was staring at me, thoughtfully. 'It's beautiful,' she agreed, 'But commuting can be exhausting.' I must have looked downcast, because she took a different tack. 'You know why you like it here, don't you?'

I cocked an eyebrow, nodded. 'Sure. Because you get more for your money. Because I lived in a big city for fifteen years, and a change is as good as a holiday. Because I can have a house big enough for visitors, and a yard for the girls.'

'That's part of it.' She looked around. 'But there's more, I think. It's how it feels, how the air smells. This isn't what I expected Australia to look like. It's nothing like the Outback. There are white fences and thoroughbreds, brick and weatherboard homes. There's even dogwood and maple trees and . . .'

'And mountain laurel,' I added, nodding in agreement. I had spied the largest mountain laurel I'd ever seen in front of the bluestone, ivy-covered Mount Macedon Uniting Church next to the Trading Post. Even though it wasn't in bloom, I would have recognised those leaves anywhere. The mountain laurel is one of my favourite plants, with its spectacular pink, white and lavender blossoms sprinkled across the wooded hillsides of Virginia every spring.

'Do you mean the rhododendron?' the real estate agent asked.

'Same thing,' I replied, enchanted.

'It's Virginia,' Lisa concluded, triumphantly, as Chris and I nodded. 'Mount Macedon could be in Virginia.'

The truth of her remark swirled and settled. 'No wonder it is so comfortable. It feels like home.'

Virginia. Victoria. Names with links to two famous British queens grafted, like foliage from the northern hemisphere, on to lands ancient and indigenous. I could see now that the terrain reminded me of the Blue Ridge Mountains of Virginia. For the first time on my journey to Australia, I felt as though I'd found a place where I might fit in. I could picture some of these houses in Charlottesville, Virginia, where I'd attended the University of Virginia, or in the state's capital city of Richmond, where I'd grown up. Whether it was the crisp, scarlet and gold glitter of that brilliant autumn day, or the strength of the flat white at the Trading Post, or most likely the sight of that lovely laurel, I couldn't say. All I knew was that I was still entranced by Mount Macedon when we touched down at JFK Airport.

But as the days passed, I experienced what photographers call rack/focus. The foreground shifted to the background, and vice versa. I was preoccupied by the mechanics of a big move—organising logistics, making lists, packing boxes. I also zeroed in on a promising school for Jacqueline, in the city's Port Melbourne neighbourhood. The beauty of Mount Macedon receded. Living in the city was the obvious choice.

But with our move just a few months away, we still didn't have a place to live. Fortunately, Andrew was headed to Australia to finalise details, and planned to check out a house to rent, just a short distance from the school.

When Andrew rang a few days later to update me on his progress, he sounded excited. Given that my husband is generally calm, I found this disconcerting, and was instantly on guard.

'How much is the rent?' I asked.

There was a pause. 'This house is actually for sale.'

I gulped. 'Weren't we talking about staying at your uncle's place, near the school, just until we were certain?'

'I've been thinking about that, and it's a waste of money. Way too small for us. Also too much chop and change, which is hard on Jac. This one is better.'

'Are we talking about a house in Port Melbourne?' I continued, anxiety increasing.

'Noooo.'

'Mount Macedon, then?' In spite of the drive, the mountain laurel might be worth it.

He sounded more cheerful. 'Not exactly. But pretty close. This is different, though. Better. It's more of a bush property.'

For some reason, the phrase 'bush property' did not sound better to me. I had visions of a wagon wheel coffee table, rusting farm implements strewn across dishevelled paddocks.

'Maybe I should have a look online?' I asked, stalling. Andrew talked on, but I wasn't listening. As I opened the site, my consternation deepened.

'Honey? Do I have the right spot? I only see one picture.'

'Yeah. That's because it's not officially on the market yet.'

'But Andrew, this is a shot of a *roof*!'

'But you can see the view. Isn't it spectacular! Twenty hectares! And private. See how it's on a ridge? And did you notice the sheds?'

I peered more closely at the photo. 'You mean the green circles?'

'Actually, no, those are tanks. We have our own water.'

'You're telling me there is no city water.'

'No town water, no. But that's no big deal. This is much better. Self-sufficient.'

That word also sounded distinctly ominous. But I could tell Andrew was gone, hook, line and sinker, all the more unnerving because it was unprecedented. I was the excitable enthusiast, Andrew the steady pragmatist. We had our roles, like every couple, and he was in violation. I felt panic rising, a sharp taste in the back of my throat.

'But Andrew, what about the people?' I asked finally. 'It's just a bunch of trees. WHERE ARE THE PEOPLE?!'

'Relax,' said my husband. 'You're going to love it.'

Somehow, I must have said yes. Because just two and a half months after that phone call, there I was, under that very roof, surrounded by boxes.

I thought back to my former hometown. I couldn't help but recall New York's famous theme song, the one which promised, 'If you can make it here, you'll make it anywhere . . .'

Did 'anywhere' by any chance happen to include the Macedon Ranges of Victoria, Australia?

4

OLD MAN EMU

Edward the emu was sick of the zoo,
There was nowhere to go, there was nothing to do,
And compared to the seals that lived right next door,
Well being an emu was frankly a bore.

I continued to read the children's story about an emu with an iden-
tity crisis to three-and-a-half-year-old Jacqueline, who sat next
to me on the yellow sofa. Still in her PJs, soft curls framing her face,
she could have posed for a cherub on a Roman ceiling. I was thrilled
she was paying attention. Jacqui had an extremely short attention
span and rarely spoke. When she did, it was a single word, mushy
and garbled. Some people assumed she was deaf, especially since we
used sign language with her. Others thought she had autism.

We weren't entirely sure ourselves what was wrong with
Jacqui's brain, but were certain we wanted to flood her with
educational opportunities. If she liked a book, we'd read it
endlessly—and right now, *Edward the Emu* tickled her fancy.
When we got to the page where Edward pretended to be a lion,
Jacqui tilted her head, looked straight at me with her china-doll
eyes, and opened her mouth wide enough to give me a good
look at her tonsils. She emitted a guttural, gargling sound.

I laughed and gave her a hug. 'Great roaring, Jac.'

We soon finished the book, and I looked at the clock. Eight a.m. Jacqui had been awake for two hours. One hundred and twenty minutes. I needed to stop converting. But entertaining a child with a short attention span had a way of making the day seem longer, because each activity only lasted for about three minutes.

'Okay, Jac, time to get dressed. You can't stay in that nappy forever.'

I instantly realised I'd made too fast a transition, because quick as Mercury, Jacqueline's cheerful mood turned tempestuous. She pulled the book out of my lap and threw it. I ducked, just in time.

'No throwing!' I caught myself, took a deep breath, and brought my voice down. 'No throwing,' I repeated, more calmly. 'We need to change you. The nappy is wet.'

I worked quickly, conscious that I was a bit rougher than I had been thirty seconds before. I took another deep breath, slowed down, tried to model some sort of Zen-like calm, despite her escalating protests.

'Shh! Daddy's sleeping. Shhh!' Andrew had just returned from London, and was jetlagged and exhausted.

Just then, the sliding-glass door to the backyard crashed open, and Sophie flew in, her mouth open as wide as Edward the Emu's, to deliver an urgent bulletin.

'Mum! I thought you said there weren't raccoons in Australia!'

'Pardon?' I replied, startled. Jacqui instantly quietened, and looked alertly at her sister.

'Rac-coons,' Sophie repeated with hyper-clarity, as though I was lip-reading. 'There *are so* raccoons here. There's one in our backyard!' she finished triumphantly.

I was already on my feet. 'Soph, that's not a—'

I scooped up the partially clad Jacqui, and hollered down the hall, no longer protecting the sacred god called Sleep, 'ANDREW! Grab the camera! Come quick!'

I'm not sure why I wasted my breath. My husband is scrupulously punctual, but makes it a point never to rush. As Dorothy Parker famously remarked about Katharine Hepburn, Andrew has an emotional range from A to B.

'Don't be a panic merchant,' he replied, as he strolled down the hall towards us, doing his own imitation of Edward, and scratching his head. 'What's going on?'

But I was already scrambling into scuffed clogs, pausing long enough to pop pink gumboots onto Jac. I hoisted her onto one hip as she opened her mouth again. I touched her lips with a finger, and shook my head, looking straight into her eyes. 'No! No bite! You've got to stop that. We're going to look and see what Sophie's discovered. Something exciting, I bet.'

We walked around the corner of the house to find Sophie, who had skidded to a stop beneath a tall gum tree. Sophie pointed to a grey bump sprouting from a high bough.

'See?' she insisted.

Her confusion was understandable. It wasn't that our former hometown was bereft of wildlife. Everyone knows about New York's pigeons, and locals were well acquainted with Gus, the famously bipolar polar bear at the Central Park Zoo. Gus's maniacal swimming bouts and deep funks prompted the city to call in a psychiatrist—it was New York, after all—who prescribed better toys. And Prozac. But if a New York child pointed out an animal, it was most likely a dog or a squirrel, or else a picture in a book. At no time during Sophie's six years in Manhattan had she encountered a marsupial on the Upper East Side, not to mention one posing for a Kodak moment in our backyard. I waited, allowing Sophie to figure this out for herself.

She squinted for a closer look. 'MUM,' she breathed, suddenly in awe of her own accomplishment. 'That is a KOALA.'

We stared reverently at the blinking, sleepy icon. Our enthusiasm, however, was not shared by a couple of cockatoos. They dive-bombed and hectored the koala, subjecting it to the most scurrilous epithets in their sulphur-crested vocabulary. Much as I liked cockatoos, they did seem to be a mite testy. Andrew arrived with the camera, and threw his arm around Sophie.

'You did it, Scruff. You spied the first koala at our new house. What a beauty.'

Our six-year-old was entranced by life in country Victoria, and began each summer morning with a wander out the back to see what sights were in store. She was a keen, enthusiastic observer, if not always an accurate one. A few days before, she'd dragged me outside to see a 'porcupine'. The pigeon-toed echidna, weighed down by all its spikes, ignored us in its single-minded pursuit of ants. Exhausted, it then curled into a pincushion under a hedge and slept for the day.

I was equally enraptured. Despite the fact that I was a dreadful photographer I kept a camera in the glove box, ready to snap pictures of the dozens of kangaroos that lived on our road. The kangaroos always seemed to hop away the second I clicked. I couldn't help but recall a comment from my dear friend Ginger, a *National Geographic* wildlife filmmaker who lived in Namibia. She pointed out that amateurs always seemed to photograph the wrong end of an animal.

Some Australians greeted our breathless reports of animal sightings with amused indulgence. Even my husband mocked me, pleased but surprised by just how besotted I was. He'd grown up with kangaroos. A farm boy, he'd even shot them. I was appalled; he was unapologetic.

'Like deer,' he said. Then, seeing my face, added, 'I wouldn't shoot one now.'

Another pause. 'Not here, anyway.'

It sometimes seemed to me that while Australians adored their unique marsupials, they could become a bit uncomfortable watching the rest of the world swoon over their continent's adorable creatures. It was almost as if the kangaroo was seen as a cliché. In the same way that I'd known Australians in New

York to wince when questioned wonderingly, 'Do you really say, "G'day, mate?"'—yet enjoy the access and attention their accents would attract—it seemed the fawning devotion of us foreigners to koalas, wallabies, wombats and Tassie devils was disconcerting. Was there perhaps a suspicion that the entire country might be taken more seriously if it had less cuddly, more ferocious wildlife? Or was the explanation that we Americans could be OTT— Over The Top? The way I figured it, if living in Australia meant being terrified by deadly reptiles, I'd indulge my desire to 'ooh' and 'ahhh' over fuzzy animals that didn't bite.

I had a lot to learn about Australia—the land, its people and its creatures. I felt frustrated that I couldn't tell the difference between a kangaroo and a wallaby, any more than I could differentiate a Kiwi accent from an Australian one. I was equally unable to differentiate between species of eucalypt, although clearly we had manna gums, because I had been told they were the species favoured by koalas. But all Australians love their eucalypts. I remember how pleased Andrew had been by the sight of the trees in California. I had even read that soldiers returning from both world wars could detect the aroma of eucalyptus wafting seaward on the breeze long before their ships reached the docks, even before the most eagle-eyed lookout could shout, 'Land, ho!'

Australia provided a sensory experience, on every level. Every night I sat on the floor of our large, empty lounge as the blood-orange sun slunk over the western rim of the Wombat Forest and dusk stole in from the valley. Then the kangaroos would emerge to nibble the remaining grass in our dusty lawn. Hesitant, ears twitching, they stared at us. I marvelled at how they balanced and pivoted on their muscular tails; at the casual improbability of their soaring leaps over fences; at their tiny, virtually useless front paws, appendages that appeared to be evolving out of existence. When they hopped away, it was the quietest, gentlest of sounds. Our front yard seemed like the Australian equivalent of an African waterhole.

I did wonder if the kangaroos would have been this brazen two hundred years before, when the indigenous Woiwurrung or Wurundjeri people had been the only human inhabitants of this region. There must have been a great deal of game here, and easy hunting, because it was estimated humans had lived in the region for up to 40,000 years. Then the Europeans arrived. I had read that John Aitken, the son of a Scottish farmer from whom a central road in the nearby town of Gisborne took its name, had been a pioneering sheep breeder who recognised that the Macedon Ranges were excellent grazing land. In 1836, he brought a flock of some 1600 sheep across from Tasmania to become the first settler in the Gisborne–Sunbury district. The journey had been a close thing; the ship foundered, and he only managed to get half his merinos across, thanks in part to the help of some Aborigines.

I wondered if those locals had ever reconsidered their assistance. It had not been many years before deadly skirmishes between pastoralists and local tribes erupted. Then, on 11 June 1851, gold was discovered in Clunes, Victoria. The combined influx of hundreds of thousands of miners in addition to other settlers resulted in the fact that by the mid-1800s, most of the indigenous people in the region had fled, or were dead. I had met no indigenous Australians locally; my primary association with the word Wurundjeri was the drive of that name in Melbourne.

I wondered if Sophie would ever come across any stone tools on this land, as I had occasionally unearthed flint arrowheads when building forts in the woods near my childhood home. It had only been the year before, in 2006, that the Victorian *Aboriginal Heritage Act* had made it illegal to disturb or destroy an Aboriginal place or artefacts. I felt an uncomfortable twinge, the delight in exploring 'our' new property tempered by the uncomfortable knowledge that it had not so very long ago belonged to others, who had been forced away, perhaps at gunpoint. As an American born in the South, I had learned that many a historical landscape included both pleasurable glimpses of epic achievements and landmines of guilt marking far less glorious deeds.

✳

It was a few days later, and Jacqui and I were once again reading *Edward the Emu*. I looked at my watch—it was only a little after six. I did wish Jacqui would sleep in. Suddenly, Sophie emerged from her bedroom, breathless.

'Good morning, Sophie. You're up early!'

'Mum, Mum, guess what! I just saw a kangaroo jumping on our trampoline!'

'Honey,' I replied carefully, anxious to disabuse my six-year-old of what was obviously a fantasy.

Sophie, still in pyjamas, her hair snarled, deflated before my eyes. 'I knew you wouldn't believe me.'

One of the many things I remembered about childhood was how often adults refused to believe something simply because it was improbable. Not impossible, just unlikely. But sometimes strange things did happen, and kids were more likely to notice. Our trampoline was unusual in that it was sunk into the ground, rather than raised; its springy mat was level with the surrounding ground, and our unfenced yard was adjacent to bush. We hadn't lived here long, and wild creatures weren't sticklers for property boundaries. Sophie was also a reliable reporter; she might gild the lily, but I hadn't known her to make stuff up.

'Sorry, Sophie. Tell me what happened.'

Her eyes lit up and I couldn't resist smiling. When you get it right as a mum, you usually know immediately. When you get it wrong, sometimes you must wait to learn how badly you've messed up.

'Well, I was on my bed, in my room, and I looked out in the backyard, and a kangaroo and joey came out of the forest,' Sophie explained. 'So I watched them. They went hop, hop and hopped right onto the trampoline!'

'Really? They must have been surprised.'

'Not really. They bounced a bunch of times. Kind of like a game. Maybe ten times. Or twenty. The joey really liked it.'

I lifted an eyebrow. 'Well, maybe once or twice, but the kangaroos did jump on the trampoline, Mum, and the joey liked it. I saw it!'

'I believe you. I only wish I'd seen it, too!'

✳

I thought we had had more than our share of peculiar animal sightings in the wonderful world of Oz, but I could not have been more wrong. A few days later, Sophie waved cheerily as she climbed into the Falcon with Andrew. We were borrowing Nana and Pa's car until we could purchase a second one of our own.

It was Sophie's second week attending a local primary school, and I noticed belatedly that her shirt was untucked, and that she had jammed her hat on so tightly it looked like a cork on a bottle. I wondered if shirts were supposed to be tucked in, or not. After the relaxed dress code of the New York City public schools, Sophie and I were both getting accustomed to the fact that Australian schoolchildren wore uniforms. Otherwise, she had made a surprisingly easy transition. Sophie told us she loved absolutely everything about her new school, including playing with gumnuts on the playground with her friend Caitlin, and writing plays with another friend, Izzy. Sophie was so pleased with her second-grade teacher that she would name one of her three fish—the only pets we owned—in her honour.

Today was to be Jacqui's first day at kinder, and I would finally test the '45-minute' commute to her school. I strapped Jacqui in her car seat, popped a new Wiggles CD into the player, and we pulled out of the drive and onto the local dirt road. We drove past horses, past the neighbouring winery and vineyard, past the local kangaroo sanctuary, and approached a paddock of black cows.

When a child doesn't talk, it's surprisingly easy to forget to talk to them. Jacqui's specialists in New York had warned me about this phenomenon, and suggested that I make sure to chat to our daughter about everything, regardless of whether or not she responded. They said giving Jacqui a play-by-play narrative of what we were seeing and doing would teach her about the world, and perhaps foster language. We'd just need to wait and see.

I had dutifully begun another one-way conversation, trying to make it sound natural, although I always felt awkward.

'Isn't it a pretty day, Jacqui? Look—the sun! Sun! And the sky is blue. Oh! See those cows over there?'

'Eeeeee. Moo,' replied Jacqui from the back seat.

'Moo?' I repeated, keeping my eyes on the juddering road ahead, startled to hear what might just be an actual word. 'Yes, moo! Cows say "moo". That's great, Jacqui!'

I glanced in the rear-view mirror, but saw that Jacqui was shaking her head no, in frustration. 'EEMOO!' she said.

Our daughter's vocabulary consisted of a handful of familiar words, such as 'Mama', 'Dada' and 'Zozo', for Sophie. I had never heard her say 'Emu' before.

'Yes, we read the book about the emu.'

But as I turned to smile, I saw that Jacqui seemed to be gesturing violently towards the window.

'Emoo!' she said, for the third time.

'Sorry, Jacqui, but there aren't any—OH MY GOD!' I hit the brakes.

'Is that an EMU?'

An enormous bird which looked an awful lot like an ostrich ran jerkily beside us. I got a glimpse of feathers and a beady red eye as it passed us. After a few stunned moments, I rolled the car forward, anxious to catch another glimpse of Big Bird. But it had darted around the bend, and off into the bush.

Jacqui was beaming, clapping her hands. In Australia, apparently storybooks came to life.

'You clever, clever girl!' I responded. 'You spotted an emu, and you know a new word!' For once it was easy to carry on a one-sided conversation. 'But I didn't know wild emus lived around here, only kangaroos. Where do you suppose it came from? What was it doing on our road?'

She looked at me blankly. I pulled over again, grabbed my phone and rang the only neighbours I knew.

David and Mary owned a lovely local vineyard called Mount Gisborne Wines. Originally Canadian, upon hearing that a Yank had moved into the neighbourhood, they'd dropped by with a bottle of their own Mount Gisborne Pinot. They had lived in the area for nearly 30 years, and if anyone knew the story behind this sighting, they would.

Luckily, David was at home, and I told him what we had seen.

'Are you in Gisborne?' David asked.

'No,' I answered, curious. 'But I could drop by there on my way to Melbourne.'

'Good. Just go into town, then turn at the fountain, and the butcher shop is on the right at the corner.'

'The *butcher* shop?'

'Yes. Just ask for Chris.'

'But, David—I don't want to—to—'

His chuckle was low and deep. 'No, no, no, Sara. Chris is Penny's son.'

I remained mystified, and asked for more details.

'Penny is a local woman, and she owns an emu farm. That emu will have escaped, and somehow made its way through the bush to you. Just tell Chris. He'll take care of it.'

It wasn't difficult to find the Town Butcher, and Chris seemed unsurprised by my report, as if it was an everyday occurrence that someone came in to discuss a Rogue Emu Sighting rather than purchase snags or lamb. 'No worries, I'll let Mum know. Thanks.'

I had had my first lesson in village protocol. No need to call a

wildlife ranger. Just ring up a neighbour. Six degrees of separation
had shrunk to one.

I pulled out of town, and onto the Calder Freeway, headed for
Melbourne.

※

The search for the right school for our three-year-old daughter
had been like a reporting assignment for me, one begun on that
exploratory trip to Melbourne with my friend Lisa. We discussed
the project with everyone we met, starting with my sister-in-law
Chris, who was a nurse at the Royal Children's Hospital. We
had relied on Chris's medical knowledge many times since Jacqui
had been born. I also interviewed occupational therapists, physio-
therapists, doctors, educators and most of all, parents. Such was
the level of helpfulness that one of the best leads had come from
the man who happened to sit next to us on our Qantas flight from
New York to Melbourne. He had a friend who knew a friend. He
made calls, a contact was relayed. It would be the first of many
times that I heard a similar refrain: 'Have you heard about Port
Phillip Specialist School?'

When I returned to New York, I called the school's principal,
who impressed me with her thoroughness.

'Do you have a diagnosis?' asked Bella Irlicht.

'Yes and no. It seems to be evolving.' I paused. 'I should
mention, Jacqui has had seizures. But she is stable now.'

'Not to worry,' Bella's voice was kind. 'We have plenty
of children with some form of epilepsy. Now, do you have
documentation?'

'Probably too much,' I acknowledged. 'New Yorkers are kind
of famous for their paperwork.'

'Send it all,' Bella suggested, 'everything you have.'

I headed for the Kinko's Copy Centre on Lexington Avenue
with cartons of files from two New York hospitals, as well as from
Jacqueline's neurologists, therapists, specialists and paediatrician.

The photocopying assignment had taken three and a half hours. Amused employees had to fix the photocopier twice.

People assume New Yorkers are stand-offish, but that's mostly an illusion. Abrupt, sometimes gruff, perhaps—given the constant cheek-by-jowl proximity—but the city's inhabitants are also eager to lean into a nearby conversation, ready with humour and advice. On that day, I was the entertainment—first at Kinko's, then at Federal Express.

'You want to send ALL this? Just so you know, that bunch of paper weighs more than two pounds.'

'Yep. All of it.'

The clerk shook her head. 'It's your funeral. And it will cost $100.'

A small price to pay, had she only known how much we had already spent. How much we would gladly have paid, had money been a solution.

✳

Our daughter was born in 2004 after a difficult delivery, which followed a complicated pregnancy. Gazing down at her tiny, beautiful features, I felt none of the giddiness I remembered in the wake of Sophie's birth; there was only overwhelming relief. Thank God, it was over and she was all right. In fact, she was perfect.

In fact, she was not.

Forty-eight hours after her birth, Jacqui had a seizure. Before Andrew and I could absorb such a shocking word, much less comprehend the terrible possibilities it suggested, she had another. And then another. Doctors came and they went, wave after wave of them. Jacqui was admitted into the NICU—the Neo-Natal Intensive Care Unit. Most newborns got well and left. Their parents beamed.

Other babies lingered, in devastating circumstances, or died. We got to know some of those parents. It was hard not to be afraid, it was impossible not to cry. We tried to remember to pretend to be happy when we were with Sophie.

There were many tests. An EEG, an MRI, a spinal tap, repeat. Then blood tests, genetic tests, one for meningitis, and on it went. There were no answers. Down, down, we fell, as if into a deep, narrow well. The hardest day was when a doctor told us that our baby's brain was simply no good. He didn't elaborate, beyond gesturing towards the EEG, folds of white paper recording the electrical patterns in our daughter's brain. It seemed the most outrageous statement, but he told me it was important that I knew, as if I could prepare myself. But the nurse who walked me to the elevator whispered that he did not know everything, that doctor. She thought our daughter had bright eyes. We should not despair.

The truth about our daughter seemed to lie somewhere between those two predictions. Jacqui's brain was not a disaster, nor did it function perfectly. We had been able to bring her epilepsy under control with medicine, and by the time she was two years old, had weaned her from the drugs. Now three-and-a-half, she remained vulnerable to a seizure if she had a fever or hit the back of her head, but we were hopeful she would outgrow her seizures altogether.

Jacqui's mysterious condition didn't have a name, but its impact was clear. Our daughter found it difficult to organise her thoughts, to speak or to pay attention. Learning anything took an exceedingly long time—learning to pronounce the letter 'f' took more than a year. And her behaviour was impulsive and could be challenging. I knew she was frustrated, and chalked it up to that. I wanted to do everything I could to help our daughter reach her fullest potential. I would be Jacqui's coach, teacher and champion. I thought she could catch up, and, in time, attend a mainstream school with Sophie. I felt sure that providing her with a stimulating environment was a key part of the prescription. And that was where Port Phillip came in.

✳

If the colourful, eccentric local wildlife we'd encountered comprised one Ozian adventure, the world of a specialist school seemed to be another. As Jacqui and I arrived, we saw a noisy procession of children marching around the circumference of the school, which along with its playgrounds, encompassed an entire city block. Some of the children wore navy uniforms, others did not. Some of the boys and girls ran, others ambled, or shuffled, or halted abruptly, for no apparent reason. One teenager was wearing a heavy black helmet. An adult pushed a smiling girl in a wheelchair. Another teacher accompanied a child who made halting progress using a walker. Some of the children had physical manifestations of their condition. They looked different. A tall young man with a dark fringe and a faraway look clutched his iPod and hummed along to 'Do you know the muffin man, the muffin man, the muffin man'. A girl with a thick mane spoke convincingly to no one in particular, gesturing to someone or something I couldn't see.

Almost everyone was smiling. There was laughter, whoops of joy, high fives and revelry. The teachers watched the circuit alertly but indulgently. This was just another typical day.

But not for me. I wasn't sure what I had expected, but I found the scene disconcerting. I stared at the boys and girls, examples of what our daughter might look like, walk like, talk like, act like, when she grew up; these were possible glimpses of her future self, in the same way that the older children on Sophie's playground gave me a glimpse into her later years. I stayed in the car, watching the procession, through a song about rosy tea and Wags the dog and waking up Jeff.

I stayed until we were spotted by a petite woman with bright brown eyes and a cheerful but commanding presence. As she made her way towards us, I scrambled to pull myself together and get us out of the car.

'You must be Sara,' she smiled. There was something about her demeanour which instantly identified her.

'And you must be Bella Irlicht,' I responded, holding out my hand.

'Call me Bella,' she said, clasping my hand in both of hers. Then she turned to my daughter, beaming.

'And good morning, Jacqueline!' Bella crouched down, and now took Jacqui's small hands in hers. 'Welcome to our school,' Bella continued, speaking directly to Jacqui, far more naturally than I did, I noticed. 'This is your first day. That's a very big day. I think you are going to love it.'

She straightened, beckoned, set off, talking over her shoulder as she went. 'No need to go through the main gate. We have a special door for the younger children. Come, I'll introduce you to Yvonne, Jacqueline's teacher.'

We entered a cheerful room with an aquarium, beanbag chairs and lots of pieces of what looked like specialised, expensive equipment nestled amid well-tended toys. Our 45-minute commute had taken more than an hour and the other parents were gone. I reminded myself that our next trip would be faster, without the need to deal with unexpected emu issues. Yvonne Miller took Jacqui by the hand, and introduced us to the other children in the room. There was a beautiful girl whose recumbent posture on a beanbag made me wonder if she could sit up. Several boys were busily scooting across the floor, while another two children sat at a desk, drawing. I suspected that, like Jacqui, these children either had limited language or none at all. I couldn't help but remember a New York friend's comment after enrolling her son at a similar establishment: 'It's the land of broken toys.'

While I was extremely grateful to have secured a place for Jacqui at Port Phillip, especially since this two-day-a-week program was one of only a handful in the state for three-year-old children with special needs, the entrance exam wasn't exactly something to brag about. The primary qualification for admittance was to have an IQ of 69 or below. When I was a child, we'd labelled such children 'retarded'. Now, the idea of calling someone such a derogatory word made me angry enough to bite someone.

This was a lovely school, I reminded myself. I just needed to get accustomed to things. But I couldn't help remembering what Sophie had been like at this age. Bright, bubbly, chattering up a storm. Learning songs about the continents, the days of the week. Sounding out letters, counting to 50, drawing wobbly stick figures with her textas, 'signing' her name with her best attempt at letters. Jacqui could do none of those things. Bringing Jacqui to school—to a special school—was yet another acknowledgment that something was wrong with our little girl. But Jacqui only had a developmental delay, I told myself, that was all. We would not be here forever.

I exchanged pleasantries with Yvonne, attempted to smile. Over my years as a reporter, I'd honed a skill for conducting casual conversations as a sort of bridge over swirling, emotionally choppy deep water. But not this day. I asked where I might find a good cup of coffee. Twenty minutes later, I was sitting on the beach at Port Phillip Bay, toes rammed in the sand, with a view of the jaunty red and white *Spirit of Tasmania* ferry berthed at the right edge of my peripheral vision. I sipped a flat white in a brown paper cup, thought about what time it was in America. I was conscious that I faced the wrong way—not north and west, towards home, but into uncharted waters. Like my younger daughter, I sat staring into space, saying nothing.

✳

Life was busy, extremely so. Hectic. Our furniture had arrived, and more boxes. A week after Jacqui's first day at school, I was unpacking the kitchen with my sister-in-law Kate, who'd brought along her five-year-old daughter Annaliese. A trained chef, Katie also possesses an organisational flair worthy of Mary Poppins. Clothes seem to fold themselves and leap into cupboards, and children suddenly look neater and have ribbons in their hair.

Kate was making quick work of setting up our new house, and offered to watch the girls while I drove to town for more cleaning supplies. I'd been gone just twenty minutes when my mobile rang.

'I don't want to worry you,' she began, breathlessly, 'but you'll never believe it. Guess what is in your backyard?'

'A kangaroo?' I suggested.

'An *emu*! By the trampoline.'

What was it with that emu, not to mention our trampoline? It seemed to be a magnet.

'It's not jumping on it, is it?'

'Don't be silly! But it's huge! Twice the size of Anna.'

'Is it dangerous?' I asked. 'I mean, do they bite?'

It sounded ridiculous, but emus had beaks. 'Or kick? Rip people open with their claws?' Weren't ostriches supposed to be dangerous if riled? Probably an emu could be, too. I seemed to remember they had long toes with sharp nails.

Andrew's sister acknowledged she didn't know much either. 'It just seems confused, not violent. But I've brought the girls inside. I wouldn't trust it, to be honest.'

'I'll go see Chris at the butcher,' I told her wickedly, knowing she would be as startled as I had been by that sentence.

But when I hung up, I changed my mind. I was a reporter. I was curious about the elusive, emu-owning Penny. How hard could it be to find her? I called directory assistance, asked for any local business that had 'emu' in the name, and was soon connected.

'Macedon Park Emu Farm, Penny speaking,' said a woman with a musical, eastern European accent.

I explained who I was. 'Have you lost an emu? Because we seem to have one in our backyard.'

'Oh thank you very much! I will be straight over.'

I returned home to find a short, bubbly, fifty-something blonde bundle of energy emerging from the front yard. 'Thank you for calling me, but she already got away,' Penny reported.

'Let me know if you see her again. Hopefully, she may come back.'

'She?'

'Yes, it is a girl.' Penny laughed. 'She is having a little fling!'

I must have looked confused. Penny continued, 'She has laid some eggs, and now, off she goes! She is very naughty, this emu. She's off to find a boyfriend!'

'But won't the eggs die?' I responded. 'You won't get any chicks.'

She laughed again. 'Oh no, with emus, it is the boy who must sit on the eggs. For sixty days! The male does all the work, he stays at home patiently waiting, while she is out frisking about.'

I was starting to have a greater appreciation of the big, ungainly bird. 'She's got a good thing going!' I joked.

Penny laughed in agreement. 'In my next life, I'm coming back as a lady emu. Come see me, my farm is just down the road,' she gestured. 'Bring the girls. And your husband. His name is Andrew, yes?' I nodded, thinking how quickly information about newcomers is known by virtually everyone in small country towns.

Like the kangaroo before it, the emu never returned to the trampoline. But the following day, I was treated to a postscript. I heard the sound of a put-putting motor, and watched in amusement as another neighbour, on a small motorbike, chased a large, flapping bird down the road. The Rogue Female had been cornered and would soon be captured. She was heading home. No more flitting about. Those eggs would be hatching soon. She needed to take care of her chicks.

5

THE MAGPIES OF WATERFALLS ROAD

In my experience, one of the many opportunities in moving to a new continent is the chance to re-invent yourself. And in my experience, one of the many traps of moving to a new continent is the temptation to re-invent yourself.

I wiped sweaty palms on my new navy blue skirt and swivelled a twenty-year-old Sledge Hammer. The Wilson racquet had a distinctive squared-off head that was a cautionary tale against purchasing trendy gear, unless you were an ace. I wasn't. We were down four games to five, the score was 15–40, and it was my second serve, after a let. I hadn't played a real tennis match in a very long time—certainly not since I'd joined NBC. Even then, I hadn't been any good.

Which somehow hadn't prevented me from signing up to play Tuesday morning tennis for the Macedon Tennis Club in the Mountain District Ladies Tennis Association. It was an impulsive decision I deeply regretted that morning. True, there were six sections, and yes, I was playing in Section Six. This was not the Australian Open. But my stomach refused to be consoled.

I took a deep breath, reminded myself of the coach's admonition to relax and let the ball roll off my fingers. I tossed the ball high in the air, my fingers sprang open early and the ball sailed out in front. I lurched forward, the Sledge Hammer connected late. The ball hit the top of the net, then plopped onto my side of the court. A double fault.

'Your game,' I said.

'Bad luck,' one of our opponents replied with a kind smile.

'Don't take it to heart,' encouraged my teammate Jenny, as we switched courts. 'It's just a hit and a giggle. Your backhand looked good, and there's still another set to go.'

I was dubious. I was anything but a gazelle on the court. More like an injured wildebeest. My skill as an athlete was the reason I had never dared to name either daughter Grace. Sure, Andrew was coordinated, but what if the girls had inherited my skills?

The biggest problem with my tennis game was my inability to serve. Everyone told me the key was in the toss. Try as I might to open my fingers, tulip-shaped, and release the ball straight overhead, it either wound up somewhere behind me, or far out in front. I see-sawed between backbends and foot-faults. Finally, I had hidden my racquet in the back of the closet.

But this was the year, I decided, when I would confront my nemesis and conquer that serve. I had signed up for lessons from a local coach, who diagnosed the problem and offered various prescriptions, including one I dreaded. Deflecting strenuous objections, he insisted I needed to join a team. 'What you need is practice. You'll learn to serve when you have to serve, in a match,' he promised.

Sophie was in second grade, and Tuesday was one of two days a week when Jacqui was in school. I wasn't working, and I was determined to exercise. There was no excuse. Somewhat piously, I also wanted to set a decent example. If I insisted Sophie not pine for friends left behind, and be willing to leap into activities at her new school, then I should do the same. I didn't want to be one of those people who moved to a new country, only to moan about missing the one they left behind.

But that wasn't all there was to it. On what was effectively my day off, I wanted to participate in an activity that had nothing to do with the world of special needs. A world where conversation revolved around tennis strategy or shopping, what sports our kids were playing or where to get your hair cut, even gardening, if someone insisted, though the local plants still mystified me. Basically, I was up for any casual conversation, and the more superficial, the better.

All of those motivations, I recognised. What took me longer to realise was that this sudden willingness to risk abject humiliation had a lot to do with the recent move to Australia. In a rush of new beginnings, it was easy to add another to the list. The world was suddenly full of tantalising possibilities. Anything could happen. Who knew, perhaps I could become a ballroom dancer, or run a marathon, or write a play. Far away from those who knew me, it was possible to imagine a new, improved version of myself, doing things I'd never done before.

In the weeks since our move, a tsunami of adrenalin had surged through me. The last time I'd felt so truly, giddily capable of anything, I was eighteen years old, leaving home for university. I couldn't wait to channel this energy into the unfinished, the undone, the could-have-beens of life.

I had met many immigrants in my years as a reporter. Many had been former refugees, for whom the horrors they had endured, combined with the obstacles of language, poverty and access, could have proved overwhelming burdens. Despite those hardships, many of these immigrants not only survived, but thrived. I had imagined the reason for that success must reflect their essential character, flowering as a result of newfound freedom and opportunity. Nature, nurture. What had never occurred to me was that there was actually a third element—a wellspring of vitality that was tapped the moment someone ticked the box marked 'Immigrating' on a Customs Arrivals Declaration. I hadn't known about it, until I'd ticked the box myself.

True, I was no refugee. Mine had been a relatively easy, well-choreographed move, because my partner and children were

Australian citizens. But we had had a comfortable life in New York; somehow knowing we'd had the initiative to leave the known and risk trying something new had ignited my confidence and convinced me I could do the improbable. If I gazed into the future, I could almost glimpse this new, improved self, demonstrating dazzling skills. I was fuzzy on the details, but I was pretty sure I saw a sizzling serve.

Or that was how it had seemed, anyway, when I had said 'yes' to play for Macedon. It was interesting to note that I wasn't the only newcomer on the team. We were all transplants, including Jenny, who had just moved from Brisbane, and Brigitte, who was originally from Switzerland; Emma and Paula also had moved to the area fairly recently. Everyone seemed to have the same motivation, to use sport to get fit and meet new friends.

With five players, we had a team and a substitute. As the brutally hot day wore on, I found myself fantasising that today had been my turn. Courtside, the kookaburras cackled, and their haunting laugh sounded remarkably pointed. But when we lost the match, I was relieved that Paula, our captain, seemed unfazed. 'It doesn't matter! Besides, wait until you see what I made for dessert!'

Win or lose, after the match, everyone sat down to lunch. The home team provided the meal, and I had been asked to bring sandwiches. I'd made chicken, lettuce and tomato, with lashings of mayonnaise. I'd also slapped together ham, cheese and lettuce. The food around me looked pretty spectacular. My sandwiches were edible, but hardly inspiring. It appeared today's competition wasn't just on the court. I would need to do better next week, when it was my turn to make dessert. Perhaps I'd bring a coffee cake, or a southern delicacy, such as a lemon chess pie.

Playing tennis followed by a ladies' lunch felt not just indulgent, but weird. I worked part-time in high school and college, full-time ever since I'd graduated from university at twenty-two. This was the first time I had played a game during what would have been a work day, and it was also my first foray into the world of community sports. I didn't know the rules, on or off the court. I was keen not to make a mistake, culturally or linguistically, conscious as a teenager switching schools of my desire to fit in.

Inside the clubhouse were a few tables, a pint-sized kitchen with a fridge, lino benchtops and hot water on demand, and a large wall festooned with the names of recent trophy winners and those from days of yore. In short, it looked pretty much like any other team clubhouse.

Paula had already taken a gorgeous chocolate cake to our table, and there was a fruit platter, a savoury tart and tea. I realised I was starving. I went to the refrigerator to collect my sandwiches, and discovered, to my delight, that someone else on our team had also brought some. I tried not to worry that theirs actually looked like something prepared by chef and author of *The Cook's Companion*, Stephanie Alexander. I hoisted both platters, harkening back to the days when I'd been a waitress, and headed to the table.

Surprisingly on such a hot day, the tea was perfect. I loaded fruit and quiche onto my plate, and one of those delicious-looking sandwiches. Scrumptious. Things were looking up. Outside, the magpies chattered. Inside, we chattered just as merrily, if perhaps not quite as musically, discussing the notable points in the match. No one mentioned my double faults, the countless ball tosses. I began to relax.

'Are you Canadian or American?' one of the women on the other team asked.

'American.'

'Oh, sorry!'

'No, we don't mind. That's only the Canadians,' I responded, to knowing, good-natured laughter. 'I'm from New York.'

'From New York state, or the city?'

'The city.' There was a polite murmur.

'I love New York!' another woman said.

'Right in the centre? I've been there at Christmas, seen the tree.'

'That's exactly where I worked!'

'From Manhattan to Macedon—that must be a shock!' the first woman said with a friendly smile.

'A bit, yes,' I replied, testing the waters.

I was intrigued by all the different ways in which my home city and home country were assessed. Everyone, it seemed, had an opinion. Some suggested I must feel lucky indeed to have left the Big Smoke, expensive and crowded, behind. They'd been there and wouldn't care to go again. Others regarded my move from New York to country Australia with a degree of bewilderment at least equal to that of my New York friends. The move was down-right suspicious—why would anyone do such a thing? I sensed a bit of cultural cringe in their assessment that New York was, by definition, superior to anything in Australia. I loved both places, and didn't feel the need to score one higher than the other.

There were still others who seemed to view me more as an oddity, an outsider; I was Conspicuously American. I could understand.

There had been that early trip to the supermarket deli counter. 'May I have a pound of ground beef and a quarter pound of turkey please?'

The flummoxed sales assistant replied, 'What's ground beef, how much is a quarter of a pound, and we don't have turkey.'

There was the fact that I spoke quickly.

'You'll slow down, after you've lived here a while,' was a comment I heard not infrequently. Couldn't they tell I *had* slowed down?

Although I did so only when absolutely necessary, any helpful suggestion I offered about a slight variation to a menu item, and any utterance of the words 'on the side' seemed to be regarded as a criticism. In New York, ordering your own variation of a dish was a time-honoured tradition.

And then there was the fact that during walks on our country lane, instead of gazing at the cows and kangaroos, I talked on my mobile phone.

'You look ridiculous,' scoffed Andrew. 'Not to mention, you're not getting much exercise.'

'It's the best time to reach people in America,' I countered.

'You do the same thing when you walk in the afternoon, when America is asleep.'

'That's when I talk to Ginger in Namibia.'

Since moving to Oz, I'd encountered only gracious, welcoming comments from those I met, genuine interest in who I was and the reasons behind our move. I was occasionally referred to as 'the American'—I was one, after all—but never, ever as a 'seppo'—except by my husband, that is. He swore it was meant affectionately, but I banned the term after I discovered it was a derivative of derisive rhyming slang for Yank. *Septic tank?* I'd had no idea! The notorious Australian sense of humour at work again, in this instance directed at a culture occasionally regarded as just a teensy bit full of itself. It seemed that while Americans adored Aussies, the reverse was not always the case.

After a month of living in Australia, perusing magazines and newspapers, watching television and chatting to locals, I learned that feelings for my homeland were complicated. Hollywood movie stars received extraordinary hype and adulation, and understandably none more so than talented Australians like Nicole Kidman, Hugh Jackman and Cate Blanchett. There was no shortage of news ink devoted to Australians of all stripes who'd 'made it' in the States.

But politically and militarily, there was an uglier image of America. President George Bush was wildly unpopular. Those I met expressed relief that his second term was drawing to a close and great interest regarding the presidential race, especially the campaign of Senator Barack Obama. America was considered the land of opportunity, to be sure, but also the land of excess, of supersize-me. Hard to argue.

Americans were seen as self-confident and well-spoken—qualities to be admired, I was told—but also could be loud and opinionated, insular and positively clueless about geography. I was told stories about Americans who confused Australia with Austria, who asked returning Australian visitors if they planned to travel by plane or car. Such stories sounded preposterous, but I was assured they were true.

To be fair, there were also American stereotypes of Australians—perhaps chief among them that Aussies were big drinkers. I hadn't heard many Australians argue the point. More contentious was the question about whether Australia was as progressive as the US. I had often been told in America that 'Australia is supposed to be just like the US in the 1950s'. Given the country's social welfare net, its well-educated population, and the fact that women received the vote in Australia nearly twenty years before their American counterparts, the statement was absurd. But there was clearly room for improvement here, both in terms of launching more women into positions of leadership, and in addressing the disturbing fact that overall, the indigenous population lagged drastically behind the rest of Australians when it came to health and prosperity.

While I was too recent an immigrant to assess my new home on any deep level, it hadn't taken long to note the lack of political correctness. I had also experienced genuine confusion on one occasion when I was told that 'the girls' were getting together. Which girls, I'd wondered? Having assumed it was an adult gathering—men were invited—I wondered if I was also expected to bring our daughters. I figured it out a sentence or two later, when the word 'ladies' was used as a synonym for 'girls'.

'Oh, you mean women!' I blurted out.

There was the briefest of pauses. 'Exactly.'

I had since heard the word 'girls' used to refer to women in a wide array of contexts, including female executive assistants, lawyers and entrepreneurs, wives and mothers and friends, and of course *Homo sapiens* with a XX chromosome aged twelve and under.

Perhaps I was hypersensitive, having just moved from a city in which words were the subject of constant debate regarding accuracy, nuance and anything deemed pejorative. I recognised that being labelled 'PC' was considered an insult, in both countries, and it was certainly possible to over-correct. But I felt equally certain that attention to language had changed lives for the better. In New York, a city of more than 8 million people, in which a staggering 800 languages were spoken—the most of any city in the world—calling a person, place or thing by the correct name wasn't just smart, it was essential. I'd been to Sarajevo. I'd seen what could happen to a beautiful, sophisticated, multicultural city, almost overnight. Name-calling had been part of the descent into madness and slaughter. In New York, taking regular soundings to ensure labels were not demeaning simply made sense.

Australia was a very different place, a more casual country where it was felt everyone, from politicians to business leaders to entertainers, should learn how to take a joke. I'd already had to learn to lighten up, not take everything so seriously. After all, I was married to an Australian, a man whom my brother-in-law jokingly accused of being the person in an argument who would 'cross the line . . . and then frolic'.

But it still bothered me to be called a girl. Churchill famously said of the US and the UK that they were two nations separated by a common language. Would the same prove true here? I figured the more I became a part of the culture, the more I listened and observed, the better I would understand my new home.

'Excuse me?' I said, 'Sorry, I didn't catch that.'

In point of fact, lost in my own reflections, I had lost track of the conversation.

'I was just saying I like the sandwiches, Sara,' said Emma.

'Thank you.'

'They are good,' Brigitte agreed. 'Did you use chutney? It tastes homemade.'

I had actually used mayonnaise. It tasted nothing like chutney. I took a closer look at the sandwich in Brigitte's hand.

'Oh! That's not mine. One of you made that platter!' I took another bite of the one on my plate. 'They really are good.'

There was a brief, quiet moment I couldn't quite decipher, but I forgot it immediately because the clubhouse door slid open and another laughing, sweaty group of women came inside, just ahead of a solid wedge of heat. I was constantly astonished at the ferocity of the Australian summer.

I turned to Jenny. 'I'm a fan of your quiche. Did you use cream? Is that why it's so good?'

'Oh, I wouldn't know,' Jenny waved off the compliment, 'I used Coles.'

One of our opponents grinned. 'Funny you should say that,' she said, conspiratorially. 'Last season I was at a game, and it was obvious that the quiche was from the shops, but when someone asked the girl who brought it, she tried to pass it off as *homemade*!'

She paused for the significance of this remark to sink in, then continued, 'Then one of the *other* girls asked how she'd made it, and she started in with how she'd used cream, and bacon and leeks—and then the first woman interrupted, and said, "You did not make that quiche! You bought it!" She was mortified.'

There was a brief dissection of this multi-faceted breach of etiquette but I had lost focus again, especially because I was now distracted by a commotion at the refrigerator, just behind us. My reporting instincts kicked into gear, along with an uncomfortable sense of foreboding.

'What is wrong?' I asked, turning around.

A mild-looking woman looked at me. 'We're just a little confused. My friend had some sandwiches here'—she indicated the refrigerator—'but someone seems to have nicked them.'

Oh, the shame.

I gulped, stood up abruptly. 'Those sandwiches—' I said, dusting crumbs off my skirt. The woman eyed me suspiciously.

'I think there's been a mistake. I mean, I think I might have made a mistake.' I gestured in the direction of the platter of attractive, half-eaten, mystery sandwiches on our table. 'Did they look like this? Did they have . . . chutney?'

The two women stared transfixed at the mutilated remnants of the delectable sandwiches.

I was speaking even more quickly now.

'I am very sorry,' I squeaked. 'I think, I mean, I know, that I took your sandwiches. Not on purpose! I mean, not accidentally either, it's just that I thought they were ours.'

I paused. Then added helpfully, 'I'm American.' As if this was some sort of disclaimer. One small mistake, and I had just thrown my entire country under the bus.

There was an awkward silence, since there was no obvious way to fix this dilemma. The shops were too far away—lunch would be over by the time I went and bought replacements. I looked desperately at our table. Most of her sandwiches were gone, but mine were virtually untouched.

'You can have these,' I offered helpfully.

Perhaps unsurprisingly, they declined. With a curt nod, one of the women collected the platter with the few remaining sandwiches that belonged to them, and strode towards the table at the far end of the room. The temperature in the room had dropped, dramatically.

I don't remember much about the rest of that lunch. I have blocked out the faces of the women from those other two teams. But I can easily see the faces of those on our table: my teammates and our opponents, all of us howling with laughter.

'Oh Sara, why did you take them?' Jenny asked, wiping the tears from her eyes.

'I thought one of you had brought them!'

'But we were bringing everything else—the fruit, the quiche, the dessert . . .'

'How would I know? I've never played social tennis, you all. Besides, I thought it was only us playing, so they had to be ours.'

'You didn't see those other teams on the court?' Paula was guffawing now. 'Remember, we are Section Six? There are five other sections, so there are other teams!'

I had not seen anyone else, and I had seen only one court—ours. I had been particularly conscious of the yawning chasm next to the service line which threatened to swallow me, every time I tossed a ball in the air. I had been counting double faults, not other teams.

'No, I did not.'

'Oh stop,' someone else said. 'Just admit it. You're American. Of *course* you are going to nick the sandwiches!'

'Exactly!' Someone else chimed in. 'We all know this is what happens in New York!'

'I always heard you had to watch your purse,' someone else cackled. 'No one mentioned anything about sandwiches.'

Our laughter deepened, mine most of all.

I couldn't help but think of the 1990s comedy *My Cousin Vinny,* in which two college students from New York wound up on trial for murder in a small town in rural Alabama, and made matters worse by hiring as a lawyer their under-qualified northern relative. In one of the movie's most famous scenes, Vinny, played by Joe Pesci, chided his fiancée, Lisa, played to Academy Award-winning perfection by Marisa Tomei, for being too obviously a New Yorker, with her brassy accent, short skirt and long nails.

'You stick out like a sore thumb,' he scolded, insisting he now passed for a local, after buying cowboy boots.

With a devastating roll of her eyes and a smack of her chewing gum, Lisa retorted, 'Yeah. You blend.'

I would continue to work on my serve. Next tennis game,

I would serve a blue-ribbon dessert. But most important of all, I'd make sure to wear my New York Yankees baseball cap. Because I could only be what I was. I was an American. I was a Yank.

6

FAIRY WRENS

The moan was low and guttural, ending in an ominous howl. Then it keened and sobbed, dropped almost to a whisper, a death rattle, before roaring back to full and furious life. The roof creaked, a gust tugging determinedly at the eaves overhead, as if, like Dorothy's Kansas cottage, this house was to be wrenched from the hillside, broken apart, tossed higgledy-piggledy. I imagined the roof flung skyward, a wall, until the tempest had clawed free the rectangular foundation, sent it cartwheeling into the black sky.

'Pretty windy,' Andrew yawned, rolling over.

'Are you kidding me?' I sat up in bed. The clock said 3.31 a.m. 'How can you even pretend to sleep?'

Suddenly, there was an almighty clang, and Andrew was sitting up, too.

'What the hell was that?' He leapt out of bed, did a lunging, speed-walk-tiptoe down the hall, past Jacqui's room, muttering under his breath at yet another calamitous crash. 'It better not wake her up.'

I was just behind him, sliding open the glass door onto the veranda, as Andrew vainly struggled to capture the culprit, an awning which was flapping, out of control. I'd lowered the awnings earlier in the day to prevent the setting sun from beating onto the veranda's red tile floor, turning the western edge of our house into a blast furnace, complete with its own clay oven. The fearsome radiant heat penetrated all the way through the glass windows, to beat against the door of Jacqui's room, which unfortunately also faced west. I'd clipped the three-metre rods which formed the base of each awning to corresponding hooks anchored in the tiles, but the wind wrenched one free, sent it flailing like a loose sail, first skippering away from the house, then crashing, like the boom of a storm-tossed yacht, against the wooden pillars of the veranda. The other shades billowed, threatened to rip up more tiles. Somehow Jacqui, and Sophie in her room at the back of the house, remained asleep. I tried to help, clutching the metal rod tightly, as Andrew winched the shade back up under the eaves. We then tackled the other four awnings in a grim, cranky rush.

'Never leave them down!' Andrew hissed.

'Okay!' I shot back.

'They have to be rolled back up every night . . .'

'I can see that!'

The wind cackled and crowed, bent on division, dissension, destruction.

The morning dawned quiet, as if nothing had happened. I looked out of our bedroom window to spy a couple of tiny blue fairy wrens flitting here and there. Where did these miniature creatures hide during such a gale? How had they not been blown from their perch? Where did they live? More Australian mysteries. Their chirps were as weightless and enchanting as they were.

Down the hall, I could also hear Jacqui tuning up.

'Muh! Muh-uh!'

I never needed an alarm.

But Andrew did. Some time between 4.00 and 6.45 a.m.—I had obviously slept through it—he'd left. Andrew had meetings at Telstra in his role as International Media Advisor. Later in the day he was off to Barcelona for a big telco conference. I hoped he could sleep on the plane.

I took a deep breath of the sweet air. The temperature had dropped 20 degrees—what was that in Celsius? I still thought in Fahrenheit, and clumsily converted when required. Regardless of what the thermometer said, the fresh, fragrant morning carried none of the brutish heat of the past few days.

So this was what was meant by a cool change. Ruefully, I realised I had once again been the victim of Australian under-statement. 'Cool change' had sounded peaceful, even melodic, the last note of a cascading C-major scale, rather than last night's *sturm und drang*, such Gothic aerial antics. I was learning that Australia was an elemental country. It did nothing by half-meas-ures. And living where we did, exposed, on the edge of a ridge, on a shard of land that jutted into forest, with sloping canyons on three of the four sides, we felt such changes acutely. After fifteen years in Gotham, I was out of touch with nature. New York humorist Fran Lebowitz put it best when she observed, 'To me the outdoors is what you must pass through in order to get from your apartment into a taxicab.'

It wasn't that I had no experience of terrifying gales, but it was mostly work-related. Somehow that was different. I'd chosen to go, and I was being paid for it. I remembered thinking I hadn't been paid enough when covering a storm called Hugo, many years before. The Category 5 hurricane had threatened to lift up the heavy satellite truck in which we cowered, and dash it into the Atlantic. But at least no one had pretended it was a 'cool change'. On this occasion, there had only been wind, not rain, but I was reminded that air was once considered one of the four basic elements. Like its brethren, earth, water and fire, it could be benign or calamitous, send kites soaring, or toss houses through the sky.

In spite of the change in the weather, or perhaps because of it, Jacqui was smouldering. She wailed as I changed her nappy, hurled her bowl of Weet-Bix across the table. I felt the bones in my shoulder stitch together, the tightness gather in my chest.

Only Sophie seemed unaffected, bright-eyed and quick as a squirrel, if also as forgetful. 'My lunch!' she squealed as we got into the Captiva for the drive to school. I waited as Jacqui, in her car seat behind me, kicked the seat relentlessly.

'Hurry up!' I barked, more harshly than I intended. I worked hard to prevent it, but sometimes Sophie bore the brunt of my frustration with her sister.

'Jacqui, please stop kicking!' I said.

Sophie was about to scramble back in, then yelped, 'My hat!'

I had already pushed the car into reverse, but she was opening the door and I slammed on the brakes, sending her lurching forward. 'Sophie, please be careful, or you'll kill yourself!'

'Mum, no hat, no play.'

'What?'

'I have to have my hat!! It's the law! I'll be right back.'

We arrived at Sophie's school to the strains of Michael Jackson singing 'ABC, easy as 1, 2, 3' booming from the loudspeaker. Her primary school played a different tune each morning just before the bell rang, a musical warning for students to climb off the playground equipment, collect their backpacks and troop to class. New York schools just rang the bell. I'd already unfastened Jacqui, so she could have a quick play, but she seemed rooted to the ground, transfixed, listening. Then, as Michael sang, 'Do, re, mi, 1, 2, 3, A, B, C baby you and me!' Jacqui began to jam. Heedless of the children walking past, she rocked, shook her curls, crouched low, butt extended, wiggling her hips, gyrating to the beat.

'Jacqui!' Sophie groaned, and rolled her eyes at her little sister.

'Wow! She's got some moves!' one of the other mums nodded appreciatively. I grinned back, tousled Jacqui's curls. My nearly four-year-old daughter couldn't talk, couldn't colour, couldn't write her name, couldn't slide down a slide or swing on a swing because she didn't have enough belly strength, but she sure could dance.

Normally, I didn't spend much time at Sophie's primary school. I didn't read with the children, like some other mums, or help out in the library. When I could, I went on a field trip, but it wasn't as often as I would have preferred. I liked the school, and would have liked to be there with Sophie, but I was always darting off to an appointment of Jacqui's. Today we had speech therapy, followed by occupational therapy.

In New York, the therapists had come to our apartment. This wasn't a special privilege; it was simply that on a small island with mass transit, it made more sense to send able-bodied therapists darting across the city than try to move children with special needs, especially since many mothers had more than one child in tow.

Living here was, to put it mildly, a massive change. Jacqui and I lived in the car. Two days a week we travelled to Port Melbourne for kinder; on the other days, we drove to Woodend for early intervention. The two locations were 75 kilometres apart. There were also other specialist appointments around the region. I reminded myself that the Melbourne commute would likely only last for a year or two; when Jacqui got better, she could go to a mainstream primary school with her big sister, nearby. But in the meantime, there was a lot of driving. Some days I wound up with a massive headache, and I had finally realised it was from the cumulative effect of so much novelty. It surprised me, because I was enjoying discovering new places.

But it could also be mentally exhausting. There was the fact that I was driving on the wrong—*opposite*, I was supposed to say opposite!—side of the road. Yet Australia, bless this trusting, kind-hearted country, had not asked me to take a road test. They'd simply looked at my New York licence, checked my eyesight and handed over permission to drive in Australia. I did not feel compelled to mention that I mostly used my New York licence as identification, since I generally travelled by taxi in the city. It had been a while since I'd had to drive every day, and back then, I hadn't shared the road with trams. Melburnians love them with an almost patriotic fervour, but I preferred trains that ran underground.

There was also the fact that Jacqui's various appointments could be all over the city, and I often had no idea where I was going. Melbourne was vast, and its traffic confusing. I was getting accustomed to roundabouts, but cursed the sadist who invented the 'hook turn', a right turn from the left lane, across multiple lanes of traffic. Exactly who thought this was a good idea? I was exceedingly careful, and never had an accident, but I often found my palms sweaty when I finally stopped.

Driving in the various villages in our area, by contrast, was positively relaxing. Free parking was limited—to three hours. Spaces were generous. There seemed to be a coffee shop on every corner, most of which were excellent. I found I was constantly comparing and contrasting the two countries, in trivial as well as important ways; noticing subtle and significant differences.

A compulsive reader, I always checked out the noticeboards while Jacqui had an appointment. I enjoyed the variety of the offerings to be found in country Victoria, compared to those back home. New York boards might proclaim: *Opera Singing Lessons, $100 dollars per half hour*; *Write Your Own Screenplay*; *Method Acting Made Easy*; or *Take Your Next Cruise on Gay Cruise Line!*

Here the noticeboard reported: *Pony for Sale, bomb proof.* That sounded intriguing. Had the pony been to Sarajevo? What exactly was a bomb-proof pony? I liked to think no one had tried. Then there was: *Wanted, Four Wheeler.* I had never been on one—I wanted one too. I could also *Learn to play the Guitar;* or sign Jacqui up for a local toddler playgroup, although it conflicted with our drive to her school in the city. I was surprised to see a notice offering *Rabbits for Sale.* Wasn't this the country of the rabbit-proof fence, bent on exterminating this introduced pestilence with the Calicivirus? Why would people raise rabbits as pets? It seemed odd.

One day, I saw a notice posted on a government bulletin board which struck me as hilarious. It detailed the existence of a hitherto unknown treasure: the Australian National Public Toilet Map. I could download my own copy if I so desired.

What a wealthy, healthy and organised country to create such a website. I could plan our next family holiday around conveniently located public facilities. Keep a copy in my hip pocket, for handy reference. Curiosity got the better of me, not to mention I had more time on my hands these days. I promptly checked out the Australian Toilet Map and discovered I could key in a street address and learn the location of the nearest public loo. I tried to imagine the US creating such a map. Impossible, because we didn't have many public toilets, a scarcity which was a frequent criticism of foreign visitors. But I had also observed that in Australia, the prevalence of public loos made it possible for many large grocery stores and trendy cafés to avoid providing facilities for customers—tricky for a mum trying to toilet train a child, as I was.

Who had researched this project, I wondered, made sure it was up to date?

Unbidden, an image occurred to me, a variation of the famous World War II US Army recruitment poster of Uncle Sam exhorting, *I Want You. You are being hired for an important job! You can help your country! Help us help you, to ensure the National Toilet Map is up to date!* Terrible puns sprang to mind, including Royal Flush, and I found myself humming a potential theme song, from Jacqui's CD of catchy Australian tunes, '*There was a redback on the toilet seat when I was there last night . . .*'

I turned away from the bulletin board to see someone staring at me, and realised I was laughing out loud. I turned the laugh into a gentle cough. I really, really needed to get out more, if this was enough to amuse me.

✳

There was a great deal to learn about Australia. There were also things to un-learn.

'Does Jacqui know sign language?' the therapist asked. Sign language was often used for hearing children who had a speech delay, to prompt language.

'Oh yes,' I said, amplifying my response with the correct sign. The therapist looked quizzical. 'Hmm. *This* is how we say "yes",' she'd corrected, instead making a fist and bobbing it up and down.

'How do you sign "more"?' she asked me.

I pinched the fingers of each hand together, then bumped them together in front of me. She shook her head slowly, then opened her right hand wide, and slid it down her chest.

'More.' She countered.

'What about please?' I asked.

Again, the signs were completely different.

Our entire family had devoted hours to watching sign language videos, including 'My Baby Can Talk'; Sophie signed to Jacqui all the time. I remembered Jacqui's first actual sentence, which had been in sign language. Never mind that she'd been trying to evade difficult core work on the therapy ball at the time. We were thrilled that she could communicate, and instantly granted her request for 'More cookies please!'

'By any chance, is this the sign for cookie? I mean, for biscuit?' I asked, demonstrating.

The therapist shook her head in amusement. 'Not exactly. You've just signed "toilet".'

I pictured Jacqui eagerly and repeatedly pushing her index finger into the palm of her hand and nodding optimistically as she angled for her favourite treat, only to be ushered to the nearest bathroom.

'You'd better show me that one,' I said. 'Sounds like we will all be learning a new language. You'd think it would be the same in the US and Australia, since we both speak English!'

'You would, wouldn't you? But in the US, the deaf use American Sign Language. We use Auslan. And for children like Jacqui, we do keyword signing, which is basically a streamlined version of Auslan. I suspect that part is the same—you simply sign the most important words in the sentence, and that helps children focus, and express their needs.

'But remember, sign is meant to be used in conjunction with speech, because we want Jacqui to talk.' She cleared her throat. 'And one more thing. It is best to speak in short, clear sentences.' She paused. 'I notice that you are, well, very verbal.'

I must have bristled, because she smiled encouragingly. 'That's fine, of course, and probably worked well with Sophie. But with Jacqui, the length of your sentence should be one word longer than the length of hers.'

'But she can only say one or two words at most, and that's only if she's very motivated. You are talking about a "sentence" of one or two words.'

'That sounds about right. So, instead of saying, "Jacqui, come on, it's time to eat your breakfast", it's best to say, "Breakfast, Jacqui". Do you hear the difference?'

I indicated my newfound knowledge. 'Yes.'

Encouraged, she continued, 'When you speak in lengthy sentences, it is confusing for Jacqui. The notes from her New York therapists indicate she has delayed auditory processing—it takes time for spoken language to get through, for her to process what you have said. That's why short sentences work better.'

As I was learning, and had been learning since the day Jacqui had been born, having a child with special needs was a daily reminder that I had absolutely no idea what I was doing. I'd found motherhood intuitive with Sophie. Verbal, like me, she delighted in word games, loved hearing animated stories, adored books. She was social, gregarious, naturally played well with others. She was also a spectacular traveller. When Sophie was one I'd taken her and a nanny with me on a month-long assignment to the Winter

Olympics in Salt Lake City. Sophie and I had taken a whirlwind mother–daughter trip to see friends in the UK when she was two-and-a-half. She had done brilliantly on both occasions. A veteran traveller, I had imagined that I could fly solo with both girls, and hoped to take them back to the US with me once a year, so they could stay in touch with the American half of their family. But I struggled to get Jacqui to the playground without shenanigans.

When it came to Jacqui, it seemed much of what I tried naturally was dead wrong. I spoke in lengthy, complicated sentences, filled with juicy words. Bad.

I was animated, both because it was my nature, and in order to gain Jacqui's attention. Bad.

I had been gently reproved that this actually *over*-stimulated her, prompted the screaming and shrieking we tried so hard to avoid. I should try to be calm, even monotone, and that would help Jacqui to be the same. I was trying.

I even had to learn how to walk. Simply taking Jacqui by the hand and strolling down the street, as I would have done with Sophie, led to disaster. Jacqui would pull away, lash out at a stranger, or simply institute a sit-down strike, even in the midst of crossing the road. She did not want to walk—it was hard work. I lived in fear that I would pull her arm out of its socket in a desperate attempt to prevent her from being struck by a car. And yet, I'd seen her walk for several blocks with her New York therapist, who was an expert in ABA—Applied Behaviour Analysis. Born from the pioneering work of American psychologist B.F. Skinner, ABA therapy employed a mixture of psychological and educational strategies to change behaviour—reinforcing desired behaviours, and attempting to extinguish negative ones. It was widely used to help children with Autism Spectrum Disorder.

'What's your secret?' I had been forced to ask, as I watched Jacqui walk compliantly by her side.

'Random positive reinforcement.'

'I beg your pardon?'

73

She had pulled a plastic bag from her pocket. 'Give her tiny treats. A piece of pretzel. A blueberry. A chocolate button. But mix it up, so she doesn't know what she's getting. The order is random, but it's always something good that she'll like. Dole them out as you walk along, and she'll walk better.'

'Would you be offended if I told you this reminds me of dog training?'

She'd leaned forward, given me a conspiratorial wink. 'Shh, don't tell. Before I trained in ABA therapy, I was a dog trainer!'

I liked our therapists, both the ones in the US and those in Australia. They were universally smart and competent, patient and kind. And I found the educational theories underpinning their successful strategies to be interesting. There was a wealth of new information about people whose brains were wired differently, and I always had a new book on the bedside table, trying to master it all. The reporter in me relished a new project, and I was learning a great deal. But the truth was that I sometimes also found it dispiriting, even humiliating. Because I knew this was much more than an assignment. I couldn't afford to fail. This was my daughter. It was my job to help her get better.

Some strategies worked, to our relief. Then I felt clever, hopeful. But many others did not, or only worked for a while. Furthermore, while every strategy seemed obvious, once an expert had explained it, it was rarely my intuitive response to a situation. Not to mention, it was easier said than done. I was not a natural. I understood how Jacqui felt. This was hard work. I wasn't sure she'd gotten the right mum.

I missed reporting, where I felt competent. Where everything happened quickly, and fast reflexes, animation and verbal dexterity were assets, not liabilities. Where there was not the crushing burden of compulsory slowness. Because when I tried to slow down, I got bored. I knew that I shouldn't, that it was wrong. I loved both my daughters to distraction. I cherished one-on-one time with Sophie. And I adored Jacqui's merry blue eyes, so full of mysteries and mischief. But I desperately wanted to find a way inside her brain in order to kick over those invisible orange cones, the roadblocks that made her path to learning so laboured and tortuous. In good form, she was a sprite, eyebrows arching to express engagement, her fabulous giggle erupting when we amused her. She was delightful as a fairy wren.

But then the wind would change, a front would blast through. Then her eyebrows weather-vaned into indignation, angled to indicate an impending squall. I found it hard to read the barometer, difficult to know when to predict laughter, what might provoke rage. And there were so many storms, so much frustration. When Jacqui arched her back in rage at some internal discomfort, or because I couldn't understand her, I found it hard not to take it personally. And most especially when she dropped to all fours and slammed her head against the tiles, again and again, or purposely stood against a wall and slammed the back of her head into it, sometimes leaving a hole, I shuddered against my own howling hurricane. I felt buffeted by sorrow, desperation and inadequacy; and, though I pushed it down, down, down, rage as well. I felt alone, alone on a mountain of lament, the wind howling.

Thus I looked forward to our appointments with the experts. I felt deeply grateful to work with women—and they were all women—trained to reach Jacqui, to teach Jacqui; yet, even as I learned more, perversely, every visit deepened my feeling of impotence and inadequacy.

I tried to keep my eyes on the prize. Physiotherapy. Occupational therapy. Speech. Early intervention. Kinder. There was a plan, there was a schedule, there was a goal.

I would do what they said. And if I did what they said, and if I followed the rules, and if I followed the plan, then Jacqui would get better.

I clung to a deep conviction that Jacqui was bright. Forget the IQ test. She was not even four. I'd seen that spark in her eyes,

I knew! Yes, there was a delay, but we all learned at a different rate. She could learn, even catch up. There were no limits, only possibilities. She would get better. She had to. And one year, not this year, perhaps, but next year, or the year after that, she'd be at primary school with Sophie. In the playground with the other children. All those smiling, happy, bouncy, perfect little children.

And yet, deep down, fear howled. Fear that trying to fix Jacqui was like trying to tame the wind.

Andrew was still in Spain. Sophie, Jacqui and I had just returned from the pool, where we'd had a late afternoon swim. Although she was only just learning to put her head under water and to blow bubbles, time in the pool was great for Jacqui. She was a water baby. But she didn't want too much direction. We had tried to take a class with other mums, but it hadn't been successful. Jacqui's attention span was roughly five minutes long. After that, she demanded change.

Fortunately, the local aquatic centre offered classes for children with special needs from a dynamo of a teacher named Leah. I was deeply impressed and appreciative that a small town found the resources for one-on-one instruction for those with special needs. Jacqui adored her teacher, and we hoped one day our daughter might actually learn to swim. In the meantime, time in the water wasn't just fun, but improved lung strength, which might facilitate more speech. Jacqui had had a good lesson, but she was tired, and a bit clumsy. Time to get her and her big sister to bed.

The phone rang. Sophie answered it. 'It's Nana,' she said.

'Ana,' repeated Jacqui.

'Nana,' I said slowly. I touched one finger to the side of my nose. I'd just taken a seminar on Cued Articulation with Rhonda, our speech therapist in Woodend, learning prompts which helped encourage children to make sounds they couldn't. It was very successful, and I was excited to try it with Jacqui.

'Nana,' I prompted again, touching my finger to the outside of my nose and pressing in gently, to indicate this was a nasal sound.

Jacqui gave me a humorous look. Was this some sort of bizarre mummy dare? Staring straight at me, she pointed her index finger and stuck it straight up her right nostril, laughing hysterically.

'Ah-nah!' she chortled gleefully. I laughed in spite of myself.

'You imp! Sorry, Nana,' I said, 'I'll explain later. Jacqui's just proving once again that any lesson we teach, she can subvert.'

Nana chuckled. 'Dear little Jacqui. How is she? And how is Sophie? I'm sure you must all miss Andrew dreadfully. Are you all right there, all on your own?'

Nana and Pa lived an hour from us, and worried when Andrew was away on lengthy trips.

'We're fine. He'll be home in a few days. He kept the trip as short as he could.' I thanked Nana, and rang off. It was 7 p.m.

'Come here, Jac, time to put on your PJs,' I said.

Sophie wandered in, wearing footy pyjamas and carrying a toothbrush. 'Can I have a story?'

'Yes, as soon as I get Jacqui to bed,' I said. Jacqui was not being cooperative, and I was tired. I tried to help her, but she took a funny step. And before I knew it, Jacqui had tripped, toppled over and fallen backwards, hitting the tile floor with a clunk. I sucked in my breath.

But it was too late. I could see that she was already shaking, violently. Damn it, she was having a seizure—the first one in many months. Technically, Jacqui didn't have epilepsy, but with her fragile wiring, the bump had been enough to trigger a major convulsion.

'Mum, what is wrong? Sophie called out. 'What's wrong with Jacqui? Is she having a—?'

'Yes, honey, but it's okay.'

'How do you know? How do you know it's okay? I want Daddy,' wailed six-year-old Sophie.

'Hush, Sophie, Daddy's in Spain.'

'I WANT MY DADDY!'

Sophie was jumping up and down, wringing her hands and crying so hard that snot was coming out of her nose. I wanted to reach out and hold her close, but had to turn back to Jacqui, lying beside me in her nappy, pyjamas tangled around her ankles. She was frighteningly pale. That was just the seizure, I reminded myself, as her right eye blinked open, shut, open, shut, sightless. Her right arm moved backwards and forwards as if she were running an imaginary race. Bubbles of froth burbled out of her mouth.

'Is she going to die? Is she going to die? Mum, is Jacqui going to die?'

'No, honey, she just hit her head, that's all. She is going to be fine.'

I struggled for calm, but Sophie was spinning out of control. I suddenly felt very alone.

'Soph, I have an idea. I have David and Mary's number on the fridge. Be a good girl and call them.'

'What about an ambulance?'

I considered. I didn't think we needed one. We knew from experience that Jacqui would come out of the seizure—hers tended to last two to three minutes. But I could see that Sophie was hysterical, and Jacqui had hit her head. I also knew why Sophie was so hysterical, and it was my fault.

'You know what, that is a good idea. Bring me the phone and I'll dial 911.'

'Triple O,' said Sophie.

'Exactly, I'll dial 000.'

As I called the ambulance, Sophie calmed down. The experts were coming.

I cursed myself internally for what had happened nearly two years before, in New York. On that occasion, Andrew had also been overseas. I'd been in our apartment with the girls, when Jacqui had taken a fall far worse than this one had been. I could still hear the sickening crack as the back of her head smashed into a coffee table. To this day, I wondered if that had in some way reignited her occasional seizures.

I'd scooped up my two-year-old daughter, who'd suddenly begun convulsing, horribly. She was frothing, had turned blue, and her breathing was short and shallow. I was terrified the fall had caused brain damage, because it looked as if she was dying. I'd shouted to Sophie to hand me the phone. But she had interrupted with dozens of questions.

Desperate, I'd said something I'd never said before. 'Sophie! Please just shut up! You must be quiet and hand me the phone!'

Without a word, lip trembling, Sophie handed me the phone.

I rarely raised my voice at my then five-year-old daughter and had never, ever dreamt I would say such a terrible thing. Even as the words tumbled out of my mouth, I felt appalled and ashamed. But there would be time to apologise later. Right then we desperately needed an ambulance.

But the ambulance took forever, and Jacqui was limp, unconscious and a terrifying colour. I grabbed Sophie's hand and dashed out of the apartment. The hospital was only a few kilometres away—we would take a taxi. I'd also rung our babysitter, whom we saw downstairs. Sherry had taken one look at Jacqui, and gasped. During the drive to the hospital she bent her head and repeated, 'Please lord, please lord, please lord.'

Five minutes later we were surrounded by experts. Jacqui's convulsions had ended but she remained unconscious. Sophie began chatting to the nurses and doctors on the other side of the drawn white curtains. Just then, my phone rang.

'Sara, are you okay?' asked a woman at our apartment building.

'Yes. I'm at the hospital with Jacqui and Sophie. Jacqui had a fall but I do think she is going to be all right. How did you know?'

'Thank goodness. There's an ambulance here, and a police officer who says he has to talk to you.'

I was mortified. 'What?'

'They say you rang 911. The ambulance arrived, but you were gone, so they called the police.'

'You're kidding, right?'

'Sorry, no. Here's the officer.'

There was a fumbling sound, followed by a gruff hello and, 'How's the kid?'

'Hello, officer. She's okay, thank you.'

'Good to hear. Don't mind saying, we were worried. About to file a missing person's report, as a matter of fact.' His tone had turned incredulous, and somewhat suspicious. 'Do you realise you left your purse? Left your front door wide open?'

'I did?' I looked at Jacqui on the white hospital bed. Still unconscious, but her colour was normal, and she looked peaceful. The doctors said she would be all right. How was it that I could be so calm in a crisis that affected others, but found it so much harder when it was my own emergency? I looked down. I'd even forgotten to put on my shoes.

'You did.'

'Officer, I am very sorry to have troubled you. We rushed to the hospital. The ambulance was slow, so we took a taxi.'

He sounded more sympathetic. Ambulances often got stuck in city traffic, and were notoriously slow.

'It's okay, I'm only saying.' After asking a few more questions, he hung up, only to show up at the hospital a half hour later. The officer handed me my purse. I knew he was checking out my story, but I still liked him for it.

'New York's finest,' I smiled.

He'd cracked a grin, patted Jacqui with a baseball mitt of a hand. 'Cute kid. Hope she gets better soon.' Then he'd high-fived Sophie, who was agog at his blue uniform and proximity, and was gone.

I'd dealt much better with Jacqui's seizures ever since, but Sophie hadn't fully let down her guard. I was reminded, again, that this business of having a child with special needs affected everyone in the family. Sophie was only six-and-a-half. Daddy was in Spain. Jacqui was still unconscious, but the seizure had ended. I was calm as I called the ambulance, and we stayed exactly where we were. Then we called our neighbour David, who dropped by and chatted to Sophie while we waited.

By the time the ambulance arrived, Jacqui could sit up, although she still couldn't speak. At least her colour was back to normal.

'Want to see the lights on our ambulance?' one of the crew asked Sophie, while the other took Jacqui's vitals.

'Cool! That would be great!' Sophie scampered down the hall in her footy pyjamas. Jacqui opened her mouth like a baby bird, but no sound came out.

'You'll be okay, darling,' I said. I pulled her close, tucked her under my wing. 'It was just a seizure. It was just a seizure.'

I wondered who I was trying to convince.

7

CATCHING PEACOCKS

I was on a trim blue launch, motoring out of the narrow harbour at Scorpios, the secluded island that had once belonged to one of the richest men in the world. From the stern, I watched the lush vegetation recede, the drooping clouds of bougainvillea. I could no longer see the house, with its art, treasure trove of books, at once elegant and simple; a home which looked as though its occupants had been here yesterday, instead of years before. This was Sleeping Beauty's island—waiting for a princess to reawaken.

We'd filmed all around the island, including the chapel, where Jacqueline Bouvier Kennedy had become Jackie O, all part of a *Dateline* story on a new book about a woman America would always remember as the Queen of Camelot. In an interview after President Kennedy's assassination, the former First Lady had likened the promise of the Kennedy era to the legend of Camelot and King Arthur. Then in 1968, in the most celebrated wedding of its day, she had married a legendary Greek shipping tycoon, Aristotle Onassis, and moved to his private island. The producer and I stared out at the brilliant blue water, talking about how inviting it appeared on such a hot day, about the luxury of having your own island, your own sea—now abandoned, no one to use it. And then we looked at one another, a glance which contained an unspoken dare. With a '3, 2, 1!' we leapt, fully clothed, into the exquisite Ionian Sea. Totally unprofessional. And so much fun.

I woke up.

Someone had recently told me that Melbourne had the largest Greek population of any city in the world outside Greece. That fact apparently had been enough to trigger this delicious dream, the latest in a series related to my former job. Each night, I was treated to a nocturnal resumé reel. It didn't matter that I was enjoying my new life. When I closed my eyes, I became a nomad, restlessly roaming. I was just like most every other mum who'd had a job she really liked before having children. We loved our kids, had wanted them, fiercely enough to make sacrifices. But loving your children didn't preclude loving other things. That was the dissonance, the tension, denied by day, dreamt by night. Each night, I sneaked out for an illicit rendezvous with my former life, former self.

But this dream had yet another layer. It didn't take a psychiatrist to recognise the significance, and it made me smile to think of what lay ahead. I had a new reporting assignment on the horizon, which would take me to another fascinating island.

Just then a sound distracted me. It was still dark, an hour before sunrise. The kookaburras hadn't begun their maniacal cackling, but I could very distinctly hear pigs snorting.

I had a flashback to that Outback adventure with Steve and Terri Irwin. We'd been travelling through thick bush in Far North Queensland, when the caravan Steve had been driving stopped suddenly, and he darted into the scrub. Our cameraman lumbered after him, and the producer and I were hot on their heels, wondering what sort of deadly creature had been discovered. Instead, all Grade Three grin and enthusiasm, the Crocodile Hunter returned cradling a piglet.

'He's cute all right, but crikey, they're a real menace,' he told us. 'Feral pigs are a major problem in the bush.'

I poked Andrew awake. 'Are there feral pigs in the Wombat?'

'Wha . . .?'

'Pigs. I'm sure I heard pigs out there.'

He rolled over, perplexed, then punched my arm. 'You woke me up for that? Those aren't pigs. They're koalas, Boof.'

'Noooo. Nothing that adorable could sound like that.'

'Yup. They sound exactly like you when you snore.'

'I do NOT snore.'

'Says you.'

I lay there, enjoying the brief indulgence of being awake without responsibility, flipping through the deck of cards with its images of my life, past and present.

There was a plaintive bleat from down the hall. I hauled myself out of bed, wandered down to Jacqui's bedroom door to be greeted by a cheeky grin, arms outstretched.

'Wee-bix!' she nodded hopefully. The Australian favourite would never be my choice for breakfast, any more than I'd ever understand Vegemite on toast, but then again, I liked a good peanut butter and jelly sandwich. I was just delighted we had a promising Jacqui weather forecast.

'Good morning, sunshine,' I scooped her up. 'Remember, lips together. No teeth.'

It had been nearly three months since Jacqui's seizure, and she was back to normal. Back to Jacqui normal, at any rate. Andrew spoke of her seizures in computer terms, as a reboot. The massive electrical discharge seemed to wipe out memory, leave her like a blank screen. Jacqui would wake up, only to stare at us vacantly. It was as if she had forgotten everything she'd ever learned. She couldn't say a single word, struggled to walk. For a day, she would cling tightly to us. Then, one by one, skills would return. And we would stop holding our breath.

I wished again that I knew what exactly was wrong with our little girl. Surely there must be an answer, if only we could discover what it was. When she was irritable following a seizure,

I feared she must be experiencing some internal static, disordered thinking or even pain, though it was difficult for her to express such concepts. For weeks after an event, she would be especially short-tempered and tempestuous. I thought of the convulsion as akin to a massive earthquake, and attributed Jacqui's instability to waves of aftershocks in the wake of a seismic event.

At least this seizure was behind us. If we were lucky, it might even have been the last one. As long as we prevented her from another fall, as long as she didn't come down with a high fever, everything should be okay. The wiring of a child's brain usually grew stronger as she grew older, which was why many children outgrew seizures. Fingers crossed.

Sophie was already at the breakfast table, buttering her toast.

'Ha Zozo,' chirped Jacqui.

'Hi Child. Hey Mum, did you hear the koalas in the woods last night?' Sophie asked.

'I sure did.'

I marvelled at how quickly Sophie was learning to decode the bush. Swimming in the warm waters of Australian culture, she was acclimatising. After initially dining out on her American accent—'the kids call me America! They keep asking me to say peanut butter and cookie!'—she had suddenly gone native. She had an Aussie accent. She spent hours in the forest with her new friend Olivia, building forts, learning about wildlife. And although she knew next to nothing about Australian Rules football, she'd suddenly announced that she was a Collingwood fan. Andrew, who barracked for North Melbourne, was horrified.

'It's not such a big deal,' I consoled him. Then seeing his face, asked, 'Is it?'

Americans adored sports, to be sure, but Australia's obsession was in a class of its own. In Victoria, the Sherrin football was practically a religious icon. Many footy matches were actually played at the enormous 'G—the MCG or Melbourne Cricket Ground—in the heart of the city. I was astonished to learn that the venerable stadium hosted an *average* crowd of 50,000 specta-tors for matches, and that often double that number turned out for major events. Collingwood, with rival Carlton, held the record for an AFL Grand Final. More than 121,000 hyperventilating fans had packed the 'G, back in 1970. Yet both teams were from Melbourne, as were the majority of the other teams in the league. The biggest crowd ever at a US Super Bowl was only 104,000 people. Was no one interested in anything else?

The importance of the footy had not been lost on Sophie, who had gone so far as to ask for a black-and-white Magpies scarf to wear to school.

'What are you going to do?' I asked Andrew.

'Leave it with me,' he answered mysteriously.

When Sophie sat down for breakfast that morning, Andrew turned to her. 'So, Soph. What's this I hear about Collingwood? Forget it. You will *not* support the Pies. Now, repeat after me, "Go, you Mighty Roo boys!!"'

Having heard tales of children threatened with disinheritance or an orphanage if they chose a different club from Mum or Dad, I was not surprised by this edict, nor by his later purchase of blue-and-white gear festooned with kangaroos and a club membership. Whatever it took.

Like me, Sophie had a lot to learn. She had been at her new school for a week when the assistant principal asked her, 'What is the constellation on the Australian flag?'

'The Southern Cross,' she replied instantly.

'That is correct,' he answered, then continued guilelessly, 'Now how did you know that? Did you see it in the sky in New York?'

'Yes!' Sophie answered, to her immediate chagrin, as the other children began laughing.

While Australia was more casual in many ways than the States, school was actually an exception, and the uniform but one example. In the US, we mostly sang 'The Star Spangled

Banner' on the Fourth of July and at sporting events—unofficially, the last two words of the song were, 'Play ball!' But at Sophie's first primary-school assembly, we discovered that students sang 'Advance Australia Fair' each and every week. Spying her confusion, the principal photocopied the words, and Sophie promptly memorised both verses. A few weeks later, at the end of assembly, the principal complimented my older daughter on how well she was doing. Sophie beamed as Jacqui and I stood by. Then, to our great surprise, the principal suddenly said, 'Ouch!'

Sophie and I whirled on Jacqui, a notorious opportunist. Sure enough, she had seen a bare arm, and—perhaps feeling jealous or ignored, or maybe just in a bad temper—had chomped.

'I am so sorry!' I told the principal, mortified. I never knew how to explain Jacqui's impulsive behaviour, which sometimes made me fret about the prospect of ever enrolling our youngest at a mainstream school. But with an understanding look for me and a smile for Sophie, the principal said not to worry. Sophie shot Jacqui a death stare.

On this particular morning, Sophie was using yet another of her coping strategies for Jacqui, one I understood but which also grieved me. She ignored her. Sophie munched her toast and read *Harry Potter and the Philosopher's Stone*, which was propped on the breakfast table beside her. As I placed a bowl of cereal in front of Jacqui, debating whether to intercede, there was an eerie howl, and Sophie instantly looked up. First koalas pretending to be pigs, now this.

'That sounds like coyotes—though it can't be, of course,' I said.

'Loty,' Jacqui mimicked, and I smiled. She was getting a few more words—or parts of words, anyway.

'Dingos,' Sophie corrected, although it was difficult to hear the word clearly through the toast crumbs.

'Hey, Soph, don't talk with your mouth full. And please include

Jacqui when you talk. She's trying to be part of the conversation. Did you say dingos? I didn't know there were any here.'

'Yep. Izzy says there's a dingo sanctuary near us—just over there,' she reported with a wave towards the ridge on the other side of the ravine. She spoke with the confidence of a White House reporter whose source is the President. I knew seven-year-old Isabel. This was indeed rock-solid intel.

'Well that's pretty interesting. Though I can't think of dingos without thinking of Lindy Chamberlain,' I shook my head. 'The dingo ate—'

'Who?' Sophie asked.

'Never mind. Before your time.'

'Mum, when are we getting a dog?' Sophie asked, seamlessly switching gears from reporter to lobbyist. Her pleas for a pet had begun when she was two, and I'd secretly saved a few of the imperious 'I want a dog!' pictures she'd posted around the apartment when she was four.

'Soon.'

'But Mum, in New York you said we'd get one when we got here.'

'I did, and we will. But not today. And before you ask, not tomorrow. In the meantime, you have wild animals. Just have a look!'

I glanced outside where several cockatoos were strutting across the veranda. Each day they seemed to become bolder, to venture closer. As I watched, one landed on the back of a chair, and stared at us appraisingly through the glass.

'Do you think we can tame them?' Sophie asked.

'I don't know. But Dad got Aunty Katie to buy us a huge bag of bird seed, even though she thinks we're crazy to feed them.'

Suddenly, Sophie leapt out of her chair, 'Mum, look what else is out there!' I followed the direction of her outstretched arm. As elegant as he was out of place, a handsome peacock was breakfasting on our front lawn.

First, dreaming of islands, and now, seeing a bird which was as much an immigrant as I was, and which just happened to be the symbol for American network NBC. A stylised peacock adorned every NBC staffer's business card, and for many years, the network slogan had been 'Proud as a Peacock'. This was a prophetic morning.

Just then Andrew walked in, and he also noticed the bird.

'Not a bad view,' he grinned. Andrew liked our property more all the time. 'Do you think it belongs to that woman who owns the wildlife park?' he asked.

'You mean Penny?' I answered, nodding. 'Sounds likely. They're not exactly native.'

Sophie and I looked at each other. 'There's one way to find out. Sophie, if you hurry, we might be able to check this out on the way to school,' I instructed.

Within five minutes, Sophie was in the car. I marvelled at the power of a potential visit to this intriguing local resident. Sophie had even remembered her hat, backpack and lunch. I buckled Jacqui in and we were off.

✳

No road trip in America was complete without massive billboards, a sight I didn't miss. The signs which dotted our region were far more pleasing: small, hand-painted, seasonal advertisements for eggs or honey or homemade jams, cherries or daffodils, even horse or chicken manure. The sign for Penny's place said simply 'Chickens for Sale/Emu Farm'. It was not far from another hand-lettered sign advertising an archery centre. I hoped there wasn't much overlap. I'd been looking for an opportunity to check out the Macedon Park Emu Farm, and this was it. The Captiva juddered down a pebbly road, which wove through the thick bush, ending at attractive iron gates set into stone pillars, already open at 8.15 in the morning. We drove through.

Tucked in among a well-cultivated garden was a quaint cottage, with Victorian flourishes. We pulled into the circular driveway, and surprised an elderly Border Collie that stretched and stood at attention, in the manner of its breed. There was a collection of sheds and fenced paddocks. A few geese honked, and what I guessed must be guinea fowl wandered by. There were waddling ducks, and the sign had promised chooks. Poultry heaven.

Opposite the house was a vast rolling paddock in which a bunch of emus was grazing. Or would that be a herd, or perhaps a flock? I certainly didn't know. Nor could I pick out the rogue female who had frolicked down our lane, but I felt sure Penny would know exactly who the culprit was. The fence appeared to have been reinforced recently, perhaps to prevent future nights out on the town. The rolling property was as neat as the back nine at Augusta the day before the Masters. Alerted by the sound of the car on the gravel, the front door opened and Penny emerged. Trotting out behind her was a small black lamb wearing a nappy.

'Good morning!' Penny hailed us cheerfully. 'Bring the girls in, have a cup of tea with Bindi and me.' She gestured towards her ankle. On cue, the lamb head-butted her. Sophie was already halfway up the steps when Penny asked, 'Would you like to meet my little one?' in her charming Macedonian accent.

'Oh, yes, please. Did you name Bindi after Steve Irwin's daughter?'

Penny smiled. 'Exactly! I like her. She is very brave.'

'Does Bindi go inside your house?' Sophie asked, incredulous.

Andrew's family ran a beautiful farm, but livestock were not given house privileges.

'Yes. She has lost her mummy and I must feed her by the bottle. She's called a poddy lamb.' There was a gust of wind and Penny shivered. 'Bindi stays inside because it was very cold when she was born, even colder than now, and she was tiny. She would have died otherwise. So until the weather warms up, she lives with me. That's why she wears a nappy!' she laughed.

'Where does she sleep?' Sophie asked.

'Why, in a cot of course,' Penny responded. Sophie stared at Penny as if Glinda the Good Witch had suddenly landed on the veranda in her bubble. The lamb butted Penny yet again, more urgently. 'Come inside, I'll show you. You can feed Bindi for me.' I glanced at my watch. Did it matter if we were five minutes late to school? How often would Sophie get a chance to feed a baby lamb in a nappy?

Penny handed Sophie a bottle with a large, rubbery nipple. As Penny heated the kettle for our tea, Sophie stroked the lamb gently, careful to keep the bottle upright. Jacqui watched in fascination as Bindi guzzled her way through her feed with the speed and gusto of a university freshman at his first fraternity party.

I filled Penny in on the peacock which had appeared on our front lawn, and she clapped her hands delightedly. 'Is that where he has gone! We have been looking for him. A dog came and scared him, and he flew away a week ago. Imagine, he has gotten as far as your house! Wait a moment, please—I will be right back.'

I took that minute to look around me, and admired Penny's spotless cottage, its honey-coloured floors gleaming. Sure enough, a portable crib, lined with piles of clean rags, sat in the living room. Bindi wasn't the only animal inside the house. There were also two languid cats, the Border Collie, who, though still on duty, seemed to recognise Bindi did not need to be herded, and a box on the counter near a fresh loaf of bread. The box was cheeping.

Sophie drew close, wide-eyed, and I kept my hands on Jacqui's shoulders, so her little hands would stay by her sides. Penny returned carrying what looked like a butterfly net, and gently opened the lid of the incubator for Sophie, who climbed on a chair for a closer look. 'Soon they will hatch and I will have more baby chicks,' Penny told Sophie. 'These I will sell at the markets.'

Penny turned to me. 'If it is all right, I will drive to your house to try to catch my peacock.'

I nodded. 'Feel free. I left the gate open, in case. But do you think your peacock will still be there?'

'He might have gone into the forest, but he will come out again this evening. I will leave this net, and you can catch him and call me.' She said this in a straightforward manner, as if catching peacocks was my occupation. I must have looked disconcerted. 'Just leave out some seed, some bread. He will come.'

I felt very uncertain of my skills at peacock roundup, but we did have plenty of seed. And Sophie would have lots to talk about for show and tell at school.

It was increasingly clear that the Macedon Ranges were chock-full of characters, and I was intrigued. What was it about this place, indeed, about all of Australia, which bred and nourished such distinctive individuals? I had time to ruminate on this question, because I was on an aeroplane, by myself, for the first time in months.

Penny was but one example, I reflected. Take Canadians David and Mary, who had created their thriving Mount Gisborne Wines after cultivating their vineyard from an empty paddock, through years of hard work and vision. They now sold their Pinots and Chardonnays in fancy hotels and local shops.

Our neighbours Mick and Kate had a different but equally consuming passion for vintage vehicles. Mick worked for an airline. Joined by his wife and two daughters, he took regular trips to the States in search of old cars and trucks to restore. In addition to the half-dozen antiques neatly displayed under their veranda, another nine automobiles, in various stages of restoration, were actually kept inside their purpose-built house. A 1954 Ford F100 pickup truck was parked by the dining-room table, a classic T-Bird nestled next to the stairway, and a third vehicle under a tarp betrayed the distinctive, muscular silhouette of a Mustang Fastback, circa actor Steve McQueen's era. There were others I didn't recognise. Cars and trucks took up virtually every square metre of the ground floor of the family home, until Kate sighed and moved the kitchen upstairs. Andrew and Mick conversed frequently and at length about manifolds, carburettors, diff locks and gear ratios, and, of course, old Mustangs, speaking a creole of Car and Do-it-Yourself.

But perhaps our most famous neighbour was the stuntwoman turned wildlife warrior who lived down the road with her filmmaker partner, Brett. Their meeting, on location, sounded unforgettable. Brett had been filming as Sue performed a particularly daring fall from a considerable height, only to see her land with an ominous crack when the boxes below her collapsed. Clearly injured, Sue had somehow remained in character and actually walked off the set, escorted by an ambulance attendant. It turned out she had broken her back in several places. When I asked her about that potentially catastrophic injury, she'd given a rueful chuckle. It turned out that over the course of her career, Sue had broken sixteen bones in all. Fit and buff, she still had the energy of a teenager. Sue volunteered countless hours for Wildlife Victoria and the Macedon Ranges Wildlife Network, responding to emergency calls to rescue koalas, wombats, kangaroos and their joeys, most of which had been struck by cars.

On one occasion, Sue was even called to Melbourne's Tullamarine Airport to rescue a kangaroo which had somehow gotten onto the fifth floor of the multi-storey car park, to the astonishment of international tourists. To dart the terrified marsupial, Sue dropped to the cement floor and fired a tricky shot from beneath a parked car. Mission accomplished, the kangaroo had been released to a wide, green paddock not far away. Some of the recuperating kangaroos wound up at the couple's property next to the Wombat State Forest. Visitors had to be reminded to drive slowly to avoid the beautiful creatures, which could be seen grazing, or, when you got closer, lounging near the couple's veranda, next to washing pegged out to dry.

Not only were our neighbours remarkable, but they were remarkably self-sufficient—another trait I'd found in many Australians who lived in the bush. Their first response wasn't to dash to the store, as I was tempted to do, but to sit down and puzzle things out. They made do, or adapted. Attempted to catch a peacock with a butterfly net.

I was certain such self-reliance was born in part of Australia's famous isolation. While the internet, mobile phones and long-haul flights made life dramatically more connected than in the days of yore, the 'tyranny of distance' could not be entirely vanquished. Living here made it much easier to appreciate how Australia's separation from the rest of the world had enabled and required this continent to develop in a unique way, unseen, undisturbed.

Early on, Australia's virtual invisibility had made it the subject of wild conjecture. I'd stumbled across accounts of Gabriel de Foigny's 1676 book *La Terre Australe Connue*—a sort of French *Gulliver's Travels*—which purported to be the journal of a European traveller who discovered a Utopian civilisation of hermaphrodites living in Australia. De Foigny had been free to make up whatever he liked, without fear of contradiction, because there were precious few facts. It would be almost 100 years before Captain James Cook arrived.

By then, Australia had been left alone far longer than virtually any place else on the planet. My reading told me the most modern scientific theory: Australia had broken away from a supercontinent called Gondwana 140 million years ago, which was why 80 per cent of the country's flowering plants and its mammals—including all those varieties of marsupials I worshipped—as well as its frogs and reptiles, were unique to the continent. A handy Australian government website also informed me that the same was true for half of Australia's birds and most of its freshwater fish; marine species also ranged from the unusual to the only-found-here. No wonder they were so picky at Australian Customs.

I knew that Australia's first people, the Aborigines, were believed to have arrived some 40,000 to 65,000 years ago. Intriguingly, no one was precisely certain how they had accomplished this remarkable feat. Scientists had theories about boats; the Aborigines had stories of the Dreamtime. I was fascinated by those tales of totemic ancestors rising out of the earth, singing into creation people, animals and plants, even the landscape.

Having been to the Outback, I could appreciate how stunned those British explorers must have been, to find the Aborigines thriving in that spectacularly inhospitable terrain—to discover their babies weren't malnourished, but plump and healthy. To discover an estimated 600 different people groups, with their own languages. It had been the longest continuous cultural history of any people, anywhere, on Earth. A history that suffered abrupt, acute and cataclysmic change when the British chose to make Australia unique in a different way—as the first European nation begun as a gaol.

As an American, it was impossible not to muse over the many connections between the US and Australia, each with links to Mother England. Both nations had a great deal to answer for when it came to the treatment of indigenous peoples; in America, there had been the additional evil of slavery. But I had only learned when I met Andrew—a proud descendant of convicts—of another link: that the British only sent prisoners to Australia because they could no longer send them to America. I simply hadn't realised that this sociology experiment in the Antipodes was the unintended by-product of the United States winning its War of Independence.

While Sophie learned about the First Fleet in school, my childhood had been steeped in lore about the American Revolution. Raised in Virginia, I could rattle off facts about our famous native sons: Thomas Jefferson, author of the transcendent Declaration of Independence; George Washington, General for the Army of the Potomac and first President of the United States; James Madison, author of the Bill of Rights; and the fiery-haired lawyer Patrick Henry, with his rousing exhortation at Saint John's Church, in my hometown of Richmond. In fourth grade, I'd memorised sections of that speech, and could still remember the thrill of saying, 'I know not what course others may take, but as for me, give me liberty, or give me death!' We'd won our liberty, and begun an extraordinary experiment in democracy.

Half a world away, Australia's modern history began just a few years later, when the *Scarborough* and the *Charlotte* and other incongruously named convict ships sailed into Botany Bay. That, too, had been a radical experiment. As much as its isolation, Australia's era as a penal colony had shaped its psyche. The country's transformation from gulag to peaceful, prosperous democracy was an extraordinary feat. Robert Hughes' *The Fatal Shore* had provided a thought-provoking, detailed account of that evolution, but it was Kate Grenville's novel *The Secret River* that made me weep with its moving account of a collision of cultures.

America and Australia were cousins: the family resemblance was unmistakable, but so, too, were their distinctions. Not all Americans would be familiar with the concept of American 'exceptionalism', but virtually everyone in the United States was raised to believe that the US was both different and special—that our history had changed world history, and for the better. And Australia's modern origins under the yoke had been character-forming, too: it had bred a hardy egalitarianism, and a suspicion of rank, privilege, power. The 165,000 convicts had only been a small percentage of this country's immigrant population, but their impact had been powerfully felt.

I had read so many books, but first-hand knowledge was always different. To live in this country was to amend, extend and alter my beliefs; I felt that I was slowly beginning to understand Australia on a visceral level. I was excited to have an opportunity to learn more about those early days.

I buckled my seatbelt, momentarily disconcerted that I wasn't also buckling in Sophie and Jacqui. On this occasion, I was flying solo. When I looked out of the window, I saw below me a tiny, emerald jewel. We would soon be landing in the most notorious Australian prison of all. Norfolk Island was dead ahead.

✳

I looked up at the majestic, soaring trees, fringing a desolate white beach that meandered into surf. The guidebooks said the conifers grew to 65 metres. It was easy to see why Captain Cook, on board HM Bark *Endeavour*, had enthusiastically suggested Norfolk Island pines be used as masts for ships. But the trees proved treacherously fragile, and the industry had to be abandoned.

Norfolk Island is now a popular tourist destination, with its warm weather, sheltered coves, fascinating history and quirky local dialect. This remote dot in the South Pacific is a paradise, but it is impossible to slough off an eerie shiver. That is the thing about an island. No matter the beauty, it is only an escape if you can leave when you want. If you aren't in chains. I could only imagine the despondence of those long ago convicts: 'Abandon hope, all ye who enter here.' To arrive here was to be consigned to Dante's Inferno.

But the dark deeds were not only from days gone by. I had come to the island to report for *Dateline* on a modern tale of treachery, the murder of a 29-year-old Sydney woman, Janelle Patton, in March 2002. The story had been of international interest because it was a true-life, Agatha Christie, 'locked-room' murder mystery. A tiny island. No way on, or off. A limited number of suspects. An attractive, appealing victim. But who had done it?

The case proved unsolvable for four years. Ultimately, police uncovered evidence incriminating a New Zealand chef, Glenn McNeill. He gave a rambling, contradictory confession that he later recanted. There was a sensational trial, right there, on the tiny island, and, in 2007, McNeill was sentenced to prison in Australia for the murder. It was a baffling case, set against an exotic backdrop—a tropical Eden, with a local population that included many descendants of those who had engineered the mutiny on the *Bounty* way back in 1789.

On paper, my trip here sounded like something of a 'boondoggle'—a 'rort' to Australians—a network-funded island holiday. The truth was nothing so glamorous. We began work early, at first light, and ended late. There was some time, but less than I had hoped, to explore those early prison origins of the island. After three days, I'd remembered that bouncing between home and work wasn't quite as straightforward as I recalled.

I'd only recently cobbled together some help with babysitting. There was a charming university student called Bethany, who looked like Snow White's little sister, and a kind local teacher named Corrina, whose experiences in the classroom and as a mum gave her wisdom that proved indispensable. Their assistance gave me the opportunity to participate more in Sophie's activities. I could take her to a tennis lesson, or karate, or Scouts—simple activities, but ones which were all but impossible with Jacqui in tow. It also made it possible for me to take this rare assignment. I had written a 'pitch' for the story, and emailed it to New York; to my surprise and delight, it had been commissioned. The producer, my friend Sandy Cummings, had flown over from the States. This was our first collaboration since we'd reported on Steve and Terri Irwin, and other Australian stories, more than a decade before.

Prior to arriving on the island, we sat down with Janelle's parents, a polite, cultivated couple, at their home in Sydney. The interview was emotionally draining for everyone, and I had been filled with horror and pity at the senseless, devastating tragedy, and its effects on their family. As the mother of two young daughters, it was impossible not to imagine 'what if' scenarios, though I consciously tried to block such thoughts.

After spending so much time with my daughters since moving to Australia, I found myself looking for Sophie and Jacqui, reflexively. First thing in the morning, expecting Jacqui's yodel down the hall. Conscious of when the bell rang, at their respective schools. At bedtime, they loomed especially large in their absence. I rummaged in my purse, found Jacqui's purple, 'P'-shaped chew toy, designed to divert her from gnawing on us, and felt a sentimental pang. I caught myself remembering to remind Sophie to get her hat for school. I'd have a momentary flash of anxiety, then shake it off, annoyed at myself. Of course they weren't here. I was working, they were home, doing well. I had wanted this assignment, and was thrilled NBC had said yes. But I had been at home so much, it felt strange to be away.

Every time the crew set up cameras for the next interview, I sneaked off to make a quick call using one of the wickedly expensive sim cards we'd purchased from the Norfolk Island telco. The calls were brief, but I got succinct updates from Andrew and breathless bulletins from Sophie. Penny's peacock had returned to our front yard, but then disappeared again. Despite offers of seed and bread, he was Missing in Action, presumed dead. The thought flattened me.

There was also a postscript. Jacqui, it seemed, had discovered the butterfly net and, in a brief unsupervised moment, carefully dismantled it. Even as I shook my head at her capacity for destruction, I found the humour—always easier, from a distance. Jacqui had some excellent stealth skills, if we could only teach her to use them appropriately. After a frantic search, a replacement had been purchased from Kmart, and the duplicate returned to Penny.

Oh, and one more thing. Not to worry, but Sophie had taken a tumble from the swing. She was fine, really. Just a graze. Although it was easier to remember the humour in Jacqui's misbehaviour from a distance, it was also true that tiny incidents and accidents seemed larger, the farther you were from home. But Andrew's sister Katie, also on hand to hold the fort, reported all was well.

I wasn't sorry I had done the story, although it had felt like a stretch, on several levels. Each hour of television required multiple hours of filming, not to mention subsequent time spent writing and narrating the script. But there was no question I still loved working in television. Scouting locations, preparing questions, recording stand-ups (pieces to camera), slipping into the chair to conduct an interview, these were all part of a craft I missed. But I decided one thing: covering true crime stories wasn't something I wanted to do any more. It felt deeply unsettling to cover this case. I spoke to lawyers, doctors and police officers who experienced similar pangs after becoming mums.

I'd seen the writing on the wall a few weeks before, when I was in my office at home doing research and Sophie wandered in.

'What are you doing?' my seven-year-old daughter asked innocently. And then, that devastating follow-up: 'Mum, why are you covering the computer screen with your hands?'

I had been hiding the document I was reviewing—the autopsy report for Janelle Patton, which detailed how she had been stabbed 64 times. How her skull had been fractured, her pelvis and one ankle broken. I was reading those dreadful sentences analytically, searching for clues relating to the murder, the murderer. And wondering what rage must have lain behind this crime.

And then my little girl wandered in, fresh from playing on the rope swing, sweaty and cheerful, pushing a strand of straw-coloured hair from her hazel eyes, and the scrim of professional detachment had been wrenched away. I saw beyond that factual report to behold a poor young woman shrieking, begging for her life, beaten and stabbed repeatedly and doubtless crying out for mercy. She must have known that she was dying, alone, on an island far from home. I stumbled, gave some sort of an answer to Sophie, but recognised my confusion as a sign that I needed to report different kinds of stories. I never again wanted to cover a computer screen to hide my work from my daughter.

At the end of that stay on Norfolk Island, there was a big dinner, and we all sat outside, under the pines. It was a balmy evening, and we relaxed and swapped stories. It was the kind of night I had missed—the chance to hang out with colleagues and friends. The irony was unmistakable. On an island that had been a prison, I felt free, unfettered.

I went to sleep. My dreams were filled with shrieking. But these were the happy whoops and cries of children, playing. Children on a peninsula, a sliver of land jutting into the Wombat State Forest. Sophie was chasing a peacock with a butterfly net. Jacqui was trying to slip down the slide. She was flat on her back, because she still didn't have the stomach strength to sit up properly. It made simple activities dangerous, and I worried she was about to hit her head.

'Come on, Child,' said Sophie, coming to Jacqueline's rescue with a roll of her eyes. 'You can do it.'

The scene faded to black.

I awoke in my hotel room, alone. And I wanted to go home.

8

THE CHESTNUT GROVE

I pulled a tray of scones out of the oven and eyed them critically. They were not as attractive as Nana's. She would have been delighted to share her recipe, and I momentarily regretted my folly. But I was determined to do things my way. I knew how to cook, how to do a lot of things, and when I wasn't sure, I knew how to extemporise.

I slid the scones onto a plastic platter, reflecting that I hadn't expected an international move would require quite so much advice. I tried not to bridle, but I found myself impatient whenever I received a suggestion—even an excellent, time-tested tip, even advice I asked for—preferring to muddle through. I was a grown-up, after all. I had held a big job in a big city.

But the truth was that the list of what I didn't know in Australia was a lengthy one. I was ignorant about the seasons; the heat; drought and water rationing; the bush; pretty much all the flora and fauna, come to think of it; the medical system; where to shop for furniture, or food, or clothes. Little things like the right shoes to go with a school uniform came under the 'I have absolutely no idea' category. I tried to wing it, with more or less success. 'Mum, the shoes *have* to be black! Not sneakers! It's *the law!*'

While suggestions were useful, it was unsettling to be

instructed about how to accomplish the most everyday things. I was accustomed to being successful and in charge, to being on the 'giving' rather than the 'receiving' end of opinion. I made a note to be less generous with offerings of sage counsel in the future.

I also found myself sympathising with ill-fated Australian explorers like Burke and Wills, or Leichhardt. I saw how it could happen. Robert, William and Ludwig might have been brave and clever, but they were intelligent fools. The substantial knowledge they possessed was largely irrelevant. They didn't know what they didn't know, and they were too proud to ask for help. They boldly set forth on grandiose missions with incomplete or erroneous plans and impractical, inadequate supplies. Not surprisingly, they died.

The stakes were significantly lower for making scones. I had felt safe to ad-lib, using a variation of a Southern biscuit recipe from my battered *Betty Crocker Cookbook*, converting ounces to grams, and throwing in extra sugar. The resulting product was perhaps not as fluffy as I would have liked, but the scones were brown and they were warm and they would do. Especially since I had a massive container of cream to go with them, and some of my sister-in-law Chrissie's delicious homemade raspberry jam.

Andrew strode into the kitchen, dressed all in white. Deep furrows creased his forehead, and his eyes looked like a page from the VicRoads street directory. Just back from London, he was jetlagged and exhausted. But there was also a twinkle in his eye, and he sported a faded maroon Muckleford Cricket Club cap on his head.

'What happened to the scones?' he asked cheerfully. 'They're flat as a sh— . . .'

'They'll be delicious.'

'Thanks for making them,' he amended, then windmilled his right arm. 'I'm the opening bowler,' he continued, clearly chuffed. He rotated his arm again, as if it were the handle of a large, invisible crank. 'A Reserve.'

I was still wrapping my head around divisions, grades, leagues, but anything with an A sounded good. He hadn't played the sport in years.

'That's great. Where do you play?'

'At home, against Daylesford. Do you and the girls want to come?'

'Home' meant Muckleford, an hour away. 'No thanks,' I responded. Too quickly.

Andrew looked disappointed and I felt my shoulders knit together. I knew that my husband worked long hours and had an insane travel schedule; the weekends were his only chance to relax. But wasn't it enough that I watched the children from 11 to 7 every Saturday, while he got to play sport? I'd even made his afternoon tea. Most weekends I simply handed him a box of Tim Tams from the cupboard. Andrew was increasingly likely to drop by the farm on his way, where Nana whipped up beautiful rounds of sandwiches or other delectables, just as she had when he was a teenager.

I handed Andrew the scones. He tucked the box under his arm and turned to leave. 'Okay, I'll take the Mustang. See you tonight.'

'Hey, wait, I have an idea,' I called out. 'Why don't you take Sophie? She can play with the cousins. Jacqui and I will find something else to do.'

Andrew turned and gave me a smile. Not ideal, but at least he would have a little buddy with him at cricket. It seemed as if the only way we could do things in our family was two by two.

✳

In America, crickets were insects that chirred and cheeped on warm summer nights. It was an appealing, melodic chorus, and the cheerful creatures had given rise to characters like Jiminy Cricket, and *The Cricket in Times Square*. On a trip to visit friends in China, Sophie and I ventured to the cricket market. We learned that in Old Shanghai, concubines had often kept crickets as pets in tiny, lacquered bamboo boxes. At night, they put the boxes under their pillows, the gentle chirping a reminder of life outside the magnificent palaces that comprised their own elegant cages. A cricket would be the only companion for a homesick country girl on a solitary night.

It hadn't been until I'd met Andrew that I'd learned anything about cricket as a sport. In America, the Boys of Summer played baseball. As a girl, I'd gone to Parker Field—later renamed The Diamond—to watch the Richmond Braves, Triple-A farm team for Atlanta. In New York, I'd jilted them in favour of the World Series-winning New York Yankees in their pinstripes, without a skerrick of guilt. North or south, it was bliss to spend an afternoon in the bleachers, to shell peanuts, eat Cracker Jacks, and sing with thousands of other fans during the seventh inning stretch. I was trying, unsuccessfully, to teach Jacqui 'Take Me Out to the Ballpark' although I'd bowdlerised the line which went, 'Root, root, root for the home team', to 'Go, Go, Go . . .!' in a nod to local linguistic complications. But while I enjoyed baseball, cricket remained as foreign, mysterious and complex as old Shanghai. Or ye olde England.

I clearly hadn't tried hard enough. My friend Ginger had also grown up in Virginia, but after moving to Africa to become a wildlife filmmaker, had spontaneously combusted into an avid cricket fan. Ginger and her Namibian husband Nad had a son, Kimber, a bright young man whose numerous talents included being a standout in the sport. Kimber had even played for the Namibian National Junior Team. Like Andrew, he was a bowler. Unlike me, Ginger attended every game. She understood the finer points, could say '6 for 30' with authority and conviction. When Gin and I chatted by phone, as we did almost every week, she and Andrew would occasionally touch base about the fortunes of South Africa versus Australia, or discuss such burning issues as the Ashes, or the Test. But then again, Kimber was Ginger's son, not her husband. I was far more likely to attend Sophie's sporting endeavours than Andrew's.

Andrew had been something of a gun as a young man, like his grandfather before him. Jack Butcher, who died shortly after our daughter Sophie was born, was the stuff of Muckleford Cricket Club legend. His name was emblazoned next to many of the records for the club, and he loved nothing better than to watch Andrew bowl. On one occasion, back when Andrew and I were dating, I had accompanied him to the cricket pitch to watch a match. A tall, broad-shouldered man stooped slightly with age, Jack Butcher stood at the edge of the ground as Andrew warmed up next to us.

'Wow, what a gorgeous day,' I said. It was a vacuous conversational opener, but I barely knew Andrew's grandfather. Weather seemed a safe topic.

'What's that you say?' Jack asked.

I paused. Then, enunciating carefully and speaking as loudly as I dared, I repeated, 'I SAID WHAT A GORGEOUS DAY.'

Jack turned to Andrew. 'What about hay?'

'She said it's a nice day.'

'*That's* what she said?' he marvelled. 'I can't understand a word she says,' he confided in a broad Australian accent to Andrew, as if I wasn't there. They proceeded to discuss square legs and a duck and other mystifying matters until Andrew abandoned us, and headed for the cricket equivalent of a pitcher's mound. There seemed to be two bowlers, but I didn't ask Jack to explain. Without Andrew to translate from English to English, we lapsed into a silence neither of us dared to break.

Andrew was a fast bowler, and his face lit up as he told stories of old matches. He acknowledged he'd never had finesse or pinpoint accuracy; his gift had been speed, and a certain terrifying, if erratic, power, when in the zone. But, as can happen, one passion eclipsed another. Andrew became a reporter, and he proved good at that, too. His budding career took him to Canberra, covering economics, then New York, to work at the *New York Post*, where we had met, then to Japan for two years, as Asia Correspondent for News Limited, then back to Canberra to cover politics. He managed to fit in an occasional game when visiting his parents for a weekend, and was contemplating his comeback, when there'd been a spanner in the works. We decided to marry, and he moved to New York in 1998.

Ten years in Manhattan had killed his cricket career, Andrew informed me more than once. Usually he said this with a wry grin. Sometimes he looked wistful, and rolled his arm around and around, holding his right shoulder with his left hand. I suggested Andrew go play with one of the teams of expat-Australian cricketers in Central Park, but he demurred.

Cricket was more than a game. It was a code for a culture, a tradition. It equalled the perfect green ground in a small country town, it signalled the arching blue of the sky and the way the sun felt on your skin. It was about being young, lithe and quick, and it was about home and family, and a legendary local who was your Pa. On nights when Andrew was feeling wistful, he would play cricket in his dreams. Just as my nocturnal wanderings reflected my longing, Andrew's reflected his. He was always at home, driving down a deserted country lane, to an idyllic field, to be the opening bowler, A Grade, for Muckleford.

Given such history and tradition, when we moved to Australia, I had been an ardent supporter of Andrew's return to the sport. But I hadn't read the fine print. I had been stunned by the amount of time cricket consumed. Not only did Andrew drive an hour each way to the game, and each game was a marathon, but counting the pre-season training, the matches, the playoffs and Grand Final (Muckleford, it seemed, was a good team), cricket consumed half of our weekends for nearly half of the year. I understood why Andrew wished we would all come to watch, and make this a family event, especially since his brother Trevor was also playing, and the cousins usually came. It always sounded appealing. 'There's a playground,' I'd be told. 'There will be lots of children. The girls will have a great time.'

But the diaphanous quality of that idyllic imagined outing quickly wilted in the harsh glare of an Australian summer's day. While Sophie might relish the opportunity to play with Uncle Trevor and Aunty Helen's children—Lloyd, Asher and Chloe— and Aunty Katie and Uncle Andy's daughter, Annaliese, Jacqui was a different matter. In part, it was her short attention span. In part, it was the heat. Then there was the fact that she was clumsy and accident-prone, and we didn't want any more falls. But the biggest challenge was her mercurial behaviour. I could usually sense when she was heading for a meltdown, and would change locations, if I could. Get home, if possible.

If I missed the warning signs, Jacqui would escalate. She might try to push another child off the slide, have a massive temper tantrum or even pull down her pants and scream. The behaviours were disturbing for children and for adults, and of course mortifying. It was better to stay in close proximity, vigilant as the military aide who carries the President's nuclear football. When it came to the loveable mini-missile who was our daughter, I had my own code book. I thought strategically, analytically. It was best to avoid confrontation and escalation; I favoured early intervention or extraction. I tried to 'read the play'—guess what she was about to do, and make a successful interception. That was my game, and it required man to man defence. Otherwise, something would happen. And a Hail Mary pass wasn't always successful.

Altercations weren't my only concern. I remembered one large family picnic at the Castlemaine Gardens where I'd briefly lost track of Jacqui as I chatted. I still remember the taste of the Mint Slice I'd bitten into when I turned around to discover Jacqui had disappeared. I searched frantically. Had she darted towards the road? I was terrified she would be hit by a car. Headed for the pond, to see the ducks? She couldn't swim. I finally found her where I least expected her. She had wandered over to a group of strangers, and seated herself at their table. They had no idea who she was and, of course, she couldn't tell them.

When I was watching Jacqui, I wasn't hanging out; I wasn't watching a game; I wasn't relaxing. I was doing a job, which was to make sure that she and everyone nearby were safe and relatively happy. It was the same for Andrew, when he was on duty. And when I thought of it that way, I was okay. But on those occasions when I let myself drift into visions of what might have been, what should have been, I struggled. When I saw other mums chatting to each other, their backs to children who laughed and played in a predictable manner, I sometimes had to look away; when the afternoon rays filtered through the trees in such a way that Jacqui's soft curls were backlit, and she turned to gaze up at me with her china doll eyes, I caught a glimpse of who she would have been, had something not gone wrong.

And then I often found myself thinking of America, of Mum and Dad, of my sisters Elizabeth in California and Susan in North Carolina. Of old friends I had known for years. I missed the luxury of not needing to explain. I missed the comfort of being with those who had known me then, as well as now. And I missed each and every one of them, as individuals. I would look up, and find it hard to believe they could be under the same sky. And I never missed them more than when I tried to pretend we were the perfect family we weren't.

It was easier, preferable, to stay at our house in the Macedon Ranges, even though I wasn't sure this self-imposed isolation was a smart choice. I was gregarious, perhaps even 'pathologically social', as a friend had referred to her extroverted husband. But isolation was preferable to life as a police-chase vehicle, following a step behind my darling, complicated younger daughter, in endless, slow pursuit. Preferable to family drives in which Sophie retreated to her books, I put my fingers in my ears, and Andrew turned up the radio to drown out wailing misery. Being a cricket widow wasn't that hard. And though Andrew wished I would come to watch him play, he no longer expected it.

Nevertheless, when Andrew headed off with Sophie, who gave a cheery wave and a 'Bye, Mum! See you tonight!', I felt a pang. I turned to Jacqui. 'Now what?' I asked. She stared at me quizzically.

I was growing weary of going to the playground or the pool on our own. The novelty of a life so dramatically different from the one we had left in New York was slowly wearing into the grooves of the familiar, if not yet the ruts of repetition. Sophie didn't mind. She now had new friends in abundance, and came home brimming with stories about Olivia, Caitlin I and Caitlyn Y, Izzys and Isobels, as well as children called Lucy and Erin and Ruby and Sophie and Sunny and Lauren. Sophie was settled, and I felt delighted and relieved. She had made an excellent transition to Australia.

I had moved before, and fully expected it would take me longer to acclimatise. Sophie's friends had nice mothers, and we were all friendly, but many worked or were busy with their own lives and commitments. I also had come to realise that the real challenge to living in country Victoria wasn't the time it took to commute to Melbourne. It was the fact that I split my time between two communities. And spent a lot of time in the car. It was not an ideal spot for meeting or getting to know people.

The result was that I pined more and more for those who lived far away. I regularly telephoned family and a rollcall of friends who were scattered, dandelion style, across the US and around the globe. It was the American way. We left home for university, then for jobs, and became a nation of rolling stones. Despite the distance, my family and friends were still there for me. They just weren't here.

I knew that when I had more pals who lived nearby, life would improve, perhaps dramatically. The Macedon Ranges and vicinity included both large properties and quaint, distinctive towns:

Kyneton and Woodend and Trentham; Macedon and Mount Macedon; Gisborne and New Gisborne and Riddells Creek and Romsey and Lancefield. The area included plenty of long-time residents, as well as many families like ours who were 'tree changers'. People who had moved away from Melbourne looking for the pleasures of a life in the countryside. The blend of locals and newcomers made for a rich brew.

Such was the friendliness of the area that we'd been invited to any number of picnics and parties when we first arrived. I knew it was up to me to follow up. But there was another difficulty I hadn't fully appreciated. Those who lived in the countryside often lived miles from one another. This was a far cry from my former life, where it was easy to walk down the hall and knock on the door of a neighbour's apartment. Or pop in a taxi for a quick cross-town trip. Getting to know new people took time, and energy. It was also a bit like picking the right time to jump into a game of Double Dutch jump rope. If I left it too long, I'd never make the leap.

Jacqui had wandered out to the trampoline, and I was mind-lessly following her. Time for action. I had a day free, and what did I have to lose? I picked up the phone before I could think any more about it.

✳

'Come on, Jacqui, let's have a look at the chickens,' Kirsty said, directing Jacqui towards a small hutch next to her herb garden. Kirsty is a tall, dark-haired woman with penetrating blue eyes and striking cheekbones. If she had lived in America, I might have thought she had Native American ancestry.

'Here you go, gorgeous!' Kirsty said, handing Jacqui a sprig of mint to chew on.

Jacqui beamed. In a small group, I reflected, she was at her absolute best.

'Did you always garden?' I asked.

Peals of laughter. 'Not at all. We lived in Carlton, opposite Exhibition Gardens. I bought gardening books, and Alex and I would drive out to the country, every weekend. That was the extent of it. Until we found this place.'

Kirsty, a former publisher for Melbourne University Press, lived with her husband Alex, a wine merchant, and their children Henry, Jemimah and Charlie on a rugged bush block in the hills. I called twice for directions en route, but ultimately found my way down a winding lane to a modern house set in the midst of a grove of ancient chestnut trees.

'What healthy transplants,' I said, touching the gnarled trunk of a tree Henry and Jemimah were climbing. I found myself remembering the pungent scent of roasting chestnuts, bought from street vendors during the Christmas season in New York. 'I'm surprised to find them here.' Kirsty hoisted little Charlie onto a low bough, where he could watch his siblings.

'Aren't they beautiful? There's a whole grove of them, going up the mountain. They would have been planted as a crop,' Kirsty explained. 'Years ago, when Alex was working in Lucca, in Tuscany, we took a walk in the hills, where chestnut trees grow wild. It was enchanting. Then, one weekend on one of our drives in the country, we took a wrong turn. We stumbled onto this block, and it was actually for sale. It was a mix of the things we love—Australia and Europe!'

'But what do you do with the chestnuts?' I asked. 'That must be a lot of work.'

More laughter. 'The year we moved in, I was pregnant. I had no idea what to do. I remembered Lucca. So I put an ad in an Italian newspaper in Melbourne, for anyone who wanted to come up and pick them. There were plenty of volunteers, and some still come each year. We also host a chestnut harvest picnic each year on Anzac Day,' Kirsty continued. 'You and Andrew must come next year. Don't forget your gloves—they have spiky casings. You can take home baskets of them.'

The conversation meandered onto books, Australian politics and travel. Jacqui held my hand as we walked through the garden with its beds of spinach, lettuces and herbs, and she watched Kirsty's children in fascination. The peaceful setting suited my daughter. She would wander down to them, then amble back, content.

'So you didn't mind me inviting us over?' I asked finally. 'I don't think I've ever done this before. But you did suggest we get together, even if it was a while ago.'

'I'm delighted you rang,' she said with her warm smile. 'I'll invite myself to your house next time! Do you have a garden?'

'Not exactly. More like dirt. I'm a very bad gardener, but I can cook.'

'I'm actually finishing up work on a cookbook. Want to see?' I nodded, and Kirsty disappeared inside to return with proofs. 'You'll have to meet my friend Peta. Though we all call her Pete,' Kirsty explained, spreading out the pages. 'She lives in the area, too. She worked with Stephanie Alexander in her kitchen garden program. Our book is called *We Love Food*—it's recipes from the garden to the kitchen.'

Kirsty also brought out warm, homemade focaccia, a bottle of wine and a pot of tea on a tray. I felt a lightness I hadn't felt in days. For Jacqui and me, this was far better than a cricket field. Andrew and Sophie were having a good day, and so were we.

✳

Andrew and I returned home at almost exactly the same time. All of us were smiling.

'Did you win?'

'Not yet. But we are looking good and I bowled pretty well. Not 7 for 38 like the old days, but I think it was enough.'

'That sounds good,' I said, though I had no idea what he was talking about.

'I got greasies,' he added, now speaking a language I understood. He held aloft a steaming paper rectangle with fish and chips.

'Lum,' Jacqui chimed in.

But Sophie was curiously uninterested. She was standing at the edge of the veranda, her mouth agape.

'Mum,' she said, breathlessly. 'Dad? Who threw wood chips all over our veranda?'

I walked quickly around the corner, to survey a scene of weird and wanton destruction. Someone had attacked our windows and torn the frames to shreds. They had carefully peeled off great strips of wood, which had been strewn across the pavers, and tossed across the front lawn.

'What on earth?' I said.

But an awful realisation was dawning, confirmed a moment later when I heard Andrew behind me.

'Bloody cockies!'

9

ULYSSES BUTTERFLY

'Look Mum. We've made a castle.' Sophie brushed a stippling of sand across the bridge of her nose. She and her new best friend Eve—whom she had known for approximately one hour and 27 minutes—were hard at work on a turret. They had constructed an elaborate set of towers, and a sturdy wall to protect against invaders. They both seemed delightfully oblivious that their painstakingly constructed defences would be breached in another few hours, when a marauding Coral Sea stormed ashore. High tide or sulphur-crested cockatoo, Australia thoughtfully provided the perfect demolition team for every occasion.

'It's fit for a princess. Here's a shell for a keystone.' I turned to Jacqui, who was digging through the sand with a small orange shovel, and carefully pouring the crystals onto her legs. She was uninterested in the bucket we had provided, but stared at the sand in amazement and amusement.

And I stared at my younger daughter. Jacqui was as calm as a *qi gong* master; even more astonishing, she was entertaining herself. The beach seemed to reveal Jacqui at her best, the way a beautiful setting enhances the fire and facets of a diamond. There was a rapt stillness, which made me swallow several times and blink.

It shouldn't have been a surprise that Jacqui liked the beach—most children do. But Jacqui wasn't usually a follow-the-crowd sort of girl. While she had a notable sense of humour and moments of real delight, Jacqui wasn't often content. Seeing her like this was as memorable as driving across the Gibson Desert and catching the first glimpse of Uluru.

The trip had been worth it. On the flight north, I'd had my doubts. An aluminium tube in which seats were packed closely together and filled with strangers, and in which exits were strictly limited, was not Jacqui's most successful milieu.

'I never thought of lip balm as an activity,' my mum had marvelled on the flight from Melbourne.

'Jacqui *thinks* it is lipstick, Granne,' Sophie told her American grandmother, shooting a superior look at her little sister.

Sophie preferred to read or watch movies, but Jacqui needed entertainment if I was to prevent her from kicking the seat in front of us. I introduced a new activity every few minutes. A few included: Play-Doh, Snack, Hand Lotion, Snack, Rubik's Cube, Walking Down Aisle, Shaking Plastic Bottle Filled with Coins, Snack, Etch-o-Sketch, Book, Mirror, Doll, Snack, Mini-Purse with Coins, Eating Coins (Unsanctioned Activity). Fortunately, my carry-on was bursting with small objects and food. Unfortunately, it became obvious I had given my daughter a few too many snacks, when Jacqui vomited late in the flight.

I reminded myself that if the other passengers didn't understand, I didn't know them and would never see them again. And any passenger who had a special kid in her own life would nod in sympathy. I recalled a woman I knew who had two children with autism. Her mum was also a carer, looking after a husband with Alzheimer's. The two of them had attended a Country Women's Association meeting where the topic had been how best to help overburdened carers. 'We just pretend CWA stands for Chocolate and Wine Association!' my friend's mum had whispered.

Chocolate, wine or sunshine. I basked like a goanna, mesmerised by the ruffled turquoise view, framed by volcanic boulders that resembled a giant pair of fuzzy dice. Behind us, a fringe of palm trees ran like a zipper along the edge of sugar-white sand.

The July air was warm, the breeze balmy, a stark contrast to the Macedon Ranges, where winters tended towards gloom, cold and untamed winds. And the sand! No sandbox could compete. For a sensory-seeking child such as Jacqui, Palm Cove was a tactile nirvana. The beach and adjacent ocean were neither too hot, nor too cold, but Three Bears perfect.

There were other factors, too. As was the case when we were in Muckleford, with Andrew's relatives, Jacqui was surrounded by a cluster of people who loved her, her extended family within metres. We walked the short distance to the beach, and back to our hotel. There was no getting in and out of the car, no dashing hither and yon. Jacqui was calmer, and it made the rest of us calmer, too. Or was it the other way around? Was she calmer, because we were?

I was learning that Jacqui created moods, but she also absorbed them. She was her own weather system—sparkly sunshine, a summer shower or a tempest—but always, our family was the jet stream. A strong, even flow could enhance and extend a good mood, even tease open a tightly coiled twister. By contrast, colliding fronts wreaked havoc. Jacqui performed at her peak in a simple, peaceful environment. But creating and maintaining such a system was easier said than done. I breathed deeply, watching her dig her toes deep in the soft, wet sand. I was soaking up the serenity as much as I soaked up the sun.

'Here's another bucket for your towers,' said Granne, as she trudged up to Sophie and Eve, carrying another load of wet sand, packed like cement.

'Thanks!' Sophie smiled up at her grandmother.

Granne had been a willing foot soldier for these two small pharaohs, endlessly ferrying material for their building project.

But she was ready for a break, and plopped down on a blue, white and aqua striped towel beside me.

It felt like a luxury to have my mother with me, as well as my daughters. As a younger woman, I'd shrugged at families who lived in one another's pockets, each child and his or her family part of a tightly knit solar system, circling the parents. Didn't anyone hanker to move on? Being a news reporter had turned me into a bit of a gypsy. But the consequences of nomadic life gave me a greater appreciation of the benefits of constellations. It was fortunate indeed to be close enough for children to feel their grandparents' love as a verb, in addition to enjoying lovingly selected presents that arrived through the post. It pleased me to see Granne's delight in her proximity to Sophie was returned in equal measure, like the small bucket being trundled back and forth, across the sand. I thought of my sister Elizabeth and her husband John, in the Bay area; of Susan and her husband Danny with their children Sebastian, Hattie and Gigi in North Carolina. They were all so far away. I resolved to make sure they got over for a visit.

I thought of a couple we knew who had learned during pregnancy that they would have a child born with Down syndrome. Despite successful careers, interesting lives, they'd immediately planned to move country, return home, to be near the support of their families. I wondered why I always seemed to reach such obvious conclusions late, why the straightforward often eluded me.

Our situation was more complex. Our move to be close to Andrew's family necessarily pulled me out of my existing orbit. I'd counted more than I'd realised on the connectivity of telephone and email, not fully appreciating factors like time zones and busy lives. I simply hadn't appreciated that I would feel the distance so acutely, like a wobbling satellite slipping deep into space. It was a challenge to maintain the signal home, and I kept in touch with fewer and fewer people. Their beeps and pings grew fainter and further apart, one by one, dropping off the grid.

Andrew had experienced the same dissonance when we lived in New York. There was no middle ground, no fulcrum to the seesaw that was our international marriage, only 'here' or 'there', on either side of the vast Pacific. We lived in the twenty-first century, and plenty of families handled such a situation. They simply boarded a plane. But I'd just been reminded of the complications of travel with Jacqui. I wasn't anxious to attempt a long haul. Thankfully, Mum and Dad had come to visit us instead.

Granne sighed, relaxed. Then she stretched her legs and said, 'Palm Cove'. A moment later, she sighed again, and repeated the name of the resort beach north of Cairns like a mantra, 'Palm Cove'. Mum was besotted by Queensland. 'It's like being in a travel brochure.'

A Connecticut Yankee, Mum had grown up on the Atlantic. Flinty, grey and frigid in winter, the ocean could be a brute. The infamous northernmost stretches were littered with icebergs— we'd shot our NBC story about the raising of a piece of the *Titanic* in the middle of summer, and still encountered high seas and formidable gales.

Latitude by latitude, the Atlantic grudgingly mellowed. On the 2300-mile drive south along US Highway 1 from Fort Kent, Maine, to Key West, Florida, the coastline also underwent as many costume changes as a Broadway chorus girl. Pebbly New England beaches gave way to the sails of Newport, the fashionable Hamptons, the fun-loving Jersey Shore; there was Annapolis, home to the US Naval Academy, then the boardwalk of Virginia Beach and the dunes of North Carolina's Outer Banks, where the Wright brothers tested their flimsy winged contraption. There were stately mansions along Charleston's Battery, live oaks in Savannah, dripping in Spanish Moss, and, finally, the firecracker that was Florida, with its sparkly fuse, Miami Beach.

An Easterner, I adored the Atlantic and its distinctive, highly regional coastline, each city and town with its own unique character and charm. But for sheer, jaw-dropping beauty, the ocean of my childhood couldn't compare to the South Pacific. It was like seating an ageing if accomplished Shakespearean actor next to a glittering, nubile red-carpet star. You'd have to be blind not to notice.

It wasn't simply that Australia's beaches were stunners—a warm aqua sea, bedecked with the gaudy lushness of tropical vegetation. But the land was sparsely populated, compared to the East Coast of the US. It was extraordinary to discover vast kilometres of beachfront that remained undeveloped; where you could, if you so desired, frolic naked and never see another soul.

I smiled at Mum. 'We still have a few more days to enjoy it.'

'Have you talked to Andrew? How is the wreck-o-vation going?'

We had all appropriated Sophie's word to describe the messy, disruptive process of renovating a home while living in it. Our family's Extreme Home Makeover had been underway for several months, and, like any contestant on *The Block*, we now questioned our sanity. There were holes in the floor tiles. Chunks of plaster, scattered like rat droppings across the lounge. The faded carpet had been ripped out, but a few patches remained to trip up the unsuspecting. Boxes were stacked higgledy-piggledy, a gauntlet to be tiptoed through on the precarious trek from room to room. In particular, Jacqui was upset by the chaos and confusion, a complication we hadn't fully appreciated. Perhaps yet another reason she liked the beach.

I paused. 'Andrew's a bit cryptic. I think it is going more slowly than he and Trevor imagined, but he keeps saying it's fine.'

Australian understatement could fool you. For the longest time, when someone told me he felt pretty ordinary, I thought that was what he meant. I had no idea I was being told he was near death's door. Given that New Yorkers were kings and queens of hyperbole, and Australian understatement was laced with irony, there were ample opportunities for miscommunication.

I wondered if Andrew's brother, a successful builder in Castlemaine, was regretting his decision to spearhead our project. He'd seemed cheerful and willing, but it was increasingly obvious Trevor wouldn't make a dime out of the deal, and the project was, to use the latest local phrase I was keen to appropriate, hard yakka. One reason we'd flown north for this winter holiday was that it gave Trevor and Andrew the chance to install our new kitchen benches, lighting fixtures, stone fireplace and windows with no one there.

The decision to give our relatively new home a facelift wasn't entirely a result of the Cockatoo Fiasco, although they'd certainly added 'window frames—aluminium', to the To Do list. If the cockatoos were tempted to become repeat offenders, they'd bust their little beaks. Yet, despite what thugs they were, I missed the irrepressible parrots and their antics. My favourite of their tricks was when they swung, upside-down, from Sophie's rope swing, apparently just for the fun of it.

But I'd become what Americans termed a NIMBY—Not In My Back Yard. In the US, NIMBYs might join forces to block a proposed nuclear power plant or mobile phone transmission tower. I hadn't heard of any uniting to ward off impending cockatoos. But this was war. I'd turned their bird feeder into a birdbath, and given away their seeds. They'd flapped off in disgust, an enormous flock of them, no doubt en route to pester some other poor, foolish transplant.

The expensive mistake had chastened me. I resolved to be quicker to accept local knowledge in the future. Ironically, as a reporter, I made it a point to seek out exactly such site-specific information. No map—not even GPS—was the equal of a canny local, especially in difficult or dangerous terrain; in war zones, it was standard operating procedure for network reporters to employ a 'fixer'—the savvy resident who knew the lie of the land, understood the people, the politics and the language.

So why had I fobbed off wise counsel from a reliable source? The answer, I was sorry to acknowledge, was plain old hubris. I preferred not to think of the number of zeros connected to my mistake. I was slowly being forced to acknowledge how very different my new life in Australia was from the life I'd led in New York. I'd thought it would be a breeze, since both countries spoke English. But moving from the city to the country, from northern hemisphere to southern, had been a greater challenge than I had anticipated. I was reminded uncomfortably of the brassy reporter in *Crocodile Dundee,* who boasted at the beginning of the movie, 'Don't worry about me, I'm from New York.'

At least I knew better than to attempt a swim with the crocs. But while I made a mental note never again to reject advice out of hand, I reserved the right to study the bartender. I'd come to see that advice was a tricky martini of fact shaken with opinion; it could be hard to separate one from the other.

'Hey, Granne, where's Opa?' I asked, suddenly on the lookout for my father, whose predilection for doing laps at their local pool had earned him the affectionate nickname of 'Sea Mammal'. 'He didn't go off for a swim, did he?'

'Why, no,' Mum responded, seeing my agitation. 'He's up there, reading.' She gestured to a palm tree behind us, under which my father was engrossed in a heavy book. 'Why? Are there Great Whites here?' For all Americans, Australia equals three things, in the following order: the Sydney Opera House, the Outback and Great Whites.

'Well, I think there are shark nets here, so I wouldn't worry, but I think Australia does have Great Whites everywhere. Not that anyone has seen them. Recently. Here. That I know of. Though there was a story on the news last night about pythons in the roof,' I continued, in a helpful digression. 'And did I remember to warn you about the jellyfish? There are signs. We're not supposed to touch them. Super deadly, actually, not just a sting, like you'd get back home. Though I don't think you will see them, because it's not the right season. At least I don't think so. Though I'm not sure.'

Not surprisingly, my mother was looking extremely confused. There I was again, sinking in the quicksand of scanty knowledge. Keen to impart information, I was long on conjecture, but painfully short on facts. I would have fired myself if I'd been acting as a reporter, rather than a daughter.

I switched gears, tried again. 'Actually, I was going to tell you about Penny.'

'The woman who owns the *emu* farm?' Mum looked even more mystified, the result of what is known in television as a 'jump cut'—an awkward, jarring leap between two unrelated images, or events.

But there was a serious link. Our neighbour in the Macedon Ranges had been delighted to hear about my parents' impending visit. But as I excitedly recounted plans to take them to Far North Queensland, to watch the crocodile shows, ride the Kuranda Train, take a visit to the rainforest and visit the Great Barrier Reef and the beaches, Penny's smile vanished, and she'd gone quiet. Then Penny reached out to hold my arm, unaccountably grave. 'Sara, you must be careful with the swimming.'

Like Granne, I jumped to the conclusion Penny meant sharks, but she had another danger in mind. A more pervasive killer that I had never considered.

'You must be careful of the reap,' she said, in her melodic accent.

'The what?'

'The reap. The reap tide.'

'A riptide!' I suddenly exclaimed. I had heard of riptides, but actually knew very little about them. 'Is it bad?'

'It is terrible,' she shook her head. 'And you cannot see it—it is under the water.' Penny put a hand to her face, steadied herself.

'Seven years ago, my husband Boris and I went on holiday up to Fraser Island with our family—just before the New Year. We were on a pretty beach; I remember it was hot. A good day for swimming. But my brother-in-law, he got caught in a riptide. Boris went to help—he got caught, too. It happened right in front of my children. The ocean, it knocked them unconscious. So many people tried to save them—they did CPR. Even the helicopter, it came. My brother-in-law survived. But Boris—he drowned.'

'Oh, Penny.'

'But Sara, I am telling you all this because there were no signs. We didn't see any signs warning of a riptide, of danger. We didn't know. My husband was a very strong swimmer, yet he died. The ocean can be dangerous.'

I swallowed, overwhelmed. 'Oh, my God, Penny, how horrible. I had no idea. I am so very sorry.'

'My youngest was thirteen years old. Suddenly, there I am, a widow. With three children. And a farm to run, all by myself.'

I thought of Penny's carefully tended property, how she raised her emus, sold their oil and their extravagant, speckled green eggs. How she raised ducks and geese and chickens, sold the duck-lings and chicks and eggs at the weekend markets in towns dotted across the countryside. She managed to raise Suffolk sheep as well, not to mention her other job, providing farm stays for inter-national tourists. Penny worked hard, incredibly hard. I thought about how lonely it would have been to bring up your children in a foreign country where people spoke a different language, all by yourself. And to lose your husband in a tragic accident. I had it easy.

'How did you make it? How did you survive?'

She shrugged. It was a very European shrug. 'What choice do you have?' Then she continued. 'My husband, he was a good man. I miss him. Your Andrew, he is a good man, too.' She paused another moment, then, 'This is why I tell you the story. When you go, it is beautiful yes, but be careful, please. Watch the children. And your parents.'

I looked out over the peaceful ocean. The sun had stretched and cracked, like a gigantic egg, its last rays gilding the palm fronds, haloing the girls. That was the thing about Australia. There was such astonishing, improbable beauty. But it could be brutal, too, and strike without warning. It was a continent that dared you to fall in love, and demanded you show respect.

A cool breeze rolled in from the palms, then out again, like an undertow. As we collected our beach bags, buckets and towels, and made our way down the path towards the hotel, there was a sudden flutter of iridescence, what appeared to be a rising of petals. A ruffling, swirling cloud of cobalt and black rose into the trees.

'Look, Mum! What are they?' asked Sophie, entranced.

At last, a question I could answer with authority—if only because I'd asked it myself, that morning, when I'd bought a coffee. Like Sophie, I'd been captivated by the sight of this swallow-tailed wonder.

'They're called Ulysses,' I told her. 'Aren't they glorious? That butterfly is kind of like you, because he's a traveller. He gets his name from a hero from a really old Greek story called *The Odyssey*. The Romans liked the story so much they stole it, and changed Odysseus's name to Ulysses. I've read that these butterflies live on every continent except Antarctica.'

'Even America?' asked Sophie.

'Even America.'

We stared at the butterflies until dusk crept in, until the cool clotted to cold, and we could no longer see the featherings of lapis and black, until we were shivering.

✳

Shivering turned to teeth chattering as soon as we returned to Victoria's Macedon Ranges.

Andrew was hopping back and forth from one foot to the other, and blowing on his hands when he met us at the airport.

'There's been a small hitch,' he said with a hesitant grin, eyeing my parents. 'It seems the contractor in charge of ordering the new windows has made a little mistake.'

Trevor was apologetic. 'The rule is, measure twice, cut once,' he said, shaking his head in disgust. 'He didn't.'

That tiny error meant that half a dozen enormous panels of glass simply didn't fit. The mistake was discovered after the old windows were removed. New windows had been ordered, but until then, there was nothing to do but cover the vast open holes with thick sheets of plastic, staple-gunned to the house. Every gust toyed and fiddled, probing the plastic in an endless search for access. Our house looked like a crack den in Bedford-Stuyvesant, New York. The temperature was eleven degrees Celsius, dropping to four at night, and the blustering wind sobbed and moaned. We could see our breath in the air, slept under piles of doonas, wore coats and hats inside during the day and to bed. With the new wood stove not yet installed, the gas heater ran endlessly, a feeble warmth, since most of the heat poured into the great outdoors.

Andrew was embarrassed, Sophie aghast, and Granne and Opa utterly amused.

'It's like camping,' Granne told Sophie with a grin.

'Exactly!' said my dad. 'Now, who would like a cup of tea?'

A short time later, Cheshire Cat-like, my father disappeared. Opa's preference for a secret hideaway, a rocking chair in the corner of the warmest room in the house, quickly earned him the nickname 'Jinx', for our childhood cat, who'd been equally adept at finding cosy hiding places.

Having our house in disarray muted my disappointment at seeing my parents leave. I would miss them, but they'd be far more comfortable in their own home than ours right now, and would quickly warm up in the sweltering temperatures of Virginia in July.

There were also a host of new, pleasant distractions and diversions. Through my friend Mignon Stewart, a former Channel 10 reporter who'd recently been hired by the ABC, I had been introduced to the producers at Channel 10 in Melbourne. One thing had led to another, and I'd been asked to do political commentary for the station's then morning show, *9am with Dave and Kim,* on the historic 2008 US Presidential Race.

Of particular interest was the fight for who would become the Democratic presidential nominee. One by one, a cast of colourful candidates had dropped by the wayside, and the Democrats were poised on the precipice of history. Either they would nominate a woman, former First Lady Hillary Clinton, or an African American, Illinois Senator Barack Obama. Neither party had ever nominated a woman or an African American to lead the ticket, and both candidates were wildly popular among Democrats.

Whoever captured the most votes in the Democratic primaries and caucuses would face Republican presidential nominee, Arizona Senator John McCain, a decorated Vietnam War veteran and former prisoner of war. McCain also made history by choosing a woman as his vice-presidential running mate, the until then virtually unheard of Governor of Alaska, Sarah Palin. Her right-wing politics and penchant for gaffes also featured in the race. It was a contest that had everything—history, controversy, characters, page-one drama and back-room intrigue, even moments of greatness.

And it gave me my first opportunity to appear on television in Australia. Suddenly, I had an excuse to telephone political cronies and colleagues at NBC to get good intel. I scoured the *New York Times, Washington Post* and multiple political-junkie websites, including *Real Clear Politics.* The chance to report on America, for Australia, seemed to provide me with a new battery pack. I felt my satellite flicker back to life. Suddenly, the signal was strong and clear, a rhythmic, steady pulse.

✳

A few weeks later the phone rang, mid-morning. It was Bella Irlicht, the principal at Jacqui's school.

'Is Jacqui all right?' I asked instantly.

'She's fine. I'm actually calling for you!' Bella replied, her energetic voice filled with promise. 'I know you have written a book,' she continued.

'Yes,' I answered, wondering where this was going.

'Well, I'd like you to write another one. About Port Phillip.' Before I could reply, Bella was off at a gallop. She reminded me that Port Phillip Specialist School had recently hosted what was called the RiSE Symposium, Re-Imagining Special Education. Special-education leaders had come to Melbourne from around the world to talk about the best ways to teach students who suffered from an intellectual disability. I'd attended the symposium, and been impressed with the outstanding programs on offer internationally, as recounted by visitors from overseas. But I'd been even more delighted and inspired to watch the teachers and students from Port Phillip present and perform. I was a believer. But I was also a mum. I'd just started reporting again, a tiny toe in the water. I was busy.

'So what do you think?' asked Bella.

'Well, I'm not . . .'

'Is that a yes?' Bella continued. I could almost see her nodding her head across the phone line, encouraging my agreement.

'I . . .'

'Good!'

'We'd need to find a publisher,' I added lamely. Surely that would bring this to a halt. You couldn't just snap your fingers and conjure one up.

'I already have one!' Bella bubbled. 'ACER. Australian Council for Education Research. Very respected.'

I gulped, caught, well and truly, in a net of my own making. Not that I'd ever really had a chance. As a friend informed me later with an impish grin, 'No one ever says no to Bella. It's actually impossible.'

I'd given it one last try, anyway.

'They might not want me. I'm not an academic, I'm a . . .'

'Reporter. Yes, I know. That's why I asked you. Now why don't you come to my office tomorrow for a cup of coffee, and I'll call the publisher to meet with us, and we'll get started? I've got these papers from the conference. They're excellent. We can just put them all together, and we will have a book.'

I wondered, considered. I had written a book. It took longer than one might think.

But I was also intrigued. I was impressed by Jacqui's school, but I didn't know it very well, didn't understand how they worked their magic. I'd no doubt enjoy the chance to step inside, peek behind the curtain, see Oz from the inside. I felt sure the school deserved to be chronicled. And what if we did more than simply include the papers from the conference? What if we actually wrote about how the school worked, including first-hand accounts from those on staff, and explanations of how things worked in the classroom, so that schools elsewhere could follow their lead? Suddenly, I was the one off at a sprint.

'Great. I'll see you then.'

As I hung up the phone, I had a momentary, alarming premonition. Bella had promised the book would be easy and quick. I hoped I hadn't found a way to make it lengthy and hard.

But it was pointless to worry. I had already said yes. I was ready to explore another part of Oz.

10

THE GRASSTREE

Andrew was sporting the look. The scofflaw look that announced risky business was afoot, that he was about to take a walk on the wild side. It was a look consistent with his choice of outfit—head-to-toe motorcycle gear—but entirely inconsistent with the afternoon's scheduled activity.

'That is a pretty strange get-up for gardening,' I observed speculatively. 'Would you like to confess what you are up to?' I asked.

'You'll see,' replied the International Man of Mystery. He gunned his KTM 450 EXC, and was off.

Our wreck-o-vation was at last complete. New windows installed, our house appeared even more like a treehouse. We'd basically kept just enough walls to support the roof; the rest was glass. There were precious few places to mount pictures, but our modern home seemed to dictate thoughts of the present and the future.

I loved the panorama of the Australian bush, complete with niche views, one from every angle. Every angle, except one. To the right of the stone fireplace, we'd added an enormous corner window, and it needed a focal point. Nothing too tall, because that would block our view of the trees and hills beyond. Not a rockery plant, either. Nor bushy, like a grevillea. But we wanted something native. Something spunky, with attitude.

And that's when the light flickered into Andrew's hazel eyes. 'I know just the thing,' he said with a grin.

Several hours later, just as the sky was growing dark, Andrew returned. He took off his helmet and jacket to reveal a flushed face and shirt drenched with sweat, although it was a chilly evening. Tied unceremoniously to the back of the bike next to a dirty shovel was a body wrapped in a burlap sack. Andrew hoisted the bag and laid it carefully on the veranda. My eyes by now had adjusted to the gloom, and I tore back the scratchy cloth.

The kidnapping victim was in fact a tree. A tree with a thick base, similar to a palm, but shorter. But what made this mystery plant so notable was its shock of Kelly-green hair. It had an elaborate whale spout of long, springy, needle-sharp fronds tufting from its stubby base, and I had an instant flashback to the troll dolls everyone had collected back in America when I was a kid.

'What on earth is that?'

'It's called a grasstree.'

'That seems kind of ordinary for something so special.'

'You'll prefer it to the old name.'

'Which was?'

'A black boy,' Andrew replied, shaking his head as I winced.

'You know, grasstree is perfect,' I said. 'Though I do wonder what the indigenous name is.' In Australia, as in the States, certain words and phrases were jarring reminders of the overt racism of days gone by. Modern discrimination was less widespread and often more subtle, but remained a troubling issue in both our countries.

'It is such a cool tree,' I continued. 'I've never seen anything like it. It's the perfect choice for outside the corner window. But what if it gets too tall?'

'I don't think they grow very fast.'

'Where'd you find it?'

Andrew looked smug. 'A little place I know. It's inaccessible, unless you happen to be off-road on a bike, in the back of Bourke. I stumbled across a grove of them one day.' He wiped his forehead with his forearm. 'There's heaps. No one will miss just one.'

'Well, it's a treasure.'

Tired as he was, Andrew got busy with his trusty shovel and soon had the tree planted.

We couldn't wait to show Sue Meli, the landscape garden designer who had planned our garden. She had excellent taste, and strongly favoured native plants. We knew she would be thrilled.

Sue was appalled.

'You dug it out from the bush?' she asked, when she dropped by the next day. 'You can't do that!'

'I did do that,' Andrew corrected her.

'Well, it's against the law.'

'Really?' I yelped.

'It's a protected species.'

Andrew's eyebrows shot up. We looked at one another.

'It was only one. There were hundreds, and they are in a spot where no one will be likely to find them. And the ones I saw at the nursery, smaller than this one, cost hundreds of dollars.'

Sue sighed, shaking her head. 'Do you know why? Because they only grow one centimetre a year,' she pinched her fingers together to demonstrate this tiny amount. 'One centimetre. A tree this tall is more than a hundred years old! Some can live as long as 600 years. Something that ancient, it isn't easy to move.'

I felt a sudden surge of solidarity with a species of foliage. Both Andrew and I examined our bouncy specimen with newfound respect. I never would have guessed. Our grasstree looked like a robust toddler, rather than a specimen that would have been a seedling at the beginning of the twentieth century. How many Wurundjeri had lived in the region when this tree sprouted? What had this tree meant to them? The traditional owners of the land had many connections to the area. I thought of the Sunbury earthen rings, north of Melbourne, and the Mount William axe quarry near Lancefield, en route to the Victorian goldfields. Old stone tools had recently been found on our road. I pictured this grasstree, quietly growing in its protected grove. Another Australian gem, tucked away.

Andrew and I looked at each other again. I felt squeamish, and could tell he did, too. But we'd already replanted the tree, and there was no way to put it back again. Besides, it looked healthy and happy and picture perfect, just outside the window. We would have extra appreciation for its beauty, recognising how precious our tiny centenarian was.

'We'll take good care of it,' I said.

'Good,' Sue said. 'I'll send instructions. And since you like them so much, we can always purchase more. But not so big next time. Remember, the younger and smaller the transplant, the more likely it is to be successful.'

※

The insects throbbed and pulsed, a shimmer of electric green, a crackle of gold. Suddenly, a ladybird appeared and flaunted her scarlet wings. She twirled and fluttered, a lyric dance, then disappeared into darkness.

A moment later I caught a glimpse of *Papilio ulysses*, although this butterfly was enormous. Its wings were like two gigantic cobalt kites, streaked with pitch, soaring high, dipping low. It was just possible to see that behind each wing was a woman. Wearing long-sleeved black shirts and black pants, their hair tied in pony-tails and their expressions neutral, the pair had dressed for invisibility. A third adult rolled the insect across the stage in a lazy series of ellipses. It was now clear that the butterfly's swallow-tailed wings sprouted from a wheelchair, which carried a quiet, long-haired girl, her neck craned up and to the side at an awkward angle. She was arrestingly beautiful.

I looked away from the stage, down to my lap, tapping away at a frantic pace. I was in the audience at Port Phillip Specialist School's state-of-the-art performing arts centre, for what was called Class Act. The annual presentation was more than a performance; it was proof of performance. Each class spent months creating and rehearsing its particular skit, designed to showcase what the children had learned. All 150 of the school's students took part in the production, supported by teachers, therapists, specialists and aides.

Class Act was the vehicle through which Port Phillip demonstrated for parents and the wider community the range of skills students had acquired during the year. I had been expecting a sort of audio-visual report card, and was surprised and delighted to discover it was actually quite entertaining. The vignettes were polished and professional, well-choreographed, well-rehearsed and with strong production values. Bedecked in extravagant costumes and skilfully made up, their smiles bright as an extra bank of floodlights, these confident children did not resemble the boys and girls we dropped off at school every morning.

For the last few months, I'd been immersed in a crash course on special education while researching the book about Port Phillip. Every morning, I dropped Jacqui off at her classroom, then wandered deep into the school. I'd sit in on morning circle, or occupational therapy, speech therapy or physiotherapy. I'd listen to the choir, or African drumming, pop by for art or drama or dance class, or sit on the pool deck to watch hydrotherapy sessions. I visited the school's psychologist, social worker, principal, office staff, head of pedagogy and, of course, numerous classrooms. Everyone was happy to talk. When I visited the school's purpose-built house to watch children learn independent living skills, while simultaneously tackling communication, reading and numeracy, I saw how hard they had to work to learn things that seemed simple and straightforward to most of us.

The curriculum was taught in a thoughtful, integrated way,

but teachers were allowed the freedom to mine their autonomous disciplines, to respond to the individual needs of their students. An inspired whim or hunch would be explored. If the idea proved sound, it was pursued; if not, it was abandoned, without fear of reproach. I often found myself thinking that many strategies employed here would improve any school—special or mainstream.

Much of what seemed casual and ad hoc was in fact carefully designed—including the separate entrance I had been directed to, back on Jacqui's first day of school. That was to provide the school's youngest students—and, crucially, their parents—a chance to adjust to attending a special school. Apparently I wasn't the only mum to feel gutted. Extraordinary Port Phillip might be, but I would have given anything to see Jacqui attend a typical school.

'It is confronting,' the school's social worker, Rosslyn Jennings, agreed. 'And in the beginning, it's also challenging for new parents to encounter older students. It's a glimpse into the future, a chance to see who their sons and daughters will become. Children learn, they gain many skills, but they don't "grow out of" having a disability. There is a tremendous amount of grief for families. A separate entrance gives the littlies and Mum and Dad a cloistered environment, so everyone can get accustomed to the idea.'

I had long since overcome the awkward, heart-lurching sensation I'd initially felt when I stepped across the threshold of the school, to depart the 'typical' world and enter a realm in which every child had a significant disability. I looked forward to my visits, to the merry wave hello from some of the children circling the front yard on large tricycles, to the shy smiles from others. 'Hi, Jacqui's mum!' I would hear in the halls, and my heart would leap. And I always found time for scones and coffee in the student-run Short Break café, beaming to see how diligently the older children prepared food, waited tables or took my order.

Navigating the warm currents of the school, I had acclimatised. One teacher told me, 'I don't feel sorry for these children.

I just accept that they are different. I think of them as if they are from Mars.'

I knew exactly what he meant. I also knew that he understood special needs on every level, having had his own son suffer a cruel, degenerative disability that had proved fatal. Many on staff had personal connections to special needs.

As for me, the school seemed, if anything, even more like the wonderful World of Oz. I often thought of Dorothy, initially bewildered and frightened to find herself in a foreign land filled with people who looked and acted in unexpected, unfamiliar ways. But she was quickly won over, hardly noticed aspects that had seemed odd before, and had even found it difficult to leave. I realised this little school had not only changed how I thought: it had changed how I felt.

Andrew nudged me, and I put down my computer and picked up my camera. It was Jacqui's turn to perform, decked out in a turquoise harem-girl outfit. Her class skit was called Magic Carpet Ride. Charmed as I was by Jacqui's dance moves, I was equally thrilled to see Sophie, in the front row with friends, cheering loudly as her little sister sang, 'Carpet, high above the town. We're up, we're up, we're up, up, up and we're down, down, down.'

But the most moving performance of the night did not involve our family. It centred on a shimmering bumblebee who was actually a boy I remembered seeing a few months earlier. He couldn't walk, and had been lying face down, rhythmically banging his head on the carpeted floor. It was a desolate sight. The teacher instantly tried to engage him by playing the piano, then by various tactile activities. I knew he had been among the students selected to participate in intensive hydrotherapy, but I had not known the outcome, until now.

As the crowd hushed in anticipation, I was stunned to see the little bee take hold of a teacher's hands, and shakily stand—a remarkable achievement. But then, to my utter astonishment, he let go, and dashed pell-mell across the stage, where he collapsed into a waiting pair of arms. I leapt to my feet and burst into applause, my claps drowned out by the spontaneous thundering roar.

'HE WALKED!!!!' I typed, when I finally sat back down, though I could barely see. 'OH MY GOD HE WALKED!!!' As if there was any chance I would ever forget that moment.

As we left the theatre, chattering, it occurred to me that even we, their relatives and greatest fans, needed to be reminded to see our special children in a different light. Like the Ulysses butterfly, they were exotic, mysterious and could be silent. We adored our children, but we didn't always understand them. On that night, we didn't need to. We celebrated who they were, as opposed to who they were not; all they could do, rather than what eluded them. Most of all, we acknowledged and admired their hard-won transformation. Like the swallow-tailed butterfly, they had each emerged from a chrysalis, a beauty to behold.

＊

The dramatic results of those hydrotherapy classes were an inspiration. I began taking Jacqui to the pool more frequently. I knew that being in the water would improve her breathing and core strength, her coordination and communication. Sophie had lessons once a week, but I took Jacqui as often as possible. She loved it.

Until she got sick.

The first symptom was the sneeze. Then a small cough. Within three days, her eyes were streaming, and the cold rattled in her chest. I kept Jacqui home from school, but there was little she could do. I watched each minute slide by on the clock, counted the minutes until I could pick up Sophie. It always made me smile to see her, hat askew, dash out of the playground with another sack full of gumnuts to bring home. She drew googly eyes and goofy smiles on them, stuck on bits of wool for hair, gave them names. Sophie made life normal and happy.

A cousin had recently given the girls a pair of rabbits, which Sophie named Jelly Beans and Snowy. Sophie and Jelly Beans watched TV together. She and her friends would comb the bunnies, dress them in doll's clothes. I had thought it silly to own rabbits in Australia, but patting their silky fur, it was hard to deny their appeal. We even had a pair of leads and harnesses, so that Sophie and her friends could take them for walks across the grass.

Jacqui continued to spiral downhill. I took her to the local doctor. 'It's just a virus. There's nothing to do but wait. It will run its course.'

Kids getting sick was just part of life. I reminded myself that at least Jacqui didn't have a fever, so there was no danger of a seizure. But Jacqui's misery was overwhelming and more contagious than the flu.

One day, after she had been ill for nearly a week, I was fed up. I rang my mother.

'I just need you to listen to this. I just need you to *hear* this.' I put the phone on speaker and extended my arm to Jacqui, who was sobbing with great deep gusts of sorrow. Usually this made me deeply sympathetic. But on that morning, I was exhausted and depleted and angry. Sick to death of misery and tears, and I said so.

'Oh dear,' Mum replied. 'Oh dear.'

'I've tried food, and TV, and holding her, and books, and driving in the car, and the bath—and nothing works, Mum. *Nothing works.* Nothing! She just cries and screams and whines and nothing I do makes her any less miserable and I don't know if I can stand it.'

'I am sorry,' Mum said, very softly. 'I wish I were closer. I really do.'

The wave of guilt smacked me in the face. What was I doing? What was the point of inflicting my misery on someone 10,000 miles away, who could do nothing to help? On my mum, who loved me, and loved Jacqui, and would now worry?

The anger, like a sparkler, had fizzled out. I took a deep breath. 'I know.'

I gently directed my inconsolable child to the couch to watch *Play School*, tucked a blanket around her, and walked a short distance away.

'I'll be fine, Mum. Promise. I know you can't do anything. It's just that I can't, either. And I don't know who to talk to. I'm not even really sure why I wanted you to hear her.' I paused. 'Maybe I just needed to know it is every bit as bad as I think it is, and that I'm not crazy,' I confided. 'Anyway, I feel better now—all beh-bah, as Jac just told me.'

Mum could sense my shift in tone, and I felt her brighten. 'It does sound awful. And I understand. I really do. You call me any time.'

✳

The seizure came without warning, a 3 a.m. blitzkrieg in advance of a fever.

Andrew catapulted out of bed at the sound of the mewling cry, to find Jacqui shaking uncontrollably, limbs contorted, drooling and choking. Andrew awkwardly cradled her, on her side.

'I tried to straighten her leg,' he admitted, when at last she lay limp, eyes closed. 'She looked so uncomfortable. But I couldn't move it.'

'You can't. I've been told the convulsions are so strong, you'd break an arm or leg if you tried to force it.'

'So there's nothing we can do.' It was a sentence filled with futility. Although I counted on Andrew's calm, stoic manner when it came to Jacqui's woes, I often thought that it was even harder for him to see our little girl ill than it was for me.

'Just what you did. Watch, until it passes. Unless it goes more than five minutes, and I have that emergency medicine.'

For Jacqui, any sudden rise in body temperature was too much for her brain's fragile wiring. A fever was the equivalent of simultaneously turning on too many electrical appliances in an old house. It would trip the circuit breaker, blow a fuse. But if we kept her temperature down with regular doses of over-the-counter medicines, we could prevent another seizure. For the next four days we were vigilant, and the virus finally ran its course. Jacqui was getting better. After two days without a fever, I sent her back to school with a big sigh of relief.

In retrospect, my relief was of the false variety experienced by the victim in a horror movie. Poised for whatever hid behind the creaking door, she relaxed when a cat walked in—only to realise too late the real danger was the monster who had climbed in through the window.

Our monster came in the guise of another seizure. But what made it so unsettling was the fact that for the first time since Jacqui had been a newborn, it was not connected to a fever or fall. Jacqui was enjoying a game of Duck, Duck, Goose at school when she suddenly turned pale, and slipped to the ground in a convulsion. It had to be an isolated event, we told ourselves. Just a bizarre, inexplicable thing that happened. But the following day, there was another seizure. And a few hours later, yet another. And I could feel us slipping back to those bleak days just after Jacqui was born, when I had gnawed on worry night and day, like a bone. And Andrew went missing, lost in a dark silence. This could not be happening again.

We scheduled an emergency appointment with a neurologist. After listening to a detailed explanation of Jacqui's case, flipping through our daughter's voluminous file, the doctor examined her, recommended some tests and summarised his findings, ending with, 'I'm afraid your daughter has epilepsy. I think we should put her on Epilim.'

I wasn't sure what Andrew and I had been expecting, but it wasn't that diagnosis. Shock is funny that way.

'But we were told she had a seizure disorder,' I said, struggling to understand. 'That's what they told us in New York. I mean, at first she was on medicine, but later we had a great doctor who managed to wean her off the drugs. And she has been fine—fine almost all of the time—for two years! Does she really have to go on Epilim? Isn't there some other way, other than drugs? She is so little!'

The neurologist cleared his throat. 'Unfortunately, sometimes things change,' he said. 'Sometimes seizures return, for no particular reason.' Then he turned to Andrew to explain further. 'It seems probable in this case that the virus prompted the change,' the doctor told my husband. 'When seizures occur, and there's no clear trigger, that's when we call it epilepsy.'

I found myself wondering if the doctor was consciously favouring Andrew. I worried that I might be coming across like a hysterical mother. It was a stereotype I feared and detested. I might be sad and confused, but I knew Jacqui's medical history inside out—in greater detail than my husband, as he would be the first to attest—and I wanted to make sure we discussed every angle.

The doctor was now looking at both of us. 'There's every reason to believe your daughter will continue to have seizures, unless we put her on medicine. It is dangerous to have uncontrolled seizures.'

It was. I knew about SUDEP, Sudden Unexplained Death in Epilepsy. There were also deaths which *could* be explained—people who had had a seizure while swimming, or in the bath, or driving a car. When I had been a teenager, my beloved piano teacher had died from a seizure that occurred after she forgot to take her medicine, following a bout of gastro. Her epilepsy had been so well-controlled, I had never even known she had it. I could still picture her sons and husband at the funeral. Epilepsy had scared me ever since.

Andrew and I left with Jacqui, and a prescription.

'Was it my imagination, or was he directing most of his comments at you?' I grumbled.

Andrew looked at me in amazement. 'What are you on about? Talk about hyper-sensitive. But I would say you went on a bit about America, how great her doctor was. It wasn't all perfect there either, remember.'

I felt doubly frustrated. Not only were we dealing with a disturbing shift in Jacqui's medical condition, but we weren't in New York, able to consult with the medical specialists I knew and trusted. I had met some of those doctors during my years as a reporter, and others were good friends. Jacqui's team included international experts in the field of neurology. Wise and collegial, they welcomed our thoughts and observations on our daughter's complex case.

But Andrew was right that it had not always been thus. Early on, I had run across a few doctors who were peremptory and autocratic, or cavalier with advice. They called the shots; it was our job to listen up. One doctor had predicted a horrific future for Jacqui. Thankfully, he was wrong.

Then there was Cowboy, as we called him, the handsome hotshot who seemed to shoot from the hip. His advice regarding medicine was perplexing. We'd resisted, he'd insisted, and we'd regretted our folly when it proved a significant mistake.

I'd learned through excruciating experience to be careful, to find the very best doctors, yes, but also to trust my own instincts and ask questions, rather than blindly obey the men and women in the white coats, no matter how smart and well-respected. Jacqui could not, would never, be able to speak for herself on such complex issues. I was her advocate. I was her mum. I was her lion.

And I was wary and distressed and pacing. This was a new country, with a new medical system, new experts, and I knew no one. The neurologist's advice made sense. We would follow his directions. I was being unfair. It wasn't the doctor's fault Jacqui's seizures had returned. It was far easier to grumble about an appointment than to confront how life was changing, under our feet. We had both been so sure our daughter's brain would strengthen with age and that she would grow out of her seizures. We had never anticipated heading in the opposite direction.

I squeezed Jacqui's hand, looked over at Andrew. 'Isn't it bad enough that she has an intellectual disability?'

'I know,' Andrew nodded. 'Poor little kid. Seems unfair she has to have a medical condition, too.'

Andrew quietly buckled Jacqui in her car seat, handed her the McDonald's fries that were her treat for a trip to the doctor's. 'Lum!' said Jacqui, beaming at us.

If only everything could be fixed with a Happy Meal.

❋

Getting the right medicine and the correct dose turned out to be trickier than we had imagined. There were more seizures. More appointments. Andrew attended when he could, but work was frantic, and I was in charge of our children's medical care. As always, it helped to treat Jacqui's case like a reporting assignment. I observed, wrote notes, kept a detailed log of her evolving condition. We needed to increase her dosage, but I was concerned because it seemed to make her nauseated. Then, one day, she vomited the red liquid.

It was a Friday afternoon. Recognising it could be difficult to reach anyone on the weekend, I quickly called the doctor's office. I was transferred to the doctor. It sounded noisy in the background, and he told me he was on rounds. I thanked him for taking the call, quickly outlined my concerns, and he offered a sensible plan. I felt much better.

But it soon became clear that what had seemed an appropriate course of action was somehow not how things were done. New York was mentioned. The doctor informed me that he had been interrupted while seeing other patients. Next time, I should make an appointment. It was abundantly clear that I had transgressed.

I felt my face flush, because I hated to be thought rude. But I did not think I had done anything wrong. I had called, but during regular hours. I hadn't asked for anyone to be interrupted. I felt duty-bound to be persistent, to get the situation resolved, because a medicine designed to help my daughter was actually making her unwell. I was a mum, and my child was sick. It was my job to help her get better.

But while I was my daughter's advocate, I did not want to be her doctor's adversary. He was a smart professional. I tried to explain, but I think we both felt frustrated, at cross-purposes. And it occurred to me, not for the first time, that it was a hell of a lot easier to be a reporter talking to a doctor, than to be a mum.

In the end, and with a courteous explanation of the rationale, he said he was referring our case on to another expert. I understood, and agreed. But I wanted to take time, think things through, figure out just who the best person was to assess our mysterious daughter. It wasn't simply that she had seizures—we knew there were other issues as well. Despite having had every imaginable test, there had been no answer.

I fought back the impulse to catch the next Qantas flight to JFK, to see the neurologists I knew in New York. But that wasn't the answer. We lived in Australia, and we needed to find the right doctor in Melbourne. This was a city of nearly four million people, with outstanding medical professionals. I would start researching, and I would find the right person to help us discover what was wrong with our darling little girl, and how to make her better. The right doctor for Jacqui, and the right doctor for me.

*

At Port Phillip's kinder, Yvonne spied me, beckoned. 'Come in! Do you have time for a cuppa?'

She was already pulling out a couple of mugs, a tray of biscuits.

'Yeah, sure.'

'How's everything going?' she asked casually.

'Fine.'

'Really? I know Jacqui's been sick. That must be hard.'

I swallowed. 'I think we have things under control at the moment. It's been quiet for a while, thankfully.'

'Are you doing much with NBC? I know you were enjoying that.'

'Not recently. I've been busy with Jacqui's medical stuff. It takes most of my time.'

'How about any work here? I haven't seen you looking all made up and glamorous for a while!' Yvonne poked me, teasing.

I made an effort to smile. 'Now that the presidential race is over, I haven't done much.'

'How's the book coming?'

'Slowly. But I'll get there.'

'Have you met many friends out your way?'

Yvonne seemed to have a lot of questions. I should have wondered more about this, but I was very tired.

'Everyone is lovely.'

I thought of all the wonderful and talented women I had met. There were my tennis pals, though I had quit playing; there were the mums of Sophie and Jacqui's friends. I'd met Kirsty and Pete, with their beautiful cookbook; Sandie, a Chinese medicine practitioner who had the best laugh of anyone I knew; Emma, who showcased her own jewellery and that of other leading Australian artists at her extraordinary shop, e.g.etal; and Jools, an artist whose paintings hung on our walls. And there were many others, sprinkled across the Macedon Ranges. I thought of our neighbours. Of Jacqui's therapists and experts. Of our friends who lived in Melbourne. They were all interesting, vibrant people.

It was just that I didn't see them very often. There was the fact that they were scattered across a wide region, and I could not seem to find time to take the next step. It was hard to turn an occasional intriguing conversation into the kind of deep friendship that could sustain me, far from all those I'd loved and left behind. I adored my husband and children, but I felt like a rootbound potted plant. I needed to go deeper, to transplant fully into the rich soil of Australia. But I seemed to live neither in the city, nor in the country. With all the driving, with Jacqui's medical issues, I was exhausted.

A dear Australian friend of mine had moved from New York to Sydney with her family not long before we moved, and I was awestruck by how quickly she had made friends.

'Must be because you are Australian,' I'd suggested.

'I think it's more that everyone and everything is just close by,' Toni had responded.

The tree-change lifestyle offered many perks, but I missed the ease and spontaneity of catching up in the city.

I put down my tea cup. 'Yup, we're fine.'

Yvonne gazed at me, seemed on the brink of saying something. But in the end all she said was, 'Well, let me know if you ever want to talk.'

❋

We dropped the two bunnies off with relatives for a family weekend away.

'Do you think they will be okay?' Sophie asked anxiously, patting Snowy goodbye. Several fish had died a short time before, the result of an overly ambitious tank-cleaning. We did not need any more traumatic experiences.

'Of course they will.'

But when we picked them up three days later, the rabbits weren't hungry. Jelly Beans lay in the cage, panting. The following morning, Sophie went out to check on them. She came flying inside, her face contorted in anguish. 'Mum! Jelly Beans is rolling over and over! I think he's having a seizure!'

Andrew and I stared at one another, disbelieving.

'Dad, he'll be all right, won't he?'

'Soph, stay inside, I'll check on it,' said Andrew, as I held our sobbing child.

Whether it was Myxomatosis or Calicivirus, both of the girls' beautiful bunnies succumbed to one of the plagues introduced in Australia specifically to eradicate rabbits. Andrew buried them in the bush, not far from the house. Sophie decorated their graves with gumnuts and stones.

There was another casualty. Over the course of a few months, our bouncy little grasstree had turned from a toddler into a haggard geriatric. Its springy hair had gone brown and brittle, and was falling out. Andrew had mixed potion after potion. The tree's 'focal point' status kept us by the patient's bedside. It moped and withered. We called the doctor.

Sue shook her head. 'I'm really sorry. It's dead. It just was too old to transplant. It never really had a chance.'

Like Jelly Beans and Snowy, Andrew buried the tree when I wasn't looking. I got into bed that night, thinking of concoctions. Of the ingredients, the proportions, necessary for my own recipe for survival. I needed to stop dreaming about far away and do a better job of living where I was. I needed to make it a point to see people who were lively and fun, to find time to frolic and play and be ridiculous. To see and do the things that made us laugh so hard we cried.

There had been too much drama. Too much sorrow. It was time to get back to doing whatever it took to give us a normal life. And then I picked up the book on my bedside table that my friend Lisa had given me, with a hug and the prescription, 'You really need something light and amusing.'

Marley taught me about living each day with unbridled exuberance and joy, and seizing the moment and following your heart. He taught me to appreciate the simple things—a walk in the woods, a fresh snowfall, a nap in a shaft of winter sunlight. And as he grew old and achy, he taught me about optimism in the face of adversity. Mostly, he taught me about friendship and selflessness and, above all else, unwavering loyalty.

And I knew just what we had to do.

✳

'You know what, Soph?' I said. 'We need to get a new animal!'
Sophie looked distinctly wary, and I pressed on before any
objection. 'Not a bunny this time. Something big, and strong.
Something that will thrive in Australia.'

Sophie's gaze was a mixture of eagerness and caution. Go.
Stop. Wait. I turned to Andrew.

'So what do you say we get a dog?' Andrew asked.

There was a squeal high enough to pierce a double-glazed
window. 'Really?!' Sophie did a kangaroo impersonation, a
hopping hug.

What had we been thinking, accepting bunnies, when we
lived in the bush? This was all Sophie had ever wanted.

'You need to figure out which breed, Soph,' Andrew said.

Sophie nodded ecstatically. 'Mum, we need to go to the
library, right now,' she directed, grabbing a notepad and pen. 'I
need to start my research.' She turned to her sister. 'Jacqui, we're
going to get us a dog.'

11

NANCI DREW

One of the revelations of parenthood is that no matter how strongly you feel, there are times to argue, and times to let go. Times when it's best to allow a child to make her own decision, and others, when it is necessary to guide and direct. Or exert your right to veto, because it is a big decision, and it's important to avoid a big mistake.

Perhaps it's supporting the wrong football team. Or considering a terrible haircut. Or choosing a vile boyfriend. Whatever it is, she'll regret it, but she doesn't know it, not yet. But Mum, with her vast experience, her superior wisdom, sees the consequences. And therein lies the dilemma—how to balance a child's right to express her autonomy and individuality, against Mum's right to protect said child against a fateful error.

As it happened, this particular calamitous choice concerned the spelling of a name.

'Sophie, Nancy Drew, the detective, is spelled with a "y".'

Eye rolling. 'Mum, I *know*. I've read about twenty of the books, remember?'

'It's prettier with a "y".'

'It's prettier with an "*i*". That's why I'm changing it,' added my nearly eight-year-old daughter.

'The "y" is traditional.'

'Then why did you spell Jacqui's name with an "i"?'

I was temporarily stumped. 'Because apparently that is how it's often spelled in Australia. In the US, she'd be Jackie. Nancy Drew, incidentally, is also American. Besides, that's not the point. The "i" is not correct. And it's going to get misspelled all the time.'

'Well, I like the "'i'". I think it's better. It's different, and *that's* the point. She's not a girl detective. She's going to be my dog.'

As I said, it was a terrible decision, but I let Sophie go ahead. Because that's how kids learn.

And because I had lost the argument.

Sophie's verbal dexterity was alarming and improving all the time.

'A future lawyer,' my mother suggested with a laugh, when I relayed conversational snippets.

With a start, I realised my little girl was growing up. In my vigilant care of Jacqui, I sometimes felt that I wasn't paying close enough attention to Sophie. Periodically, I'd catch a glimpse of my elder daughter which took my breath away.

I watched Jacqui so vigilantly, so microscopically, she never seemed to grow a minute older. But Sophie's development was like a series of snapshots: I could practically hear the shutter drive on the slide show in which my American first-grader transformed into a confident Australian child on the doorstep of Grade Three. Not for the first time, I reminded myself to pay close attention, because Sophie's childhood would be fleeting, everyone said so, and I didn't want to miss a moment. It was easy and delightful to spend time with Sophie, yet Jacqui, with her complicated array of challenges, always pulled focus.

Now that we had help with childcare, I found as many opportunities as I could to escape with Sophie, one on one. I hoped she would notice, appreciate the time. Regardless, I did. I took her for scones at the Trading Post after tennis practice, or to a friend's home for a play. And, on one magical day, Andrew and I took Sophie to check out a litter of puppies.

The visit was the culmination to her research project. Sophie had checked out dozens of books from the library in her quest to select the best breed of dog. My one restriction was that the dog needed to be kid-friendly. She had given us nightly updates, stretched out on the carpet, chin in hand, staring at her books. She regaled us with the relative merits of Cocker Spaniels and Border Collies, Dalmations and Blue Heelers, Saint Bernards and German Shepherds. In her considered opinion, the best prospects were a King Charles Spaniel, a Labrador or a Golden Retriever. 'In case anyone pulls its tail,' she said.

We were all mindful of our family wild card. Jacqui might be perfectly well-behaved with the dog, but if, on the odd occasion, she sat on it, pulled its tail or ear, or in any other way bothered the family pet, we wanted a dog that would respond with indulgence and amused tolerance.

In the end we found a breeder of Golden Retrievers in Woodend. The puppies would be available in January. Andrew and I took Sophie, who brought along her friend Olivia, for consultation. The pair sat down on the grass, to be instantly surrounded by a bouncing, furry commotion. A small golden pup with a pink ribbon walked straight up to Sophie, wagging her tail. She bit Sophie on the finger, gently.

'This is my favourite!' Sophie told us, smitten.

'I think she has chosen you,' the breeder smiled. 'She is the smartest, by the way. It was very easy to teach her to sit, when I come with food.'

The dog seemed a bit Marley-esque to me, but I liked spirited animals.

As we waited for six-week-old Nanci to grow old enough to leave her mum, Andrew called a mate to build a fence around the back garden. The enclosure would not only be for our pet, but a much-needed safe haven for Jacqui, too. I was always worried she would wander off into the bush, go missing in the thousands of hectares of forest that surrounded our home. One night, we'd all been outside having a barbecue, when I realised Jacqui was missing. I knew she couldn't have gone far, but it was pitch black, and there was no answer when we called her name. We'd grabbed flashlights and begun to search. On a hunch, Andrew had gone to the rope swing, a fair distance from where we had been. And there she was, holding the rope, standing quietly, alone in the dark. I was trying to teach her to say, 'Cooee', that useful Australian call, which carried well across vast distances, but her responses were erratic.

The fence meant there would be no more kangaroos jumping on the trampoline, nor wayward emus wandering by. But on the plus side, Jacqui would be safe, and the chunky brown wombats from which the forest took its name would no longer be able to surreptitiously snack on our newly purchased flowers and shrubs in the middle of the night.

Next to the enclosed backyard, we added a kennel and run with an extra high fence, for Nanci Drew.

'Is it secure?' Andrew asked his mate.

His mate snorted. 'I haven't had a dog escape yet.'

Immediately adjacent to the dog kennel, we added another fenced area for chickens. We were debating what kind of chook house we needed to buy when our neighbours Mary and David rang with an inspired substitute. 'Anybody there want a cubby house?'

A family he knew was getting rid of a small child's play house, and he had thoughtfully rung us. Sophie was particularly amused that the cubby had an old telephone stapled to a wall inside. 'The chooks can call us if they get hungry!'

Our friends Sandie and Jack's children—Sebi, Jessie-Rose and Lola—joined Sophie for a children's DIY paint-a-thon. When they had finished, the henhouse was a bright blue, with white trim, and gaily decorated Easter Eggs painted on the front door.

Now all we needed were the chooks. But after the debacle with the rabbits and the fish, I was uncertain of my skills. I talked to my sisters-in-law.

'It's not hard,' Helen told me. She pushed aside her long brown hair, and stepped into the yard. I admired Helen's quiet strength, and her competence in so many areas. Trained as an accountant, she juggled raising children with doing the books for Trevor's business. She could also ride a horse or a motorcycle, and was a keen hockey player.

'What are those!' I asked. They had spectacular feathery crowns, like a powder puff, and the softest of feathers. 'They're Silkies,' Helen told me, patting one. 'My favourite. They're very gentle. Jacqui would love them. The eggs are smaller, but aren't they lovely?'

The chickens were indeed so attractive and unusual, they hardly looked like chickens.

'You could also mix in some Isa Browns,' Kate said, 'Or Rhode Island Reds. I can get you half a dozen pullets. You can start there.'

'That sounds good,' I agreed. 'What is a pullet?'

Kate looked at me, to see if I was joking, then shook her head with a smile. 'Okay, we are starting at the beginning! A pullet is a young female chicken. That way you'll have them laying for longer.'

'What do they eat?' I asked Helen and Kate, 'and how often?'

'You'll find they are very easy,' Helen said reassuringly. 'Just give them any scraps you have.'

'And then layers pellets,' Kate added. 'And shell grit.'

It was starting to sound complicated to me.

'What's that?'

'To make their shells thicker, so they don't break.'

'What about a rooster?' I asked

Kate stared at me to determine if I were pulling her leg. Married to a farmer, and a farmer's daughter, she found it incomprehensible that I could be utterly ignorant of such basic matters as chickens.

'Not unless you want to wake up really early! Don't worry, we'll get you started,' she said, throwing her arm around my neck. 'I'll bring you some of my Golden Yolk Layers Pellets, and then you can top up from the pet shop. There's nothing to it. Even you can't mess it up!'

To my delight, Helen and Kate were right. The chickens were surprisingly easy and clearly one of the world's best bargains. I gave them old rice, the rind of a melon, the tops from strawberries and curry that had sat in the fridge too long, and they devoured the lot as if it were gourmet fare. In return, they gave me glorious eggs. Not only did they reduce our family's waste, but they were such excellent producers that soon we had too many eggs. When invited over for dinner, especially if it was in the city, I was as likely to take a dozen eggs to our hosts as a bottle of wine.

It was Sophie's job to collect the eggs each morning, and when she brought them in, some were still warm to the touch. I discovered that freshly laid eggs tasted different from those bought at the store, even those which were organic and free-range. For some reason, the yolk of fresh eggs sat up quite high, and was round as a dome; it was also a very bright yellow.

Chooks also turned out to be polite and predictable. When we let them out in the afternoon so that they could enjoy being free-range ('Don't let them out in the morning, or they lay their eggs all over the place, and you'll never find them,' Kate had counselled), they filed back to their cubby house promptly at dusk. I had never known.

'Wow, chickens coming home to roost! I get it!'

Andrew shook his head, sorrowfully.

But one morning, after we'd owned the chickens for several weeks, I looked outside early one morning and saw the entire flock contentedly scratching for bugs in the front garden. I'd not realised, until that moment, that we'd neglected to lock the gate after the chickens had retired to their perches the previous evening; at first light, they'd spied the open door, and flown the coop. After delightedly pondering more chicken-related expressions—hunt and peck, feeling peckish—I recognised I somehow had to get the chickens back in their enclosure. We dared not leave them out all day, because of the foxes that patrolled the forest, and the wedge-tailed eagles that flew over the valley. Andrew had already left for work, so it was up to me to be a Chicken Jackaroo, and herd them back into their pen. How hard could it be?

I put on my Blundstones and purposefully strode towards one hen. This was no doubt one of those situations where you were supposed to display who was the real Boss Chook.

The chicken knew exactly who was boss. She was. She took off at a dead sprint.

'Okay, missy, have it your way,' I panted, after she'd disappeared into a grevillea. I turned to spy a second chook ogling me and took off in pursuit. She proved equally speedy and evasive. I returned to the house to ponder tactics, and picked up a broom. I proceeded to chase after the remaining chickens, which scattered in a squawking profusion of feathers, wings and attitude, leaving me worse off than I had been before.

As I stood in the yard, broom aloft, staring in frustration at the darting chickens, Sophie wandered outside, rubbing her eyes, still in her pyjamas.

'Mum, are you trying to murder the chickens?'

'Certainly not!'

'Then why are you chasing them with a broom?'

'I'm rounding them up.'

Sophie, turned, went inside, and opened the cupboard under the sink, where we kept the bucket of scraps. 'Want some help? Watch me, Mum. It's easy!'

Sophie pulled on her boots, and wandered into the front yard, holding the scraps in front of her and crooning, 'Here, chooky, chooky, here chooky, chooky.'

It sounded ridiculous. No self-respecting chicken would ever fall for such an obvious ploy.

A beak poked out of the grevillea. Another chook ventured out from behind a gum tree. Slowly, they followed the pied piper with the pail.

'I think they are a bit ruffled, Mum,' Sophie said politely, after she'd gotten four of the chickens in the pen. The other two refused to budge. Sophie slowly walked towards them, deftly scooped one up and tucked it under her arm, holding its talons with her other small hand. She unceremoniously stuffed it into the nesting box Andrew had added to the side of the chicken house, and firmly closed the lid. Then she set off to capture the final wayward chook. Within a few short minutes, all six chooks were placidly wandering around their yard. Sophie came inside to wash her hands for breakfast.

'French toast for you, chicken wrangler. How'd you learn to do that? Did Pa teach you? Or Aunty Helen or Aunty Katie?'

Sophie looked at me quizzically. 'I didn't learn, Mum. It's just what you do. It's obvious.'

Not to me, it wasn't. And having subsequently witnessed other adults foiled by rascally poultry, I stuck to the theory I'd adopted soon after arrival, when I had watched Sophie fearlessly help Pa clip the wings of a chicken. What was obvious was that farming was in her DNA.

✳

December was sunny and hot and filled with family activities, but it was an odd season for an East Coast American. Fake snow. Sweaty Santas. Instead of ice skating at Rockefeller Plaza, fortified by hot cocoa and mulled cider, or skiing in the mountains of upstate New York, we went to the beach with the aunts and uncles and cousins, dove into the surf. The waves were a welcome relief from weather that was brutally hot and dry. There was talk of the old days, of swimming in Nana and Pa's dam, but the dam was nearly empty. Pa shook his head. 'It won't fill in my lifetime,' he pronounced.

Christmas cards arrived from America. Sophie's friend Mary Ben in an apple orchard. Her friends Phoebe, Zoe and Nadine in autumn leaves. Cards from family and friends, across America, arrived every day in the post, filled with photos and greetings and news. It was impossible not to think of family. I pictured them, gathered in Virginia. Mum, seated at the Steinway, playing Christmas carols; Dad accompanying on his trumpet. I saw Elizabeth and Susan singing 'Deck, the halls with boughs of holly!' while the brothers-in-law, John and Danny, sat engrossed in conversation. I could picture Susan's children, little Sebastian and Hattie, examining the presents under the tree. A judicious poke. An inquisitive shake. Waiting was so very hard. Outside, the sky would be the colour of Paul Revere pewter. Snow was coming.

Instead I was in shorts and a t-shirt on a picnic blanket in the park, where we listened to Sophie and her classmates sing, 'Silent Night' and 'Rudolph, the red-nosed reindeer'. The traditions jangled. I made gingerbread men, only to find it too hot to decorate them. The roast dinner for Christmas lunch was delicious, but all I wanted was salad. But as I opened my enormous pillow of a stocking from Nana and Pa, and as the girls squealed with delight at their piles of presents from grandparents and aunties and uncles, and as the cousins ran outside shrieking, I got into the spirit of the day. I knew Australians loved Christmas in the summer, and I felt Scrooge-like for my Bah, humbugness. But I just needed to get accustomed to it.

When Christmas was over, I couldn't wait to take down the spruce Andrew had thoughtfully purchased at a tree farm near our home. Its needles had turned brown in the ferocious sunshine that poured in through what I had nicknamed the Ginger Window, since my childhood friend had been the one to suggest the extra large pane of glass next to the fireplace. It made for a beautiful view, and was worth the extra heat in summer. I took off a favourite ornament, a glass oval with a sketch of our old weatherboard farmhouse in upstate New York. It set off a pine needle cascade and an avalanche of memories. I pulled out the vacuum cleaner. Had we really lived in Australia for nearly a year? It was inconceivable.

A highlight of December was a visit from some overseas friends. I'd met Julie Bruton-Seal years before, when we had both lived in North Carolina; she now lived in the UK, but Julie and her mum and dad were Australian. Des hailed from Queensland, Jen from New South Wales, and Julie had attended boarding school in Australia. But her envy-provoking upbringing included extended jaunts all over the world, to stay wherever her parents were filming. Jen and Des were Australia's answer to David Attenborough—a talented pair of wildlife filmmakers who'd shot more than fifty nature films on virtually every continent. Their still photographs had appeared in *National Geographic*, and their Emmy award-winning films had aired as *National Geographic* specials, as well as appearing on the BBC and countless other television networks around the world.

They were far less well-known in Australia, having lived overseas for decades. I found it surprising, especially since Jen had been a budding tennis star before exchanging her racquet for a camera. She'd served against Margaret Court, been a doubles partner for Rod Laver, even played at Wimbledon. Then she'd met Des, and they'd headed off to Africa, a move she said she'd never once regretted. They were friends with the Leakeys in Kenya, as well as other fascinating explorers, naturalists, anthropologists and filmmakers who lived and worked in Africa from the 1960s through the 1990s. The couple had recently retired, and were back in Australia for a long overdue chance to catch up with relatives and old friends. Julie and her husband Matthew had accompanied them.

'I can see why you moved here,' Julie smiled at me, as we took a long walk through the property and down the lane. An expert in botany and a fine vegetarian cook, Julie was also a registered herbalist. She and Matthew were writing a series of books on how anyone could use local plants as pharmacy and food. They'd just finished *Hedgerow Medicine*, and were snapping a few photos, including one of our pantry, for their next book, *Kitchen Medicine*.

'Can I eat this?' Sophie interjected, a tattered leaf in her outstretched, grubby hand.

'Only if Julie says so,' I told Sophie, 'because she is an expert.'

'That's sheep sorrel,' Julie answered, 'and yes, you can. You, too, Jacqui,' she added. She bent down, handed Jac a small flower even I recognised. 'And dandelion has loads of uses. I'll pick some leaves for the salad tonight, and I can also show you how to make dandelion tea.'

'Are you sure you don't want to move back to Oz?' I asked, holding Jacqui with one hand, and linking the other arm through that of my friend. 'Just wait until we take you to the cherry orchard down the road!' I continued.

'Lum!' Jacqui nodded excitedly, patting her stomach. I smiled. It was good to see Jacqui doing better. We'd switched Jacqui's medicine from a liquid to tablets—Andrew had taught her how to swallow them—and she was no longer nauseated. Jacqui was an enthusiastic eater, especially when it came to cherries. I was trying to teach her to discriminate between the fruit and the pit, but she was as speedy as she was voracious. She generally swallowed the stone.

'Cherry pie for dinner, perhaps?' Julie responded.

'Sophie, come take a look at this wombat spoor,' said Des, squatting on his haunches. He had the enthusiasm of a boy, though he was close to eighty. 'Can you tell the difference between this and kangaroo spoor?'

'Wow! It's kind of square! That's cool. But what's spoor? Isn't that poo?' Sophie asked, soaking up every bit of information from our naturalist friends.

'That's right,' Des nodded. 'Just a bit more scientific, but exactly the same. You can track an animal following its spoor, or discover what he's been eating.' He stood, turned to me. 'Sara, you must like this much better than living in New York. I never could see how you lived there for so long. All those people! Much better living right here in the bush.' He opened his arms wide, as if to encompass the entire Wombat State Forest.

Julie grinned. 'Remember, Sara likes people!'

'She likes wildlife, too,' Des countered. 'I remember when she came with you to Namibia. You enjoyed that trip, didn't you, Sara?'

'It was unforgettable.' Visiting Julie and her parents, as well as Ginger, whom they'd helped get started as a filmmaker, had been a magical experience.

'Victoria is very pretty,' Jen said, returning to the previous conversation. 'I hadn't spent much time in this part of the country before. The bush is beautiful. Dry, though. You will need to be careful.'

'You mean snakes?' I asked.

She shook her head. 'You know they are more frightened of you than you are of them. I meant bushfires. You wouldn't have learned much about them, living in New York.' She shook her head, and I looked at her quizzically. She said only, 'They're impressive.'

I nodded slowly, musing. Everyone seemed to be talking about bushfires of late. Thirteen years of drought was hard to comprehend. Everything looked fine to me, but farmers like Pa shook their heads and looked exceedingly grave when discussing the weather. There had been any number of Total Fire Ban days during the previous month. I'd had to learn that these were days in which no one could light a fire outdoors, not even the barbecue, because the risk of starting a bushfire was so great. But otherwise, it was life as usual. Andrew didn't seem alarmed. I figured if there were a fire, we'd just leave.

Just then, Sophie let out a yelp. 'Look! Look, Mum!' Above us, peering down inquisitively, was a large, healthy koala.

'Good spotting, Sophie,' Jen said with a smile.

'Look who has come to see the wildlife filmmakers!' I grinned.

✳

The Captiva rattled so teeth-jarringly across the washboard road that I had to slow down. I found myself swallowing, reflexively, the result of the dust catching in the back of my throat, even though the windows were rolled up, the air-conditioner at full blast. When was the last time it had rained? I couldn't remember. Some time in early December? Once?

It was a stunning day in early February—the sky bright blue as a fairy wren. But the field next to the road was parched and pale. I juddered down our drive, to discover the local water supplier was filling the tanks.

'Isn't this the second time he's had to deliver water this summer?' I asked Andrew, as he peeled off several hundred dollars in fifty-dollar notes.

'Third,' Andrew corrected, but waved a hand dismissively. 'She'll be right. It was like this when I was a kid. Years where it rained, years when it didn't.'

'Do you ever worry about bushfires?'

'Nah. We'd get plenty of warning. Look.'

From our spot on the top of the ridge, we had a commanding view of thousands of hectares of trees.

'I'm off to get the pooch,' Andrew said.

✳

A few hours later, Andrew rang from the car. 'Get the camera ready!' he said, in a conspiratorial tone. 'And get the girls! I'm about to come around the corner.'

'Hey, Soph,' I called out. 'Can you come help me set the table?' I had the camera behind my back.

'Wha tha?' Jacqui asked, trying to discover what I was hiding, as Sophie entered the living room, and gave me a suspicious look. But she was instantly diverted by the sight of Andrew cradling a small, soft, yellow ball of fluff.

'My dog!!! DAD, YOU GOT OUR DOG!!!' shouted Sophie, 'NANCI!!!'

She dashed to the dog so quickly, scooped up the puppy so instantly, that the photo of the moment was a blur. But Sophie's smile was megawatt special. I patted Nanci, patted Sophie. Jacqui came over for a closer look.

'She's a bit car-sick, Soph,' Andrew explained, attempting to loosen Sophie's fierce grip on the newest member of the family. 'Here, put her in this little pen, by the back door. Look, I've got nice, soft rags in it. Nanci can see us through the glass. When she is bigger, we'll put her in her kennel.'

As if on cue, Nanci howled and I had a momentary pang, a premonition.

Sophie was wordless, cradling her pup as Nanci wagged and wriggled and carefully licked Sophie's face. As we watched our new puppy, we were all blissfully unaware of the mischief she'd get up to in just a few short weeks. But most of all, we were oblivious to the horror which was about to engulf the region just a few weeks later, in the first week of February 2009.

12

THE LYREBIRD

'Oh, he's absolutely gorgeous! Just spectacular! You have done an amazing job!'

There was a moment of stunned silence. Andrew had informed me I sometimes went on a bit. But I was originally Southern, after all, born and raised in a region with etiquette as flowery and formal as in Japan.

'Can you carry it?' the butcher asked. 'It's heavy.'

'I think so,' I reached out for the platter laden with an enormous salmon. Early that morning I'd dropped off homemade stuffing—fennel, onion, dill, a hint of garlic—but the butcher had done the rest. He'd slit the fish, stem to stern, filled it, then bound the salmon back together again with twine. I would put it in the fridge, and in a few hours, all I needed to do was cook and serve—a foolproof and easy main course.

'When's the party?'

'Tonight.' I glanced at my watch. How could it already be 9.30 in the morning? 'Yikes, I'd better get going! Thanks again!'

A fleeting glance flickered across his face. 'You're staying?'

Stay or go, defend or flee. It was all anyone in the Macedon Ranges could talk about. As an East Coast American, I still felt woefully under-informed. The experts suggested leaving early, but that word seemed to be open to interpretation. Should we have left last night? Or at first light? Or were we okay to wait until we heard a troubling news bulletin, or saw a faraway wisp of smoke?

'Actually, we're leaving as soon as I put this in the refrigerator. Then it's off to family near Castlemaine,' I replied. 'But assuming the forecast is a big fizzle, we'll be back in time for this dinner.'

His cocked eyebrow rose higher. As I listened to our 'Fire Plan', it sounded not only unorthodox, but downright insane. Flee, but return in time to host a dinner party. But we'd had our plans disrupted too many times this summer. We were eager to go on with life as usual.

'Well, good luck then,' he said.

'You, too.'

The bell jingled as I left the shop. After just a few seconds outside, I thought I might spontaneously combust. You had to push through this heat, breast-stroke through thick waves of it.

I looked around. Woodend was a ghost town. The streets virtually deserted, houses shuttered, drawn tight. If we were near the coast, instead of near Mount Macedon, it would appear the town had battened down for a hurricane. But there was no deluge, only extreme heat. And an extreme forecast.

I had been looking forward to this Saturday evening for weeks. It had taken more than a year, but by early February 2009, our wreck-o-vation was finally finished and the garden planted. We had invited a few friends from Melbourne for a dinner that would be our unofficial 'open house'. These Melburnians were keen to see exactly what had prompted us to lose our minds and move to a dirt road in the middle of nowhere, and we were now ready to show them. But one couple had just pulled out, and I could understand why.

The first warning sign had been a phone call from Andrew's mother the day before. 'Have you heard about the Total Fire Ban for the 7th, Sara?' she asked, sounding uneasy.

'Yes, but we've had oodles this summer. Isn't this just more of the same?'

'I don't think so. They're saying this day is very different. I'm not sure what 45 degrees translates to in the old temperature, but it's extreme.'

I had learned from the cockatoo fiasco to pay closer attention to the advice of locals, especially family. I now took regular soundings, plunged my pole into the river of opinion to check the depth and the current, to probe for shifting shoals I couldn't see.

'So we should be worried, then?'

'Too right!' Nana replied in a flash. 'I think it could be a terrible day, if the wind is as bad as they say. You weren't here for the Ash Wednesday fires on Mount Macedon, but we will never forget them. I don't like the thought of you staying where you are. Why don't you come to the farm, be with us?'

To me, heading further into the Victorian countryside sounded a bit like out of the frying pan and into the fire. But then again, the Butcher homestead, set well away from the forest and in the centre of wide, grassy paddocks, had stood for a century and a half, unscathed. Our house had been built less than a decade ago—long after those devastating fires of '83. As I considered my options, for a moment I fervently wished we'd just moved to the city, like everyone recommended. What a simpler, saner and safer life that would have been. I knew cities and understood them. The Australian countryside still baffled me.

'Let me call Andrew. I'll get back to you.'

But I'd scarcely hung up from Nana when the phone rang again.

This time the caller was our friend Cameron Stewart, Associate Editor of *The Australian*, and an award-winning reporter for the paper. He'd know the scoop. More crucially, he and his gorgeous wife Mignon, an anchor for *ABC Asia,* were among our presumptive dinner guests.

'Hi Sara, about tomorrow night,' said Cam. 'I assume you're cancelling?'

Cameron Stewart is one of the most polite men I know. I'd met him in Manhattan, when Cam had served as *The Australian*'s New York correspondent from 1996 to 1999. If he assumed dinner was off, it wasn't because he had doubts about my ability to cook fish.

'Actually, no. Not yet anyway,' I answered. 'But are we crazy? What do you think, from talking to the experts? Is it really that dire?'

'Have you seen what the Premier says?' I heard rustling, as Cam shifted papers on his desk. 'Here, let me read you the quotes from Brumby: "It's just as bad a day as you can imagine and on top of that, the state is just tinder dry. People need to exercise real commonsense tomorrow."' Cam continued, 'The Premier says it's expected to be the worst day of fire conditions in the history of the state.'

I felt my stomach do a series of Olympic gymnastics manoeuvres.

'Rightio. Give me a sec and I'll call you straight back.'

But when I reached my husband and raised the news reports, he'd already seen them. 'That's what the politicians always say. We've had these days before. I grew up here, remember. It's just part of living in Oz.'

'Andrew, your mother rang, too.'

'My *mum*?! Of course she is worried, that's a mum's job!'

I found myself wondering how many couples were having this same conversation, how many alarmed men and women were being told to relax by a more nonchalant partner. I tried a third time. 'But Cam says this day is different. And you know it's not like him to be a panic merchant.'

I thought I'd gotten through. Andrew hesitated. Then he said, with the air of a defence attorney revealing the mystery witness at a murder trial, 'But the cricket's still on.'

I rolled my eyes, thankful he couldn't see me. From what I could tell of those who played cricket, years of standing in a field under a brutal sun cooked their brains. I was silent. Apparently silence did the trick.

'Look, I think we would be fine where we are,' Andrew relented. 'We have great visibility. But if you're that worried, we'll go to Mum and Dad's for the day. If the day turns out to be a shocker, we can cancel later—these are all old friends. But it's not easy to coordinate everyone's schedules, so let's not be hasty. I'm telling you, 99 times out of 100, these things are a beat-up,' said my husband, the former reporter for a tabloid newspaper.

I hung up, by that time worrying if I was over-reacting. Over the years, Andrew's calm good sense had served us well, and never more so than during the months of September and October 2001. Andrew had been at work, and I had been home with our new baby, when those two planes struck the Twin Towers, one after the other. On that surreal day, as we listened to reports that yet another aircraft had crashed in Pennsylvania, and still another had struck the Pentagon, there was confusion, incomprehension and a yawning terror, eclipsed by that cataclysmic collapse.

Andrew and I both worked in media, which is predominantly based in Midtown Manhattan, and we lived on the Upper East Side, about eight kilometres from the Twin Towers, located on the west side of Lower Manhanttan. We were shaken but fine, and a flurry of phone calls and emails revealed our closest friends were safe. But there was no one in New York, indeed the entire metropolitan area, who didn't know at least one of the victims, either directly, or by a half a degree of separation. Our country, our city, had been attacked. I returned to work the next day.

The smouldering inferno burned on, a furnace too hot to extinguish. As we walked past the photographs of the missing, past the teddy bears and the candles, and the daily funerals for the hundreds of New York fire-fighters killed fighting the blaze, as we heard the sobbing of bagpipes outside Saint Patrick's

Cathedral, across from NBC headquarters, we found ourselves sleep-walking through an apocalyptic time. The ash from the burning buildings settled on the terrace of our apartment, like a light drift of snowflakes.

Nearly 3000 people died in those four terrorist attacks, a horrific toll. It was as if someone had wiped out a small town; as if more than half the population of Woodend had simply vanished, in an hour. And every one of them had been someone's mum, or baby, someone's lover, or brother, or friend. Overnight, New York shrank and gentled, as everyone, from those wealthy beyond imagination to those who owned little more than their dreams, came together, bound by that legacy of loss. It seemed to me that the horror of 9/11 lapped outwards, in concentric circles of trauma and despair, to reach even the farthest stretches of the globe. But the heart of darkness was that blazing wound, that point of impact, Ground Zero.

Amplifying our fear in America that autumn had been a little remembered postscript—a deadly string of anthrax attacks that began one week to the day after 9/11. Letters filled with anthrax spores had been mailed to several newsrooms nationwide, including Fox News, in the News Corporation building where Andrew worked, and NBC. In all, five people would be killed and seventeen infected by the weaponised anthrax.

One of those infected was the assistant to then NBC anchorman Tom Brokaw. I was serving as a back-up anchor for Tom's news bulletins when he was out of the office. We watched dumbfounded as workers wearing spacesuits arrived to clean up the contamination. Those of us who had been in the vicinity of the spores were at risk and immediately prescribed powerful antibiotics. Because I had happened to take Sophie to NBC, to show off my new baby to friends, including Tom, our six-month-old daughter had also been in the wrong place at the wrong time. We found our family in the middle of the investigation by the FBI and the Centers for Disease Control and Prevention, or CDC.

Our daughter was tested for anthrax infection by doctors wearing masks and long plastic gloves. To our overwhelming relief, the tests came back negative, and Brokaw's assistant made a full recovery.

But it had been a terrifying time, and I'd appreciated Andrew's steadiness and calm. In this case, Andrew knew far more about the Australian bush and its bushfires than I did. If he wasn't worried, I'd try not to be. Besides, bushfires were a natural phenomenon. Somehow, that seemed less alarming than terrorism.

Still, I was curious to find out more first-hand details. With the girls in tow, I headed to a nearby Country Fire Authority station to find out more for myself. There were several CFA trucks parked, nose out, sparkling, freshly washed and polished. Inside, scanners chattered. A clutch of men stood around a table, analysing maps, gesturing, plotting. A dozen pairs of boots were neatly lined up, along with fire suits, masks, helmets and other assorted gear. The girls stared wide-eyed, enjoying the commotion. I could tell they picked up the intensity, which was palpable. It was a sensation I'd encountered many times, in many places around the globe. This CFA station hummed with the purposeful air of a team engaged in the last-minute planning that precedes a major mission, and I suddenly had the feeling I could be at the fabled New York station known as 'The Pride of Midtown'.

Midtown Firehouse 54—Engine 54, Ladder 4, Battalion 9—was a firehouse on Eighth Avenue and 48th Street, just a few blocks from Rockefeller Center. It was a unit dedicated to fighting fires in high-rises, and the ladder trucks had raced to the Twin Towers on 9/11, sirens screaming. And when those mighty towers had collapsed, that one firehouse alone lost fifteen of New York's bravest.

As I watched these volunteers, my stomach lurched. I wondered if they had any idea what might be in store, if the following day turned out to be as serious as predicted. I saw a young man, clearly a recent volunteer, who stood just outside the scrum of grizzled veterans. He was keen to chat.

'I think what has everyone a bit worried,' he told me, 'is that they had to invent a whole new level for the day.'

'What do you mean, a new level?'

'You know how they rate the days in terms of danger? Severe, or high, or Total Fire Ban? Well, they say tomorrow's conditions will be worse than any of that. They're calling the risk catastrophic.'

I nodded, and turned to leave. It was time to pack.

✳

It took the rest of the afternoon to load the car. Papers, documents, ATM cards and chequebooks, credit cards, passports, birth certificates, computers, mobile phones and chargers. All the things you needed if you became homeless, all the things I knew from covering other disasters that were difficult and time-consuming to replace after a fire or flood, tornado, hurricane or earthquake had destroyed your home. I also packed several changes of clothes for everyone, and Jacqui's supplies of medicine. I put in bottles of water, a battery-powered radio, torches, blankets, VicRoads maps in case we needed to follow back roads. I was always getting lost.

It took longer to choose which of our treasured possessions to take. I loaded cameras, photo albums, special pictures the girls had painted, family jewellery, Sophie's favourite stuffed animal, Jasper, and *Edward the Emu*, still Jacqui's favourite book. I looked around. Our house had only just begun to look like a home. Every room contained reminders from my travels, and Andrew's: colourful rugs from Pakistan, Afghanistan, Jerusalem and Namibia, and ones I'd inherited from my grandmother. Baskets I'd picked up, ceremonial beaded vests and detailed carvings from Somalia and Sudan, Kenya, Egypt and Zimbabwe. I grabbed a few silks and old puppets from China; a pewter service I'd purchased in the Loire Valley; a tooled silver cake server from Sarajevo; a sequined voodoo flag from Haiti; and Andrew's lovely collection of ceramics and linens from Japan and North Korea.

And then there was the rock. It was a heavy grey stone, inconspicuously placed next to the fireplace. It was my favourite souvenir, given to me by the crew of the deep-sea submarine *Nautile*, after we'd been to the bottom of the Atlantic to the wreck of the *Titanic*. That rock would survive anything, I figured.

There were wedding gifts, from Australia and America and from friends who lived in other countries overseas, each with its own story to tell. There were the pieces of antique furniture I'd just polished, in anticipation of our party; some we'd bought, others we'd inherited from my family, and carefully shipped across the Pacific. And there were beautiful items from Andrew's ancestors, including a gold and white tea set from Japan, and a fabulous old clock that told time inconsistently, but chimed melodiously. There was my piano. Andrew's old cricket trophies. Mine, from public speaking. His Mustang in the garage. And all of our books, books which seemed like old friends.

I walked around the house for a long time. It wasn't fashionable to care about things, but possessions could be imbued with memory and meaning, with history. They were pieces of home, when home was far away. It was foolish to dismiss them, to pretend you wouldn't miss them, if something were to happen. I chose a few small items that packed easily. Just in case. I knew from experience that no one ever returned after a disaster desperate to find their plasma-screen TV, but rather the picture of their great-grandmother, the baby shoes of a child long grown, or the hammer their father had given them as a nine-year-old boy. I could still picture the man who had searched for that hammer, discovered the metal head, in the midst of utter devastation. He had wept for joy. A few cherished mementos would need to be enough.

I retrieved the camera from the boot of the car, and took pictures of each room, then closed the front door and locked it. I made sure there was plenty of water for the chickens, and left the gate to their little yard wide open. Having done everything

I could do, I felt instantly better. Even our puppy, Nanci Drew, would be at the farm where she'd been born, which was the best place for her. And Andrew and I would be with the girls. Besides, nothing was going to happen. We'd be home in time for dinner, a good dinner with friends in which we'd toast the catastrophe that never was.

✳

'It's pretty hot,' Andrew said lightly, when we arrived at his parents' home in Muckleford. 'I'll give you that.'

He appeared more fascinated by the weather than frightened of it. It occurred to me that his stint overseas meant that the last time Andrew had encountered a day of fire danger, he'd been a teenager. We were standing behind the house, and every step felt like wading into invisible magma. A short time before, the predicted northerly had struck, and the winds were clocked at more than 100 kilometres an hour. I kept my head down. It was hard to breathe, hard to think.

'It feels ominous.'

He nodded. 'Yeah, be good when it's over. I'm off to cricket— guess it's not a great day to come watch us.' I started to make a snarky comment about heat stroke but realised he was joking.

But Andrew wasn't smiling when he returned a short time later. Hearing the unmistakable rumble of the Mustang, I walked out to check what was wrong and learned the game had been called off. Given the 46-degree temperature, this was inevitable, but Andrew was annoyed.

'Sooks,' he groused. Standing outside had gone from unpleasant to unbearable. I wondered how many people, desperate for a weekend break after days spent in meetings, found it hard to accept the fact that on that day, nature had other plans.

And then I found myself thinking, inconsequentially, about the salmon. What a ridiculous entrée I had purchased, given the forecast. What if this God-awful wind knocked over a power line and cut off our electricity? Fish would spoil in no time.

Just then Andrew interrupted my thoughts with a pronounce-ment: he would drive home to get ready for the evening's dinner party, and the girls and I could stay where we were, to return shortly before our guests arrived. Phrased as a helpful sugges-tion, it was an obvious escape plan. It was clear he thought I'd over-reacted, and he was finished with this forced evacuation. My objections fell on deaf ears.

'But we'll be separated,' I concluded. 'If something happens.'

'Just for a few hours,' Andrew replied.

I had no intention of taking the girls back to our property until the promised 'cool change' had blown through, until the combination of plunging temperatures and nightfall extinguished the extreme fire risk. But that was hours off. Irked, I headed back inside with a terse goodbye to my husband. Which was why it took me a minute—exactly one minute too long—to notice the sound of the engine, rattling down the drive. It was not a thumping, vintage V8, but a gurgling diesel. Andrew had driven off in the Captiva. Which meant he had inadvertently taken all the crucial items I'd so carefully packed for safe-keeping. I had Jacqui's medicine in my purse. But if we had to leave in a hurry, I would need to take one of Nana and Pa's cars, and there would be no car seat for Jacqueline. How unbelievably irritating! Thank God this would all be over soon.

✳

Nana, Pa, Sophie, Jacqui and I were idly chatting. The old house creaked in the dry gale, but there was no sign of danger. We hadn't even bothered to turn on the television. The phone rang.

'Hello, Norm!' said Nana, in the delighted tone she always adopted when her younger brother rang. I instantly tuned in. Norm Beaman was something of a legend in Melbourne news circles, a veteran reporter who'd worked in virtually every television newsroom. That Saturday was his day off, but the dire predictions meant every newsroom was operating at peak capacity. Norm was acting Chief of Staff for Channel 7. Given his role deploying crews, we'd soon have the most up-to-date information.

Nana looked shocked. She was gripping the phone.

'*A fire where?*' she asked. 'Bert! Flick on the wireless!' she commanded urgently, and as Pa hastily complied, I caught the unmistakable sound of the 'sting'—the brief, urgent tune, like a musical cluster of exclamation points, designed to warn listeners they are about to hear something big. Usually something bad.

'Norm says there's a bushfire on Mount Disappointment! And Annie is there!'

There was a bewildering kaleidoscope of information: in the foreground, ABC bulletins with word of a rash of fires, with mention of Kilmore, Wandong and Mount Disappointment; in the background, details which made it clear that Norm's wife was among those in mortal peril.

'Where is Annie now, Norm? Call us back, the second you know!' Nana turned to us, wide-eyed and shaky. 'Annie's rung Norm. She saw the fire—he says she told him it was miles off—and tried to get out. But it was just too quick. The fire leapt, and it's surrounded her.' We all stood, staring, as Nana reiterated, 'She's trapped up there, on that mountain.' Pa put an arm around Nana, pulled her close.

'Is Aunty Annie going to be okay?' asked Sophie, suddenly tuning in, the emotional current acting like a magnet.

'Norm will tell us,' said Nana. 'We'll have to wait.'

'She's very clever, Soph,' I said, reassuringly. As if surviving a fire could be solved by intelligence alone.

I took a deep breath, reminded myself that Annie was also extremely capable and that she and Norm kept their home and surrounding property well-cleared, and were prepared with hoses and even had fire-retardant suits. But the expressions on Nana and Pa's faces were exceedingly grave. A barrage of reports from the

ABC mingled with reports on television, as we surfed channels: 'We repeat, there is an imminent threat;' 'The following communities are under ember attack'; 'Prepare to enact your fire plan'. I tried to ring Andrew, but his phone was engaged. I pictured him, flicking on the radio in the car. He would hear the news, instantly call his uncle. And I had no doubt what would happen next.

The house phone rang again, splintering the hush.

'What?!' exclaimed Nana, in an alarming tone, 'No, no, no.' It was hard to catch the words, for she spoke softly now. 'Norm just heard from Annie again. She. Had to jump. In the dam. And that's when she—that's when her phone cut off.'

'She will ring back,' I said, with more confidence than I felt.

'He's tried to call. There's no answer.'

Kind-hearted Annie, beloved of the entire family, was trapped in the middle of a raging bushfire. Tears streamed down Nana's cheeks and Pa shook his head slowly, back and forth. Tears gathered in his dark eyes, too, and then I knew. He did not think she stood a chance.

I could picture the house, the grounds and dam, set on the crest of Mount Disappointment, which was not far from Whittlesea. The home had a spectacular view which had been further improved by Annie's passion for gardening. Many years before, when Andrew and I were dating, we'd visited Norm and Annie, and first talked of perhaps one day buying our own hilltop home.

The origins of the mountain's unhappy name dated back to 1824, when the Hume and Hovell Expedition out of New South Wales had hacked through thick bush to the summit, in hopes of spying Port Phillip Bay. Instead, the exhausted explorers saw only thousands of hectares of undulating forest, in every direction. They exacted their revenge and it had been called Mount Disappointment ever since. The region was still thickly wooded, and although the mountain was a perfect place for a four-wheel drive adventure, it was a terrible place to be caught in a fire. As far as I knew, there was only one rutted, winding road up or down the mountain.

'Mum, what's wrong?' asked Sophie, tugging on my arm. 'Why is Aunty Annie in the dam? She'll get all wet.'

'She'll be okay, Sophie, you'll see,' I said.

The lies adults tell children. The lies we try to hope into truth.

❋

My mobile rang with the number I'd wanted to see.

'I'm going to try to intercept him,' Andrew said without preamble. 'You know my uncle. There's no telling what he'll do to get Annie.'

'I know,' I said. 'You're doing the right thing.'

'Everything okay there?'

'We're fine.'

But as television and radio made clear, many others were not. We listened, though we turned off the television so as not to alarm the girls. And for some unspoken reason, as if responding to an atavistic taboo, we refrained from saying Annie's name. As the news reports flared and billowed with the expanding fire, we acknowledged her often, but carefully, and by extension.

'Still no word from Norm?'

'No.'

'She's very strong. And brave.'

'She is.'

❋

Some people fight fear. Others attempt to tame it. I try to give it a border. Ever since I became a reporter, I've found that it is easiest to face fear if I look at it through a lens. By closing one eye and peering through the viewfinder of a camera, it is possible to shrink the world to a tiny box, to confine terror to a predetermined field of vision; with practice, it is sometimes possible to detach from emotion altogether, or at least prevent it from contaminating everything else. This doesn't always work, of course, and it never works forever. There can be fallout from such wilful suppression of feeling, down the track. But in an emergency, it is a useful tool for self-protection, even if such a restricted field of vision makes it possible to step closer to calamity than is wise. I had covered frightening situations as a reporter. I had been in war zones. But sitting in a pleasant kitchen, with nothing to do but think about how badly I wished I could spirit our daughters far away from the threat of fire, was far more terrifying than being a reporter. At times, being a mum could be the scariest job of all.

It was clear the scope and scale of this emergency were overwhelming. I also had a memory bank stocked with images of other disasters from all those years as a reporter. I could picture what came next, a little too clearly. I carefully pushed those images aside, and took stock.

Our immediate circumstances were secure. No flames, no smoke. We were out of harm's way, unless the wind shifted, or a new fire started. Those were distinct possibilities, of course. I had none of the provisions in the Captiva, but Nana and Pa were both well prepared and experienced. For now, the electricity worked. We had phones, water, food, air-conditioning and batteries for when power failed. Pa had hooked up the hoses, repeatedly watered the house and the lawn which surrounded it.

Sophie and Jacqui seemed delightfully oblivious, devouring crackers, cheese and almonds at the polished red gum dining-room table, and I was thankful they were still young. Pa headed out to do another check of the hoses, to give yet one more dousing to the shrubbery. Nana was organising supper. I was suffering the poisonous pressure of anxiety, a by-product of toxic worry combined with nothing to do. I envied Andrew—not just his native unflappability, but the fact that he had a rescue mission and could channel fear into action. But perhaps there was something I could do, right here.

I picked up the phone and dialled.

Four p.m. Saturday afternoon in Australia in February is 2 a.m. Saturday in New York. It is the weekend, it is the middle of the night, and any network is at its lowest ebb, in terms of staffing. I figured the best place to ring would be our main international bureau, where at least it was just turning 7 a.m.

'NBC London,' a harried voice answered.

The London Bureau is the largest hub outside NBC Headquarters in New York. It deploys producers, correspondents and camera crews around the world to cover international news. It's a busy world, and the London Bureau is a busy place.

'Hi. It's Sara James in Australia.'

There was a pause. 'Who?'

It was only a year since I had left New York and it was a bit painful to think I'd been forgotten already. But then again, I'd been based in New York, not London, and the desk assistant sounded young. This was no time for wounded pride.

'Sara James. I'm an NBC correspondent. In Australia.' No matter that I hadn't done a story in months, I was still on the network website. I had an NBC computer, my recording gear and two decades of experience.

'Oh, I'm sorry!' he said instantly, tone changing. 'What's up?'

'Are you guys up to speed on the wildfires?'

'I saw something about them cross the wires,' the desk assistant replied. 'Sounds pretty hairy. But you know it has to be huge for us to cover fires overseas.'

'This will be. It's heading for horrific.'

The desk assistant sounded distracted. 'Look, I'm not seeing any mention of fatalities.'

I thought of Annie. Please let that be the case. Please, let no one die.

'None confirmed, but given what I'm hearing, I think there could be. Wait till you see the vision. It's like Armageddon.'

But it was early, and no vision had been fed to London yet. The harried desk assistant had to keep track of any number of breaking news stories. News was like triage—the worst cases got attention first—with the added caveat that every nation on earth cared the most about news concerning its own.

'Thanks for calling, and let us know what develops,' he said.

'Will do.' But it was time to be a bit more assertive. 'Look, would you mind putting a note in the hot file? To flag this? And could you let New York know? I'll give you my mobile number to include.'

'Sounds good. Do you have a crew?'

I didn't have a camera, much less a cameraman, and I couldn't deploy.

'Not at the moment. We've had to evacuate, and I'm not even at home. But you've got my mobile, and I can do a phoner, if they need it.'

Given that a phoner is a report by telephone, and that television is a visual medium, I doubted the shows would want one, but it was all I could offer at present.

I hung up feeling better. I'd done my job. And then I shook my head at the irony. A job I wasn't paid for. A job I used to have, and somehow still thought I did.

I had one more call to make. To my surprise, I actually reached Cam Stewart on his mobile. 'It's Sara. Sorry to bother you. I know you're on deadline and this is blindingly obvious . . .'

'No problem. We'll get together another time. But how is Annie? I saw Norm's live cross on 7.'

'Still waiting. Andrew's gone to intercept Norm.'

Cam sighed. 'It's terrible everywhere. I can't believe how bad. I hope everything turns out okay. Let's talk later.'

When I rang off, I glanced over at the girls. Nana was reading a book to Jacqui, and Sophie was engrossed in Nancy Drew's Parisian adventure, rather than being fully aware of the drama playing out in her home state. It was better that way.

But I was desperate for an update.

✳

'We're at the bottom of the mountain.'

'So you managed to intercept Norm?'

'Roger that,' Andrew answered. 'I'm with Norm and Cam,' he continued, referring to his cousin, Norm and Annie's 21-year-old son. 'We got stopped at a roadblock, all piled in Normy's car.'

'And the cops just let you through?'

I could almost hear the smile. 'Yeah, no, not exactly. We kept probing the perimeter, shall we say. Till we found a reasonable cop. He told us which way we definitely could not go, then suddenly had to walk away to make an urgent call.'

I laughed for the first time that day. It was a relief. 'But what about Annie?'

'The cops won't let us up the mountain. The fire front has passed through, but the mountain is still ablaze. They say it's too dangerous.' He sounded frustrated.

'Norm and Cam must be frantic. I'm glad you're there.' Suddenly a thought occurred to me. 'But Andrew, if you're with Norm . . . where is the Captiva?'

There was silence on the other end of the phone, as the penny dropped. Andrew had completely forgotten that he had taken the vehicle loaded with all our valuables.

'It's back at the roadblock. It's locked. It will be fine.'

'I'm sure it will.'

As I hung up, the image of our marooned car struck me as a tiny window on the way in which the speed and magnitude of the disaster was dictating events. People had been surprised, forced to make split-second decisions, on the fly. There had been no time for thought—only reaction. When people made instantaneous decisions, the chance of error increased exponentially. There would be mistakes. Some might prove catastrophic. I shuddered. I didn't care if a fire incinerated our car, with everything that was inside it, just as long as our family was safe. Just as long as everyone was accounted for, including Annie. Compared to people, things were irrelevant.

*

The hours passed slowly, the violent temperatures of the day slowly melting into a heat that was more bearable, then an acrid-smelling dusk, then night. But more fires were on the rampage. The horror was far from over. From the upstairs veranda, we could see orange flames on the horizon, from Eaglehawk, near Bendigo, bright against the vast black sky, but the wind fanned the flames away from us. 'It's the cool change,' Nana explained. 'We won't have to shift. We are lucky.' Others weren't. The new wind direction sent existing fires in new directions, expanding, extending, as if invisible archers were at work with blazing arrows. Exhausted fire-fighters hardly knew where to turn.

Andrew's sister Kate rang. Her husband Andy, a farmer, was also a CFA volunteer. Kate was home alone with their six-year-old, Annaliese. Aside from worrying about Andy, there was no way she could defend their property alone, so Pa left to be with them. I thought about the family. Helen and Trevor and the kids were at their house. Andrew was with his uncle and cousin. Pa, with Kate and Anna. Chrissie, at her home in Brunswick. And I was with Nana and the girls. Like many other families that night, the events of the day had pulled us apart. We faced the same danger, but in separate locations. All hoping everyone else was all right.

We had lost power. I wondered how many people had, and what the consequences might have been, although it was clear spoiled food was the least of it. We had no way of knowing then that so many people would die, the majority of them from the Kilmore East fire, which ravaged Mount Disappointment and other communities, including Kinglake. All we knew was that the howling heat would turn any spark into a galloping, deadly inferno.

And as I put the girls to bed by torchlight, it was clear to every-one that the scale of the disaster was unprecedented. I stayed fully dressed. I would not sleep that night. Nana and I huddled next to the battery-powered radio, listening for the latest news. We were safe. It was the ultimate blessing. Because countless others were not.

✳

'She's alive!'

The words were as thrilling as they were difficult to believe. But the elated, husky voice continued, 'She's just fine, actually. In fact, she just won't stop.'

We were leaping with elation, abuzz with questions. 'But how? How on earth did Annie survive? Did she jump in the dam?'

'Actually, she wound up running into a burnt-out paddock instead—there was no time to get to the dam. She says she thought she was a goner, more than once,' Andrew continued, full of details. 'She got so lucky. There were a few of them, you see. A few neighbours around when the fire struck, and they worked as a team. They would shelter in one house, defend it, then fall back and defend the next. The wind kept shifting, and they had to race from spot to spot to keep from being burned alive. That's when she wound up in the paddock.'

'Is she injured?'

'Not badly,' Andrew said. 'Considering.' There was pride in his voice. 'Her face is red—I reckon she has second-degree burns. Her eyes are practically swollen shut, but she is unbelievable. She was hacking down a burning tree with an axe when we arrived.'

'Thank God they all made it.'

His voice dropped a register. 'Not everyone. Someone was killed—and not far away.'

'That's terrible!'

'It is. I'm surprised anyone got through it, to tell the truth,' Andrew said. 'When we finally got here, hours after the front passed, the shed was still alight. Remember that old fire truck of Uncle Norm's? It is incinerated. It's like a lump of metal. The wood pile is too hot to put out yet, but we'll try with buckets later. We don't want the house to catch now. But we can't use the water from their tanks—it's still boiling, from the radiant heat! The fire even melted the water pipes underground.'

Andrew might no longer be a reporter by trade, but he reflexively noted details, analysed the mechanics of a monstrous event.

'It's such a random thing, this fire,' Andrew continued. 'A lot of Norm and Annie's neighbours have lost their homes, even though they were more fireproof, and had sprinklers. But Norm and Annie's house is wood, and it's untouched. Annie and her neighbours were able to save it. They just kept hacking down trees, racing from place to place. I was buggered, just from getting up the mountain, but Annie won't quit. She has more energy than the rest of us, put together.'

'She must be buzzing with adrenalin.'

'Too right. When we drove up, the forest was unbelievably hot, and there were still trees on fire. Norm and Cam and I had to push burning logs out of the way. A couple we couldn't move—too hot to touch—so we had to drive off road, around them. I can't imagine what the heat was like when the front came through. I don't know how they made it, I really don't. I can't believe she . . .' he paused to collect himself. 'I am just so glad she survived.'

I tried to lift his spirits.

'Why does it sound like you are eating?' I asked.

He laughed. 'Because I'm having a Magnum. Next I'm having a mint one, maybe then some vanilla.' Andrew told me that they were devouring everything in the freezer, starting with the ice-cream, and downing litres of water. I relayed all the information to Nana, who was getting her own bulletins from her brother Norm.

It was good to smile, because somehow, the danger almost seemed more frightening now that Annie was safe. We could not stop thinking about all of those who were not. It made me remember those hours and days after 9/11, reaching out to everyone we knew, checking in. The pain of uncertainty, as well as of fear. To have a miracle in our midst was almost too good to be true. It took time for relief to seep in, to open the lungs, to unclench the jaw and to still our pounding hearts.

✳

On Sunday afternoon, we returned to our house. The Captiva, still packed, was parked in the driveway.

'Daddy!' the girls squealed, as they ran in the front door.

The fires were still raging, but we were among the lucky ones. The Macedon Ranges had been spared. From the front yard, I looked out across the grey-green expanse which was the Wombat State Forest. There was nothing but beauty, and stillness. Except for the acrid scent in the air, there was no sign of what was still unfolding, no sign that this had been the worst disaster in modern Australian history.

I thought of the American tradition of Thanksgiving. People in a new land, giving thanks, because they had cheated death, thanks to help from the locals. We had abundant reasons to be thankful. I saw no reason the tradition could not be moved forward from November to February. I called the neighbours. And on that Sunday night, 8 February 2009, we had a Thanksgiving dinner. Instead of turkey, I served an enormous, stuffed salmon.

✳

My mobile rang on Monday at 8 a.m.

New York.

'We've seen the pictures,' said a foreign editor, an old friend from 30 Rock. 'It's as bad as you said. We'll take a spot for *Today*, and one for *Nightly News*. Aren't you in Victoria? How close is this to you, Sara?'

'We're fine. But my husband's aunt is lucky to be alive,' I answered, and explained.

For the next few days, along with a cameraman hired by NBC, I reported on Black Saturday and its aftermath, and among those I interviewed were Andrew's aunt and uncle. I had already known how lucky we were to have Annie, but when I drove up the mountain, and surveyed the devastation, I could only hug her, then hug Norm and Cam. Then hug everyone again.

Annie was surprisingly bright and upbeat. It might have been the shock, but it seemed more as if she were humming with electricity, acutely aware of the astonishing fact of being alive, against overwhelming odds. Annie and Norm were busy helping their neighbours, some of whom had lost everything. They were unperturbed about damage to property and vehicles, though saddened by the devastation of her once beautiful garden. 'And then there were our cattle,' Annie said. 'It was just a small herd, but they were so lovely. They all have names of course. But there is no way they could have survived this,' she reflected, arm outstretched to the scorched hill, smouldering forest. As far as the eye could see there was uninhabitable desolation. The blackened corpses of naked trees. Earth, scorched grey-black, gritty. And there was that smell. The stench of things that burned, which were never meant to. Scent is our sense most powerfully linked to memory. I was suddenly in New York, in the days after the eleventh of September. I had to pull myself back to the present.

One hundred and seventy-three people had been killed on Black Saturday—a horrific toll. In addition, hundreds of thousands of animals had died. A picture of an injured koala being fed from a baby bottle had gone viral. Domestic livestock, cows and sheep, horses and family pets had also been injured or died. None had been immune, and some people had perished trying to rescue beloved animals. We felt fortunate that Nanci Drew had been in an area untouched by the fires.

But Annie wasn't finished. 'And then there was the lyrebird,' she continued. 'They're very rare, you know. We were so lucky to have him here on the property. I'd hear him crashing through the bush, and then spy him, preening. He put on such a show, flashing that beautiful tail.' She smiled wistfully.

The lyrebird was flightless, I knew, and endangered in no small part because of feral cats. Introduced animals were a menace, and although Sophie would have loved a kitten, I could never own one in Australia. But at least a cat might be avoided. A flightless bird would have had no chance against such a terrible fire.

'Have you ever heard one?' Annie asked me.

'No, never. I've only seen pictures of them, in my bird books.'

'They are the most glorious mimics.' She looked down. 'I will miss him.'

Uncle Norm, red wine in hand, simply watched Annie. Wherever she moved, he was a silent shadow. More than once he reached out to touch her, as if she were an apparition he feared might fade if he turned away. 'I thought I'd lost her,' he said, then turned to their son Cam. 'I really thought we'd lost her.' And Cam nodded.

Tucked inside their cozy cabin, sitting on a kitchen chair, facing Norm and Annie on the sofa, I felt strange—I was inter- viewing relatives—but the feeling passed in a moment. Annie had lived with a reporter for more than two decades. She understood the drill. I unfolded my sheet of questions.

'When was the most frightening moment, Annie? Can you tell me about that phone call to Norm? Why did you go to the paddock? Can you describe the fire front for me—what it looked like, sounded like, smelled like?' And then I paused. 'Annie, I have to ask. Did you think you would survive?'

She took her time, looked at Norm and Cam, then answered. 'No,' she said simply. 'I didn't.'

✳

Later, we stood on the crest of that blackened hillside, the tele- vision lights for the live shot angled to burn away a patch of darkness, reveal the contours of the shell of a home which had belonged to Norm and Annie's next-door neighbours. I thought about how Annie and her friends had escaped by the narrowest of margins, and only because they had one another. That was the thing about the countryside, about Australia, about the bush. You needed your people, your tribe. It was virtually impossible alone.

I struggled to write the live intro and tag which would wrap around the recorded story I'd already fed, with its interviews and vision. Reporting excels at providing the outline, the contour of an event, as well as the raw emotion and stippling of details that make us care. Television reporting can provide context and analysis. But reporting is designed as a third-person exercise—someone with objectivity, on the scene, providing an eyewitness account. I felt myself popping between two worlds. I was a reporter, outside the event, and I was a local resident, reporting on people I loved, my own family. I was smack in the middle of this story.

The soundman hooked up the lapel microphone as I fiddled with my jacket. It was surprisingly chilly after the cool change, impossible to believe the scorching temperatures of a few days before.

'Are you a righty or lefty?' the soundman asked.

'Righty,' I said, and he tucked a small earpiece called an IFB into my right ear. Immediately, I could hear the chatter of voices in the Control Room for Studio 1A, 16,000 kilometres away at Rockefeller Plaza. It was astonishingly familiar. A different kind of family.

'Hey, Sara, it's Erica at *Today*! Can you hear us?'

'I sure can. Hi, Erica.'

'How's it going, Sara?' asked Joe Michaels, the director.

'Thanks, I'm doing fine. We all are, thankfully.'

'Good to hear. Scary. Glad everyone's okay.'

'Hey, Sara, it's Billy in audio. Can you count to 10 for me? I need to check the delay.'

'Sure. 1, 2, 3, 4, 5, 6—'

'Got it. It's a four-second delay, FYI. And we're coming up on 10 minutes to the *Show* open.'

'Hi, Sara. It's Jim.' Jim was Jim Bell, the Executive Producer of *Today*. 'Those pictures are unreal. You'll throw to Matt Lauer, okay?'

'Will do.'

The surreal sensation intensified. I was standing in front of a camera on Mount Disappointment, in Victoria, Australia,

100 metres from Norm and Annie's house. Our satellite dish would beam a signal that would send a live transmission from this camera to a satellite in space, which would in turn relay that signal to the *Today Show* control room in New York. After a four-second delay, because I was halfway around the world, my report would be broadcast live, across America. And I would report on Black Saturday, on its impact on Australia, and on what had happened to my husband's family. And I suddenly remembered the line of scripture from the Book of Ruth, in the Old Testament, a line used in many wedding ceremonies: 'Where you go, I will go, and where you stay, I will stay. And your people will be my people, and Your God, my God.'

And I felt the truth of those ancient words. These were now my people. They were my family, as well as Andrew's.

Perhaps I was thinking too much. Or maybe I was tired. It was late at night, and I had been working around the clock for several days. At any rate, I muffed a word in the live tag. New York was unconcerned. 'All clear. Thanks for the hustle, Sara. Glad everyone's okay and best to everyone.'

But my television reporter uncle was highly amused. 'You blew it!' he cackled, when I stepped away from the camera. He mussed my over-sprayed hair. 'What's the trouble, your first live shot?'

More laughter. 'I thought you were a bigshot network reporter, but you actually blew the last line!'

'I did not!' I shot back. 'Besides, you made me nervous, standing there, lurking! Who could concentrate?'

Norm gave his trademark giggle and hugged me fiercely. 'Come inside, you great big failure. You and your crew. It's time for a drink.'

✳

The dry, hot weather continued, and as the days passed, my uneasiness deepened. My reporting assignments over, I had lost the crucial border that helped keep anxiety in its box. It bloomed, a toxic vine. I reviewed our fire plan. Bought more supplies. Worried.

The country seemed different to me. I had known to expect snakes and spiders, as well as sharks in the ocean; that was travel brochure Australia. Such extreme species were actually part of the continent's allure. And although reptiles still scared me, I was beginning to understand their patterns, and found these creatures less of a danger, the longer I lived here. By contrast, the danger posed by bushfires was one I'd never anticipated. I had not understood the country's dark secret, had not comprehended that this was a land of fire. How had the Aborigines managed? They'd had no weather forecasts. Where had they gone?

The fires and 9/11 balled up together, somehow, in my head, in my chest. I would drive by Mount Macedon, and it suddenly looked brooding and sinister. It made me feel marginally better that everyone in the region, indeed everyone in Victoria, was rattled and on edge. Friends called to check on us, not just from elsewhere in Australia, but also from overseas. This fire had been unprecedented, and Andrew was among those chastened. Like many people on Black Saturday—especially many men—he had underestimated the danger. But he insisted on context. It had been an extreme, probably even a once in a lifetime event. And he also reminded me that we had left. We had relocated to the farm. Never mind that he had left; the girls and I had stayed put, and all of us had escaped, unharmed.

'You'll see. These things go in cycles. That's Australia, Sara. It's an extreme place. You need to get used to it. But the drought will end, it has to. And then something else will happen.' He gave a rueful shake of his head. 'But it doesn't help to be a panic merchant.'

I would not, I said, and I tried to believe him. But mostly I just waited for that long summer to end. One day I ran into Norm and Annie's son, Cam, at Channel 7. We had a good catch-up, during which I asked about his mum and dad's cattle.

'Just wondering, did they ever find them?'

'Actually, they did!' he said, shaking his head at this astonishing tale of survival. 'You won't believe it, but only one died. The rest found shelter down in the valley. Mum says when they found them, the look in their eyes was just terrible. They had been so afraid. Their hooves were burned, and she and Dad took food and water to them every day for weeks, but they made it.'

'That is absolutely incredible.'

'It is. But there's another amazing thing,' Cam continued. 'Did Mum tell you about the lyrebird? Well, it's back, too. She's not only seen it, but heard it singing.'

I practically leapt. 'You are kidding! I'm calling your mum!' I hugged him.

I felt a sweet, budding shoot of happiness.

And for the rest of that day, and the day that followed, and the one after that, I smiled whenever I thought of the lyrebird. How could it be? How was it possible that a flightless bird had escaped such an inferno? Like Annie's survival, it almost seemed impossible.

But that was Australia. The impossible was always happening. It made the continent at once terrifying, and beguiling. No wonder they called this place Oz. The country had such bewitching otherness: hopping animals with babies in their pockets; ostrich-sized birds that laid enormous teal-green eggs; obscenely deadly reptiles and spiders and jellyfish; birds that fanned their plumage in the shape of a lyre to woo a sweetheart; and a giant mountain in the middle of a desert which was, in fact, an enormous rock. Collectively, all that glorious oddity exerted a magnetic pull. It was a country you had to see to believe. And it was a country you had to live in to understand.

I'd surrendered to that pull, left the beloved land of my birth. The return of that lyrebird was like an unspoken promise. If it could survive, so could we. The fires would end. The cycle would break. And if the lyrebird could hang in there, so could I.

13

POSSUMS AND WOMBATS

'Sophie, I thought I asked you to lock Nanci in her cage,' I said.

'But Mum, I did!'

My friends Sandie and Kirsty were over for a visit with their children. But Nanci Drew was darting about, knocking everyone over. She wasn't mean or malicious, just hyperactive and wildly disobedient. In the interests of child safety, she had been banished to her kennel.

'I think you forgot,' I suggested.

'I'll do it again,' Sophie sighed.

'I've got ham off the bone from Sitka, and some beautiful cheese,' said Sandie, unpacking a bag.

'I've got pineapple, straight from the can,' I replied, to laughter. 'But I also have a pizza stone. And I can make the green salad.'

'I've brought Persian feta, some tomatoes and herbs from our garden, and I picked up these pizza bases in Woodend,' said Kirsty. 'I also made Pete's banana and chocolate cake from our cookbook for dessert.'

It was shaping up to be a feast.

Our conversation was interrupted by the sound of screaming

from outside. I dashed to the door to see Jacqui on the ground. Thankfully, she'd fallen face first—no seizure danger, at least.

'Bad dog, Nanci!' I said, helping Jacqui up, to take a closer look. Nanci Drew, who had grown from a fluffy yellow puppy into a large and powerful dog, as is inevitable if the breed in question is a Golden Retriever, wagged her tail in a friendly way.

'SOPHIE!!!!' I called out for my invisible eldest, with more force than I had intended. Jacqui was always tumbling, and fear could bleed into—and amplify—my reaction. I recognised the problem, but wasn't always successful at preventing the emotional equivalent of a secondary infection.

'Let me have a look,' said Sandie, coming over to check on my younger daughter. As a Chinese medical practitioner, Sandie not only had knowledge, but a healing touch. Jacqui, although dirty and frightened, wasn't bleeding or seriously hurt.

'Good as gold, I'd say,' Sandie reported, and gave Jacqui a cuddle. 'Let's clean you up.'

Just then, Sophie came galloping around the corner of the house, tawny hair flying.

'Mum, I did lock Nanci up, I swear it, I did lock her up, I did! It's all Jacqui's fault!' Sophie glared mutinously at her sister.

'How exactly is it Jacqui's . . . never mind.' Jacqui got extra coddling, because every fall could be dangerous. Sophie understood, but was aggrieved.

'Everything is all right. No one got hurt. But Soph, you didn't lock up Nanci, you couldn't have. Because here she is, and her kennel is wide open.'

Our Retriever watched us, obedient as a show dog awaiting the judges. She cocked her head, staring at us soulfully. Was it her fault Jacqui didn't have great balance?

It was also true that Nanci was only one and a half years old and didn't get enough exercise. I simply didn't have the time. At least Sophie and I had taken her to puppy school, for all the good it had done. Nanci had never gotten over being car sick. Nausea, coupled with an innate reluctance to do anything that wasn't her idea, resulted in a less than stellar report card.

'Was Nanci Drew the worst in the class?' Sophie had asked when the puppy class had ended.

'Not exactly the worst,' I'd replied.

'Which dog was worse than Nanci?'

'I can't remember.'

Although Nanci knew *how* to heel, she seemed to regard the command as a suggestion, and complied only if she desired. Her idea of 'retrieving' was to catch the stick or ball and run away. We had watched *The Dog Whisperer*, had read our share of training manuals. We knew that we needed to spend more time working with our dog. Be consistent. But a more apt description of Nanci Drew could be found in the pages of *Marley and Me*, especially when visitors arrived, and she morphed into Hyper Dog, into a Hollywood Stunt Dog.

Desperate to impress, Nanci did vicious figure-eights through the back garden at Mach 1, cut turns as tightly as a Nascar driver, showered us in plumes of mulch. She leapt over the newly planted red-hot poker plants like a champion pole vaulter, did wheelies around the birdbath, disappeared into the grevilleas, only to emerge sneezing and snorting, and ready for her next trick, a touch-and-go landing, into and out of the covered sandpit.

If inclined, she was perfectly capable of running up the wooden ladder to the children's playhouse, although she preferred a dazzling leap to the ground, rather than bothered with the slide. When finished, a breathless Nanci would tuck her head in a modest half-bow, then flop to the ground, panting. Some children clapped in glee at her performance. Others ran in terror. My friend Jools simply burst into laughter.

'Of *course* you would have a dog that is out of control! With your life, how could you possibly have any other sort?'

Nanci's exuberance could be excused, barely, but not her other habit: 'Mum, Nanci is trying to take a piggyback ride on me!' had become a familiar refrain, whenever a child under the age of ten came to visit. Sophie or I would rush to extricate the victim from Nanci's inappropriate embrace. All in all, it was best to keep Nanci on her lead, or exile her to the kennel while the kids were playing outside.

The trouble was that ever since that first night at our house, when she'd slept in a portable crate just outside the glass door, Nanci had been certain her place was next to the house, watching us, not in a fenced enclosure metres away. When we had first introduced her to the clean, snug kennel, with its spacious dog run, Nanci had whimpered. Then she'd begun tearing at the mesh with her teeth. When that failed, she'd begun digging, only to discover the hard-packed earth was unforgiving.

And then she had howled. Great, mournful, desperate howls. To her great surprise, and ours, there had been answering calls from across the ravine, on the next ridge. As Nanci quivered with excitement, we listened to the responding chorus of what we later learned was a litter of pups at the dingo sanctuary about four kilometres away. Perhaps they told her not to give up. More likely, it was simply her nature. Nanci had returned to her tunnelling, in earnest. We'd surrendered, and given our dog free run of the backyard, except when we had visitors with young children.

'Sophie, please do me a favour, and try one more time. She just needs to stay in the kennel until dinnertime.'

With a last bitter look, Sophie marched Nanci to the kennel. I heard the sound of the latch click shut. The canine inmate was safely locked into Cell Block C.

'Mum, I have an idea!' Sophie said, as she turned around. She threw one arm over the shoulder of Sandie's son. 'What if Sebi and I go *spy* on Nanci?'

Sebi was already nodding excitedly. 'Yeah, we'll find out how she does it and let you know.'

Like Kirsty and Alex, Emma and Bernard, and many of our friends, Sandie and Jack had moved to the Ranges from

Melbourne. As was the case with Sophie, Sebi seemed to have the country in his blood. A budding poultry farmer, he and his younger sisters, Jessie-Rose and Lola, often attended the Gisborne Market to help out Penny. Sebi had even convinced his parents to buy several of Penny's baby emus, which grazed in a paddock next to their home, along with dozens of wild kangaroos.

Sophie loved any excuse to play outdoors with local children. But for Jacqui to be involved, I was learning that it worked best to host everyone at our place. I often had a babysitter, and it was far easier to control the variables, to ensure that Jacqui was safe. Jacqui was also at her best in familiar surroundings.

It was a spectacular day, and I saw no reason to deny the pair their Mission Impossible. 'Off you go then,' I said, bringing Jacqui inside, where the other children were beginning to work on the individual pizzas.

It had been more than a year since Black Saturday, and the Macedon Ranges had returned to normal. But for once, no one was complaining that it was cold. To general delight, there had also been rain—quite a lot of it. But the sun was shining, there was a fire blazing in the fireplace, and I was in my kitchen with friends. I realised with a start that I was really starting to feel at home. An abstract thought drifted into my mind. I'd learned that in our area, bare root-stock trees, as well as flowers and shrubs, do best if planted in winter.

'How's the book on Jacqui's school going, Sara?' asked Kirsty.

'Ah, the book,' I replied.

Kirsty had only just left her job as a publisher. Balancing the demands of a high-pressure Melbourne career with three young children and a tree-changer lifestyle had proved challenging. Buoyant and resourceful, Kirsty chose to use her skills in new ways. The book she had been editing with her friend Pete, back when we'd first met, now had a colourful cover and a copy was propped on my kitchen bench. Another friend, Jacqui, an award-winning photographer who lived in Macedon, had taken all the photos.

All three were now friends of mine, as was Pete's sister Kate, a physiotherapist who had worked with our Jacqui in a program run by the Riding for the Disabled Association of Victoria. Pete and Kate's mum, Barb Heine, was a pioneer in hippotherapy in Australia—a treatment for those with brain damage which utilised physio, occupational therapy and speech therapy, in conjunction with horseback riding. Barb had won the Order of Australia Medal for her work with the community; tragically, she had recently died from cancer. Pete, Kate and their brother Marc continued the foundation Barb had begun, and Kate ran a special camp for children with acquired brain injuries and their families. As I looked around the kitchen, I realised my new friends all seemed to understand Jacqui, and our family, intuitively or professionally.

'I liked doing the research,' I finally answered Kirsty's question. 'But I'm way behind. I just want it to be finished, like your book.'

We Love Food not only showcased Pete and Kirsty's recipes, using produce from their backyards, but reflected how Victoria's Macedon Ranges were a garden of a different sort. This was fertile soil for a wide variety of intriguing enterprises, as hardy local species and recent transplants cross-pollinated. Relationships in the tightly knit region linked back, doubled up, crossed over and intertwined in myriad ways. I was meeting more people, all the time, each linked in multiple ways.

'Are you doing it all by yourself?' Kirsty asked.

'Not at all. We've got teachers and specialists at the school who are writing chapters, too. I thought that would make things easier, but it's the opposite. The work load is shared, but various people need to sign off on everything.'

'Are you glad you agreed to do it?' asked Sandie.

'I am, I think. The school's approach is revolutionary, and I'm learning heaps. But I haven't had time to pitch stories to NBC in forever, and I miss reporting. Working on a nice, short two-minute story sounds pretty good right now.'

As we put the first batch of pizzas in the oven, I ruefully remembered thinking this book project would be quick and easy. Somehow I'd found a way to make it lengthy and complicated. I'd wanted to do more than include a collection of articles from a conference. I'd wanted to put together a book that could serve as a blueprint for others in search of how to create an outstanding school for children who learned differently, or who had an intellectual disability.

Practically speaking, it meant that I'd been attending special school for nearly as long as my daughter, although I didn't sit in on her classes. But it was like having a crash course in special education, which had obvious benefits for me. Gaining a better understanding of how the school worked buttressed intuitive strategies we'd slowly developed to enjoy life with Jacqueline, as well as to instruct her. Somewhere along the way, I'd found that I no longer tried to act as Jacqui's teacher all the time.

And if I had considered my rapid speech and over-caffeinated New York persona as demerits for Jacqui's carer, it was good to know that singing, dancing and performing with her was beneficial, as well as fun. Trying to communicate with and encourage someone whose brain works in a radically different way is like trying to break into Fort Knox. Port Phillip had taught me that my love of music and theatre were gifts I could harness for the benefit of both my daughters, and in Jacqui's case, the equivalent of the safecracker's special case of tools. The more I learned, the less I worried. Maybe it would be enough for Jacqui that I was her mum, and loved her to distraction.

Yvonne, Jacqui's first teacher at the school, had worked in the field since the bad old days of institutions, and I often dropped by to see her over a cup of tea.

'You know what they say, Sara. "As the carer goes, so goes the family",' she told me one afternoon.

'A couple of people have mentioned that. What does it mean?'

'There's extra stress on a family which has a child with an

intellectual disability,' Yvonne had replied. 'And since the carer is the person most responsible for that child, she feels it most. I say she, because usually the carer is mum. As you know, it can be an exhausting and demanding job, and it can wear people down. Then the entire family can fray. The stress can break up couples, too.'

'I keep hearing that 80 per cent of marriages where there's a child with a disability end in divorce. Eighty per cent! That's pretty scary. Is it true?'

Yvonne hedged. 'It's very high, and we see it all the time. We believe it's our job not just to support the student who attends our school, but his entire family. That's why we try to make sure we know how everyone is doing, especially the carer.'

'So, in the nicest possible way, you spy on them,' I said. Yvonne's warm brown eyes crinkled at the edges.

'That's not it at all. It's more like we make ourselves available, approachable, in case anything is going on, or anyone wants to talk.'

I was suspicious. 'What about those cups of tea you and I had, when I first moved across . . .'

'Yes?' she replied, all innocence.

'I'm guessing that wasn't just social chit-chat. Were you checking me out?' I was astonished, and genuinely curious.

Yvonne said nothing, gave me another of her twinkly smiles.

'Yvonne, were you worried I could handle things? I thought I was doing pretty well!'

'And you were. It's nothing personal. Think of it as a service that we offer to all the families,' Yvonne said, and her eyes were kind. 'Having a child with special needs can make the world feel small sometimes, or even dark. It's not always so easy to have play dates, that sort of thing. Not everyone understands.'

I kept my head tucked. Pressure on couples. Kids not getting invited on play dates. It was just a little too familiar. Having a kid with an 'ID' sometimes felt like living in a parallel universe.

'But it's also true that people have their particular situations. Take you, for example. You moved here from overseas. You didn't have any of your own family here, or any friends nearby. You had left a career. And then you move to a dirt road in the middle of nowhere. That's a lot of change.'

Yvonne had been ticking items off on her fingers. There weren't a lot of fingers left.

As much as I felt like I'd won the jackpot to have our daughter attend Port Phillip, the drive to and fro was becoming harder and harder. Jacqui cried and wailed if we were stuck in traffic. Sometimes, on really bad days, she intentionally wet her car seat. We both needed a change.

Andrew couldn't help with the driving. He'd recently left Telstra to start his own media consultancy firm. It was a big step, but one that made sense. Andrew was able to use the skills he'd learned and contacts he'd made in Australia and overseas, first as a reporter, then as Rupert Murdoch's spokesman, then in senior management at one of Australia's largest corporations. Though he had left Telstra, he had kept the company as his first client. Andrew had a business, and had no business being a chauffeur.

There were challenges to starting a new company, but I could tell Andrew found it exciting and liberating. He had a swanky new office in the heart of Melbourne's CBD. What had once looked like a bowling alley had been transformed into a light-filled loft decorated with modern art; more than one visitor mused that the office looked like it belonged in SoHo or TriBeCa, in New York City. Old friends shook their heads in surprise, even wonder. They still remembered the copy boy from the *Herald Sun* who wore daggy clothes and was straight off the farm. What I knew, that some of them did not, was that he still dressed like that at home. And that the office had been renovated, not by a fancy city team, but by what I sometimes called Butcher, Inc. This consisted of Andrew, his dad and his brother, working on the project for weeks on end, only hiring the few subcontractors for jobs they could not do themselves.

I was most impressed by the resourcefulness, the capacity for hard work and the all-for-one, one-for-all attitude of Andrew's family. I was proud of Andrew's new job, and his new role. But it was also true that I was a little envious. My husband was coming into his own professionally. I loved being a mum, but being a carer was tough and time-consuming.

Professionally, I was on ice. I had skills I rarely used, and could almost feel them getting rusty, ossified. More to the point, I still loved the craft of reporting and telling stories and wanted to work. I missed my old life, the life I had led in New York, where it had been far easier to balance work in television with being a mum.

But how could I do my former job as a correspondent while I was on the equivalent of a giant hamster wheel, endlessly running to keep the big wheel rolling south and north along the Calder Freeway? Was the only answer to move to Melbourne? To call it quits and chalk up this attempt to live in country Australia as a failed experiment?

I baulked. There had to be another answer. I had finally made friends, and I wanted to get to know them better. The interesting mix of people reminded me not just of my native Virginia, but also of the Hudson River Valley north of New York City, where we'd had a weekend home. I looked around me. Home was to be in the kitchen, looking at the faces of the children, intently decorating the tops of the pizzas. Home was to watch the afternoon rays slant through the windows. To watch the sun ignite fairy-floss clouds, as cockatoos screeched their goodnights. Home was to . . .

'MUM!!!!!!!!!!!!!!!!!!!!! Mum! Mum! Mum! Come quick!!!!!!!!!!!'

The cries of jubilation made us dash outside, just in time to see two child-sized possums leap from a large tree, in pursuit of a bolt of yellow fur that looked an awful lot like our dog.

'WE CAUGHT HER!!!' they shouted, although Nanci, pink lead dangling, remained very much at liberty, fast as the colt from old Regret.

'We saw her!' sang an exultant Sebi, more accurately.

'She got out!' added blonde Jessie-Rose and Lola, in unison.

'She escaped!' cried little Charlie as he, Jemimah and Henry all gathered to the fray.

'Come look, Mum, come look,' said Sophie, her eyes bright as sparks, grabbing my hand. 'We caught her in the act!! Red pawed!!'

There was a babble of explanations, as we were hauled in the direction of Exhibit A, the large paperbark gum near Nanci's kennel.

Sebi: 'We were way up high!'

Sophie: 'So Nanci couldn't see us.'

Sebi: 'And then she did it!'

Sophie: 'Wait till you see how, Mum, just wait!'

Exhibit B was the re-enactment. As we watched, Nanci was confined in her kennel and the gate latched. Sherlock Holmes and Watson told us we need only wait.

'Just walk a little bit away,' they instructed. 'And turn your back to Nanci, so you're not watching. It doesn't take her long.'

We did as commanded, only whirling around when the pair shouted, 'Now! Look at her now!'

Sure enough, Nanci was standing on her hind legs, her front paws pressed against the gate. She was not quite tall enough to reach the latch. But to our astonishment, she extended her tongue as far as possible, and pushed up first one, then the other of the two metal pieces of the simple latch, to unlock the gate. The pressure of her paws did the rest. The door swung open, and the convict was free. Tail wagging, Nanci trotted out to greet us. Her expression said it all. No more kennel time for her. Nanci had won.

'Four seconds!' I said, impressed. 'She escaped in less than four seconds!'

'Good dog, Nanci,' said Sophie, patting her dog, beaming. 'See Mum, I told you I had locked her up, like you told me. She just let herself out, because she hates that old kennel. You clever girl. You just wanted to be closer to us. Mum, she's a real girl detective! Isn't it perfect that we named her Nanci Drew!'

It rained and rained and rained. The showers which had been pleasant and welcome became monsoons which clattered down on rooftops, sheeted against the windows, pelted into downspouts, and poured into our water tanks. In New York, I'd never paid much attention to how much rainfall we received. Here, we checked the rain gauge every day. Twenty points. Fifty points. One hundred points! And still it came, day after day. Our tanks were full. More remarkably, so was the enormous two-hectare, 80-megalitre dam on the Butcher family farm. The dam Pa feared wouldn't fill in his lifetime was overflowing. It was the stuff of legend, the stuff of ancient memory. The rain turned the leaves of the gum trees a silvery grey. The kangaroos' pelts were wet and they looked sodden and miserable, but they took shelter in the forest, only emerging for an early morning or late afternoon feed. The water pooled and puddled, turned the dusty road to a muddy, rutted, clotted track, and suddenly dozens of rabbits could be seen nibbling the tender green grass. Old-timers smiled. Then the smiles flattened. Enough was enough. When would the rains stop?

One morning the phone rang. It was Nana. Andrew hung up, grinning. It was a Saturday, and we had nothing on, but Andrew was in motion.

'Get the girls, come quick. Mum says the Muckleford Creek has flooded!'

'I didn't know there was a creek. Do you mean that dry riverbed?'

'Not any more. It has flooded, for the first time in years. Mum says we have to see it to believe it. Let's go!'

The Butcher family homestead in Muckleford stands atop a gentle rise, with paddocks stretching in all directions. Across the country lane is flat grazing land. Or there had been. Now there was a vast marsh, leading to a swirling, bustling stream.

'Isn't it amazing,' breathed Nana.

Just then Andrew's brother Trevor arrived. 'I've got two kayaks. Keen for a paddle?'

I had a sudden flashback to some of the weekends we'd spent in Manhattan. Sightseeing might mean a visit to the Egyptian mummies at the Met. Or checking out the dinosaur skeletons at the Natural History Museum. But when a massive snowstorm blanketed the city, New Yorkers on cross-country skis could be seen schussing down Broadway. Big natural events weren't to be missed. And now, here we were, in a raggle-taggle collection of farm vehicles, bobbing through thick gurgling mud, testing the depth as we went, getting as close as we dared to the rushing, cascading marvel that was Muckleford Creek.

'Many a mickle makes a muckle,' I remembered hearing. The creek had taken its name from the many mickles, or fords, which had crossed the creek, back when prospectors panned for gold here in the 1850s. But I had never seen the creek flow.

The kids were laughing excitedly as Andrew and his brother removed the kayaks from the roof of Trevor's Land Cruiser and climbed in.

'When was the last time you kayaked, Andrew?' asked his brother, as Andrew bobbed unsteadily.

'Not real recently,' Andrew replied.

'Wouldn't think so. Not a lot of time to kayak, working for Rupert in New York,' Trevor goaded.

'I'll be right, mate,' Andrew shot back, climbing in. 'I'm off like the proverbial bride's nightie.'

Still sparring, the brothers were off, as Chris, Helen, Katie, Andy and I discussed who would go next. I pulled out my phone to videotape the scene of cousins, aunts and uncles and grandparents, horsing around in their gumboots, splashing and leaping and frolicking. After thirteen years of drought, rain was far more than precipitation. It was a novelty. An activity. A lark. We couldn't stop smiling.

Jacqui tried to find her footing. I held her hand as she reached to touch the wet, and nearly tumbled in. She looked up at me, smiling.

'Mum, what's happening?' Sophie asked, her anxious voice capturing my attention.

I looked up, pointed my phone at Andrew, who did not look like he was having as much fun as he'd expected. The kayak was rocking this way, then that, and spinning unpredictably. Andrew tried to use his paddle to steady it, but appeared to be finding it difficult to navigate around the trees which were right in the middle of the swollen stream.

It happened in less than a second. With a sudden splash, Andrew's kayak was upside-down.

'Where's Dad? Where's Dad?' Sophie asked, hopping from one foot to another.

I was laughing. One of them was bound to go in, and it would have to be Andrew.

'Don't worry, it's a kayak. They pop right back up,' I replied.

'They're such a couple of idiots,' Kate said, shaking her head, and I cheerfully concurred.

Camera rolling, I shouted to my husband, 'Pretty funny, Andrew! Time to come up!'

Seconds passed. And more seconds. I dropped Jacqui's hand, and took a first tentative step towards the creek bank. I could see Trevor trying to paddle upstream, a difficult task at the best of times, and impossible against the swift current. It seemed Andrew was actually in trouble. That thought refused to connect to real action, although my feet seemed to be moving. But what exactly could I do? The kayak was closest to the far bank, and the raging current was of unpredictable depth.

Sophie kept pace, squelching beside me. 'Is Daddy going to drown? Make him come up, Mum!'

She had grasped the gravity of the situation, faster than I had. I counted on Andrew to get into scrapes, and always to come out of them okay. She knew only that boats were not supposed to be submerged, upside-down, with people inside.

And then, with a mighty splash and an audible gasp, Andrew's head popped to the surface. I took a huge breath, and squeezed Sophie's hand in relief as we watched Andrew grab a tree. He clutched the trunk and kicked free of the kayak, which speedily bobbed downstream, then hauled himself onto the bank. Trevor, bobbing a short distance away, shook his head.

'You dill,' was all he said.

'What happened?' I asked, when my waterlogged husband reached us, shivering and shaking like a large, wet dog. 'Why couldn't you pop back up?'

'I was stuck under branches, underneath. And my gumboots got caught. I couldn't get out of them.'

'You wore gumboots. In a kayak.'

'Not my best idea,' Andrew shook his head. 'To tell the truth, I thought I was a goner.' He wrapped his arms around his chest. 'As I was upside-down I was thinking, how stupid is this? I'm going to cark it, right here on the family farm. I'm going to drown in the bloody Muckleford Creek, under blackberry brambles.'

'On Father's Day,' I added.

I had stopped laughing. I'd been videotaping harmless hijinks, a lark, an escapade. And as it turned out, a near-fatal catastrophe. It had really not sunk in, until it was too late to help, that Andrew might be in real trouble. This was how it happened, then, those silly pranks that ended in tragedy. You didn't even realise it was happening, and suddenly it was all over.

Another thought occurred to me. In Australia, I was always using Andrew as my reference point, even my canary in the coalmine. But the truth was, he was rediscovering the land of his birth. He'd moved overseas as a young man, and those years in America and Japan had shaped and changed him.

Furthermore, we had both been shaped by becoming parents. I looked at my husband, and thought about how the pressures of a fast-moving stream could separate a pair, as well as obscure all that happened underneath. All too often, Andrew and I were forced to paddle independently, each focused on the challenges of our respective responsibilities—mine as carer, his as provider. It was easy to be envious of his autonomy, and aware only of my burden. But beneath the trimmings, the trappings, his responsibility was every bit as great as my own. It was why we each did what we did.

I looked at the girls, splashing in the marshy paddock. Still so young. But our darling Sophie would grow, and sooner than we might imagine, there would come a day when she was ready to set forth, and ready or not, we would have to wish her Godspeed. As she sailed into her future, we would be there, always, and adore her, always, and would remain that sheltering harbour that is home. But it was inevitable that she would grow up to have a life, and a home, of her own. That was the way of the world, and always had been.

But our younger daughter was a very different kind of child, and her future was mysterious and unclear. Although our little girl would grow, and learn, and change, no amount of love would alter the fact that her complicated condition made it unlikely she could ever live on her own. She would need a carer. For a very long time, perhaps always. She would need support.

But we would not always be here to watch over her. And beneath the façade of Andrew's new job and his fancy office, the reality was that he felt compelled to work hard, driven to put aside money for that time when we were no longer here. We wanted Jacqui's future to be secure, and we wanted Sophie to be able to have her own life, and to enjoy Jacqui, as a sister.

I reached out to take my husband's freezing hand. We followed an unspoken script, in which we tried to stay positive, both for ourselves, and for one another. But I suspected he might feel as I did at times. In a kayak, upside-down. Poorly prepared, rusty and with the wrong equipment. Recognising that when you're weighed down, it's harder to pop to the surface. And yet the stream looked cheerful and serene, as it burbled and babbled along.

*

'You're here, you're here!' I threw my arms around my sister Elizabeth, who had arrived from the Bay Area for a visit. She had a chic new haircut, was lean and buff, but otherwise, exactly the same. We talked non-stop about her life and mine, about Mum and Dad, and our sister Susan, who had just had her third child. I couldn't wait to meet baby Gigi, and was relieved by Elizabeth's report that she was thriving. Susan and Danny's middle child, Hattie, had been born premature, and had still been in the NICU when we moved to Australia. My sister-in-law Kate had also had a close call recently. After a pregnancy filled with rare complications, in which Chris's medical knowledge had once again proved invaluable, Kate had been rushed by ambulance to Melbourne for an emergency delivery. Little Laura had been born so premature that her dad's wedding ring fitted around her upper arm. Thankfully, like Hattie, Laura was bright, healthy and happy.

Because Elizabeth and I lived on opposite coasts in the States, we had seen each other infrequently, and usually at large family gatherings. This was more time together than we had had in years, and we cocooned. I smiled to watch Elizabeth play Play-Doh with Jacqui, Cluedo and Scrabble with Sophie, instruct both girls in introductory yoga.

'That is a very interesting downward dog, Jac,' my sister observed, cocking her head. We did simple things, and it was perfect. Both of us had been fearful that living so far from one another might pull us apart; instead, it brought us closer together. It was a boon to be able to have my sister near enough to see the contours of my life, literally and figuratively, as I tried to figure out how to make our family life work more smoothly.

'It's a great school, but what a drive!' Elizabeth noted, as we sipped coffee after drop-off. 'Does she always spit and kick the back of your seat?'

'She's not exactly a model commuter.'

'Isn't there someplace closer?' she asked. A question that resonated, after she'd flown home.

✳

It was November 2010 and I had lived in Australia for nearly three years when my first overseas friend came to visit. And she came not from New York, but from Namibia.

As with Elizabeth's visit, there was something grounding about having someone who had known me for so long be with me in my new home. Someone who knew who I was, and who I had been. And no friend knew me better or had known me longer than Ginger. We'd met at the age of twelve, and our lives were tied together in such a remarkable number of ways that we'd wound up writing a book about it. I often had to write about things, in order to work them through. *The Best of Friends* had been published just a few months before I'd left New York. Among our many points of intersection was the fact that one of Ginger's sisters had epilepsy and an intellectual disability. Gin understood what our family was facing, on many levels.

Nevertheless, although we spoke of many things, it was several days before Ginger broached the topic my sister had raised. 'You do a lot of driving.'

'I know. I feel like a taxi. I sit in a café and work on the book after I drop Jacqui at school, but it's still a colossal waste of time.'

'It doesn't seem sustainable. Are you sure you don't want to move to the city?' Gin had asked.

'I don't know what I want.'

And we'd gone through it all again. In the end I said, 'It's not just that Andrew is from the country. Sophie hates the idea of moving.'

'And what about you?'

I thought about that question. 'I don't really want to move, but I hate the driving. And I also need to have something to do which has nothing to do with special needs. Something fun.'

Ginger looked at me with a familiar smile. 'What about having a party?'

Ginger and I made her sister Dona's shrimp dip. We made guacamole and Southern baked beans and grilled steaks and chicken and devilled eggs. We bought wine and beer and started making calls.

A large crew came, and the house rang with laughter and good cheer. It was an awfully good party house, I realised. At the end of the evening, Ginger and I sat on the sofa talking it over.

'I have to say, I'm delighted,' Gin confessed.

'Why?'

'Because I'm your oldest friend, so I want to make sure you have good friends here. And I liked everyone! I see why you love it here.'

'I just have to see more of them.'

Ginger looked at me. 'Well, if you can't move, perhaps Jacqui can.'

*

There was a hushed whisper, near my ear.

'Sara, come quick!'

I awoke, eyes adjusting to the dark, trying to get my bearings.

'What is it?'

'Quick! The front lawn!'

As I crept towards the living room, it felt as though I was actually in a lodge next to an African waterhole, and had just been awakened by the guide to spy a rare leopard on its nocturnal prowl. But it was Andrew.

'Stand by the window and wait,' he instructed. 'Don't move, or it might see you. It may just be a kangaroo, but I think it's what you have been waiting for.'

He flipped on the lights, and there, right in front of me, was the creature of my dreams. The marsupial that gave the adjacent forest its name.

'A wombat!' I exclaimed. 'An actual live wombat!'

The chunky wombat, with his chocolate-brown pelt, stubby legs, small eyes and tapered nose, looked to my American eyes a bit like a bear cub crossed with a beaver and a baby seal. Though that was all wrong; it didn't begin to capture this animal, because what it really looked like was a wombat.

As I watched the charming creature, who was dazed by the bright light from the veranda, I reflected that we were all both beneficiaries and prisoners of our experience, and our sight was not immune. We saw what we wanted to see, and it could be hard to see something new, and appreciate it for just what it was. No more, no less.

Because what we saw was far more than colour and shape and movement. Sight was also about comparing and contrasting the observed with the remembered, attempting to catalogue and categorise, to understand the exotic and unfamiliar, by relating it to the known. As I stared at the wombat, so familiar, so foreign, I could fully appreciate why those sketches of kangaroos by early British and French explorers looked an awful lot like large rats. I tried to imagine arriving here, 200 years ago, to a place so wantonly foreign. Trying to make it home. It could not have been easy, but associating one animal with one remembered might have offered a bit of comfort.

The wombat was chewing at our grass contentedly.

'He's a marsupial, right?' I whispered.

'Yes. But he could be a she. Did you know their pouches are upside-down?'

I turned, tried to see my husband's face in the darkness, to see if he were kidding.

'No way.'

'Yes, way.'

'But if she stands up on her hind paws, her joey falls on the ground?!'

Andrew snorted. 'You boofhead. She doesn't stand on her back legs. She's a digger, remember? You've seen all those wombat holes, all over the hillside. She's a little Aussie digger. And when she burrows, if the pouch were right side up, then the joey would get a mouthful of dirt. So the pouch is upside-down.'

I looked at the wombat again, with even greater respect. Nothing remotely like a bear cub. The adaptation of a species. What a continent.

Andrew started in on echidnas, and how they were monotremes, and how their young licked milk from between their spikes, all of which sounded a bit repulsive. I was still thinking about wombats. And their crazy ways of caring for their young.

I wondered how my adaptations would appear to this contented creature—my young tucked into the Captiva, trundled back and forth to Melbourne. I was doing my best to adapt to local circumstances, local terrain, doing what I thought I needed to do, although I suspected that it might look as ridiculous and even crazy as an upside-down pouch.

Did life really need to be this topsy-turvy? I thought about what Elizabeth and Ginger had said, as well as Andrew. And Port Phillip, too, for that matter. They had all suggested that we give the specialist school near us a try. I was hesitant. But if it worked, then life could be a little less frantic. And if life was a little easier, that might make Jacqui happier, and then maybe I could get a little more of my own life back, too.

I had almost finished doing the reporting for the book on Port Phillip. Most of the rest could be done from my desk at home. And maybe I could even do a little reporting for NBC again, if I could get our life sorted out. The only way to know was to try.

14

THE ROSE GARDEN

I smoothed out my new skinny black dress, added another dash of red lipstick and stared through the glass windows at the familiar glittery spangle that was New York City, at night. Car horns blared, sirens wailed. An inviting cacophony. I linked arms with my friend Andi.

'Do you think they'll come?' I asked.

Senior Producer of the United Nations television division, Andi Gitow had worked as a producer at *Dateline*, where we'd met. Andi is a woman of many skills. She's earned a string of Emmys and other awards for her television producing, in hostile places like Darfur and Sarajevo. She speaks French, and has worked in Paris for *Vanity Fair*. Andi knows how to bargain hunt for designer clothes, and has been known to bring a crystal chandelier home in her carry-on. She also just happens to be a trained psychologist.

'Of course they will,' she responded soothingly.

There was a gentle 'ping', and the elevator doors opened onto the fourteenth floor of Bookmark's Lounge.

And out walked the first instalment of my former life.

'Sara! Welcome home!'

Within minutes, the bar was a crush of men and women, dear faces suddenly near again. I saw pals who were actors, writers, reporters, doctors and lawyers, and those who worked in television—many former colleagues at NBC. It was exciting to see old friends not just doing well, but soaring. Glamorous, witty and down-to-earth, *Dateline* correspondent Hoda Kotb had won her battle with cancer and was now co-hosting the fourth hour of the *Today Show* with the irrepressible Kathie Lee Gifford, to universal acclaim. Ellen Mason, who had produced one of my first stories at *Dateline*, was now second-in-command of a new magazine show being launched by the network. To be back in New York was to be back in the centre of the action, the centre of the goss—and it couldn't have been more fun.

Two years before, almost to the day, I had been in the sweltering heat and terror of Black Saturday. Now I was enjoying the cosmopolitan whirl of a sub-zero New York night. But inside this bar, it was snug and warm, inviting and lively.

I was throwing a party for myself at the signature bar on the top of the Library Hotel on Madison Avenue and 41st, just a short stroll from NBC. On a chilly Thursday evening in early February, the party was timed as a post-work get-together, a drink on the way home, before dinner. Wine flowed. Appetisers made the rounds. There was laughter, and snatches of multiple conversations sketched scenes from the latest chapters in interesting lives. I listened, storing up those stories, and the sight of their faces, memories to take back to Australia.

I looked around the room, at the giddy, animated swirl of black and gold. Many of these men and women I had met through work. Others, through life in the city. I had been away from New York long enough to recognise that, collectively, this was a high-powered, talented group. But that wasn't who they were to me. They were simply old friends. I had missed them. I had missed this. I had missed New York.

'Happy Birthday!' said Bridget, and gave me a squeeze.

'Mum's the word,' I replied, in a mock conspiratorial whisper. 'It's just a get-together because I'm in town.'

My birthday had been a few days before and I'd told Andrew that all I wanted was to have a party in New York for my old friends. He agreed with the plan, then bought me a stunning pearl necklace from e.g.etal, designed by my friend Emma herself. I'd declined to wrap the party in the trappings of another year passing, since television is an industry in which no one ever acknowledges growing a day older or a pound heavier, despite any evidence to the contrary.

A cluster of girlfriends had gathered around.

'How are Sophie and Jacqui?' asked Ellen.

'How's the cute guy with the funny accent?' asked Nancy.

'Andrew must be so happy to be back in Australia,' said Susanna, who remembered my husband from his motorcycle days.

'Are you enjoying it?' Stacey asked.

'Everything's great,' I responded.

'Love the dress,' said Angela.

'It's perfect,' added Lisa.

'Thanks, I didn't eat in order to squeeze into it.'

'Wait till you see the gems I have for you,' Sharon trilled, a former reporter whose new passion was jewellery design.

I could not stop grinning. New York had been my professional base, a city of wit and culture; but I realised it had been the company of this sisterhood of warm, talented and delightful women that had made New York so difficult to leave.

Late that night, I was at Andi's apartment, off 5th Avenue, my home away from home in the city. And I couldn't wait to ring home.

'Hi, Mum!' Sophie answered. Her cadence was very almost-ten, but her cheerful voice still sounded like sun spilling in through an open kitchen window.

'You are so clear, you could be next door!' I said happily.

It had been the wrong thing to say. 'I wish I was. When are you coming home? I miss you.' Sophie's voice was younger now.

My ribs constricted. Now that the homesick feeling for New

York was sated, I suddenly craved the family I'd left in Australia. But the trip was short and I knew it had been the right thing to do.

'And I miss you. I'll be back very soon—in just a few days—before you know it. How was school?'

Sophie gave me a quick briefing before handing the phone to my husband, who asked about the party.

'I think it just might have been a big success.'

'Told you.'

'You did. Sophie sounds good. How is Jacqui going at her new school?'

I crossed my fingers in my lap, twisted my new bracelet from Sharon. It had only been a few days.

'No worries. Seems like a nice place.'

'That's goo—'

'Bit of strife on the bus though.'

I stopped. Not the bus. Please, not the bus.

'Meaning?'

Andrew chuckled. 'Apparently, on their drive to the pool, for swimming, she decided to stand up in the middle of the aisle and do some dance moves, then giggled her head off.'

I burst out laughing, relieved.

'Dangerous, but at least she's entertaining. Was she singing her theme song?'

'Dunno.'

Increasingly, Jacqui was not only talking but even singing, developments that thrilled us. Her expanding vocabulary proved that Jacqui listened to everything anyone played during those long car trips to Melbourne. Our daughter knew her share of nursery rhymes and Wiggles tunes, but she was a rocker at heart. Her current, hands-down favourite, was P!nk's 'So What'. Jacqui's version was picked clean of consonants, but when our six-year-old daughter belted out, 'So wha!! I still a woc stah! I gah mah wock moves!' it was a crowd-stopper.

'They're not going to kick her off the bus, are they?'

'Nah. It's special school. But they did say from now on she'll need to travel in that car seat you gave them. And use some plastic clip, to prevent her from unbuckling her seat belt in traffic. But don't worry. She'll settle down.'

I got off the phone, beaming. All in all, a good report. If Jacqui could not attend the same school as Sophie, at least she could attend a well-respected special school in our area. After years of commuting, it was luxury to have the bus pick Jacqui up at our front door at 8 in the morning, and drop her off at 4 in the afternoon. Life was a lot simpler. It had made this trip possible. While there was still extra work for Andrew when I was gone, especially since Jacqui was an early riser, I'd arranged for babysitters to help out, including a thoughtful university student called Kayla whom both girls adored. And Nana was also there, cooking meals and spoiling everyone rotten.

When we had moved to Australia, I'd pictured travelling home once a year as a family, as expat friends of mine did. But that idea had proved easier in theory than reality. We had tried it once, at the end of our second year in Australia, with a green light from Jacqui's doctors. But despite our best efforts, Jacqui had a seizure within 24 hours of landing, in the middle of heavy traffic on the Los Angeles freeway. Emergency calls and consultation with the Royal Children's Hospital back in Melbourne ensued. We had needed to increase Jacqui's anti-seizure medication, permanently. For the rest of our trip Jacqui had been miserable and cantankerous, both because of the seizure, and because she was out of her routine. Her behaviour had been, in perhaps the greatest understatement in the world of special needs, 'challenging'.

As much as everyone wanted to see her, as much as Andrew and I both wanted our family to be like everyone else's, it was abundantly clear that travelling to the US was not a good option for Jacqui. That annual trip home had been a crucial component of how I had planned to make Australia work for me, for us. Cancelling it was hard to accept, and sometimes I would have a sudden, intense pang, as if I would hyperventilate from the distance. It had nothing to do with where I was living. It had everything to do with everyone I'd left behind.

Unless and until Jacqui could make the journey, Andrew and I agreed I would take Sophie to the States, once a year, to make sure she stayed in touch with her American roots. Andrew missed out, which pained both of us. But there didn't seem to be another option. And there were also occasions when I would go back to the States alone, as on this trip. I made such trips very short. I was accustomed to jetlag, and I could accomplish everything I needed to do in less than a week.

For I had business on my mind.

✳

My decision to fly to New York had been prompted by a conversation with yet another old friend, Linda Pattillo. A former foreign correspondent for ABC and CNN, Linda had downsized her life when she had her son, Ryan. She and her husband David now ran a boutique photography business, splitting their time between Atlanta and Maine, when they weren't snapping weddings overseas. But Linda had never lost her nose for news, nor her ability to pose a succinct, uncomfortable question.

'When was the last story you did for the network?' she'd asked recently.

It had taken me a moment to remember. 'Oh! I did a *Today Show* piece on that Qantas jet engine,' I said, referring to the November 2010 emergency landing of QF32 in Singapore, after one of the new A380's four Rolls Royce engines had exploded and shattered shortly after take-off. Thankfully, the experienced pilot had managed to return to Changi Airport and execute a safe landing. NBC London had called me at home, and I'd dashed to Melbourne's Tullamarine Airport to interview passengers arriving after their ordeal.

'Why do you ask?'

'I just thought it had been quite a while. But that was only a few months ago.'

She knew as well as I did that before the Qantas story, I'd not been on air for ages. 'I've been busy writing that book on the school!' I squeaked. Even I knew I sounded defensive.

'I know, I know. I'm not trying to give you a hard time. I'm the one running a photography business, remember. It's just that you don't sound satisfied. I used to work at the network, too. We both know that if you want to stay in the game, you've got to swing for the fences. Otherwise, you will disappear. You know what I mean.'

I certainly did.

I had been in Australia for three years now. Initially, I'd been consumed by trying to get everyone settled after the huge move. There had been the commute. Jacqueline's medical situation had flared up, and her needs had become complicated and acute. And there was the book.

But now, the girls seemed settled. Andrew's new business was thriving. We had babysitters. And as for the book, I was almost finished. Almost. My sister Elizabeth teased me that she'd heard the word 'almost' so frequently, she would believe the book was finished when it had a cover and a publication date. Regardless, I was out of excuses. If I wanted to restart my stalled media career, I needed to give it a try.

It took a while to recognise that what was holding me back was fear. A fear far greater than I'd ever experienced as a freckle-faced 22-year-old, fresh out of university, ready to scamper off to a Central American war zone on my own nickel. Back then, I'd been confident the network would want me, even though I'd barely landed my first job as a cub reporter. Youth came with a large helping of magical thinking, but the fact was that those who believed in the impossible had an uncanny knack for making it come true. I knew a whole lot more now than I had known back then. I had a string of awards to prove it. Yet self-doubt gnawed, sharp-toothed as a rodent. I had stepped off the fast track. Would I still be good? The technology had leapt forward. I was older. What if the door to a fascinating and sometimes glamorous life had closed—forever?

My friend Linda's call made me wonder if there was another possibility. Even if the door were closed, it might not be locked. What if all I needed to do was to reach out and turn the handle? What if I was being as big a sook as the Cowardly Lion? What a shame it would be if I allowed myself to lose something I loved, now that I could do it, based on the illusion that it was gone forever.

I would need to find out for myself. The answer could only be found in New York, in a Goliath of a building, with a golden Atlas at its base. All I needed to do was walk through the revolving doors of that 65-storey colossus, a building with so many people that it had its own postcode, and take the elevator up to the fourth floor.

That was, if my ID badge still worked.

✳

The morning after my party, I donned a new suit, borrowed a pair of killer black boots from Andi, and hailed a taxi, blissfully happy not to be driving. I arrived to see skaters twirling on the skating rink, as the flags of myriad nations blew stiffly in the breeze.

I walked inside, headed for security, and gently slid my card across the magic eye.

The metallic arm slid open. I resisted the urge to high-five the security guard and sailed through.

But before heading to the main offices, I made a detour, heading backstage at the *Today Show* for the makeup room. The makeup artist and hair stylist hugged me, then took a closer look. Mary and Laura tsk-tsked and pushed me into a chair. Forty-five minutes later, I was five years younger, and had had a full night of sleep.

Reinvigorated, I made the rounds at the *Today Show*, *Nightly News* and the front office, feeling a renewed confidence, and brimming with story ideas. I was ready to focus on something that had absolutely, positively nothing to do with special needs. A job where I would be asking questions, ferreting out answers, meeting deadlines and telling stories. A job which might once again take me to homes in towns and cities all over the world. Oh, how I had missed it. To my delight, the conversations seemed to go well.

I realised I felt a bit like Rip Van Winkle. Things looked familiar, although there were subtle changes, and I'd need to brush up on a few skills. But the trip had strengthened my resolve. I would not give up. I was officially flipping over the sign that said 'Back in 5'—to proclaim, in clear, bold print, 'Open for Business'.

Later, as I boarded QF108, en route from New York to LA, then switched planes at LAX's Tom Bradley International Terminal to QF94 for Melbourne, I wondered how it would all work out. I might have taken a match to my metaphoric 'Gone Fishing' sign, but it was clear I'd embarked on a fishing expedition of a different sort. I'd set my hook, and cast the line. Now I had to do the hard part. Sit back, relax and hope I got a bite.

It was 22 February 2011, and I had been home for less than two weeks. New York was a silvery memory, like a beautiful, lunar metropolis which could only be glimpsed if I stared hard enough at the midnight sky.

But it was daytime—a summer afternoon—and I was sitting in old shorts and a t-shirt at my office desk, staring out of the window in search of inspiration, watching frayed strips of eucalyptus bark flutter and rattle in a tepid breeze. The desk was littered with notebooks, education treatises and notes from interviews. Somehow, it all had to moosh into a book.

My mobile chimed, a welcome distraction. I noticed that the area code was 212, and reflexively converted the time. One a.m.

Who on earth would ring from New York at this hour?

'Hi, Sara. It's Geoff in New York. Are you watching what's happening?'

I scrambled out from behind my desk, banged my hip on the corner and splashed tea on my shorts in flight to the lounge. I flicked on the television remote, scrolled to Sky News.

No wonder NBC was on the line.

'I am now.'

'It's a big one. Six point three, and centred near Christchurch. Do you know the cathedral?'

'Of course. Actually, Andrew and I went to New Zealand on our honeymoon.'

'Well, the spire fell. There are going to be casualties.'

'Right.'

'When I saw you in New York, you mentioned you were free to do some work. How fast can you get to New Zealand? I don't need to tell you that you're a lot closer than anyone else.'

I looked at the clock. Just after 3 p.m.

'Can you give me five minutes to check a few things?'

'Call me back.'

I hung up, immediately dialled Andrew, thankful my husband was a former journo. My call sounded like a text, our conversation like an exchange of World War II telegrams.

'Hi, love. Big earthquake. New Zealand. Okay if I go?'

'Big?'

'Six point three. Christchurch.'

'Big. Go.'

Andrew knew all about earthquakes, from his years in Tokyo. I had been anchoring on the news desk of the *Today Show* on 17 January 1995 when an urgent bulletin had crossed the newswires that a magnitude 6.9 earthquake had struck Kobe. Andrew and I had been dating long-distance, and I'd instantly rung to alert him, waking him up. Although he'd been cranky at first, I had always been pleased that I had gotten the news to him faster than his news desk or his Japanese translator.

'Need help booking a flight?' asked my husband. I could hear typing. I knew Andrew would already be 'reading in', checking the internet for the very latest.

'I'm all right, thanks, and I'll organise babysitting. I'll be gone a few days.'

'Good luck. And be careful, Boof.'

'Will do.'

One minute down. Four to go until I was supposed to ring NBC. But it was the middle of the night there. I figured I had a few extra minutes up my sleeve.

I rang Qantas to check for the earliest available flight, while I ransacked the closet. I pulled out jeans, shirts, a zip fleece, light and heavy jackets in bright colours to show up against the black of a middle-of-the-night sky, as well as hiking boots, toiletries and a water bottle.

'I've got a flight to Auckland at six,' the agent told me, hesitant. 'But that's international. You need to check in two hours before. You've barely got time even to purchase this. Are you certain you can make it?'

'Are there later flights?'

'Tomor—'

'I can make it. Book me on that one, please.'

I gave her my NBC credit card details, and rang off.

I had 30 minutes until I would need to leave, but I knew I also needed a TV cameraman.

I noticed that my breathing was quick and shallow, and I was pacing. Slow it down, slow it down, I told myself, you've done this hundreds of times before. Breathe. Be calm. Prioritise.

Breaking news was always like this—you were sitting somewhere having a mug of coffee, with a resting pulse of 49, and suddenly you were catapulted into heart-thumping action, speeding to catch a plane, scrambling to get details, uncertain when and where you'd wind up. But I had the flight booked, and I could ring NBC Travel later to organise a hotel.

Priority one was getting a cameraman. As a television correspondent, I'd be precious little use without one.

'Hi, Zoomer. It's Sara. That earthquake in New Zealand? Can you get me a cameraman, preferably with a dish?'

'Zoomer' was Peter Morris, an ex-Channel 7 reporter who also lived in the Macedon Ranges, and who had recently started his own production company. Zoomer knew everyone. If I could hire a cameraman who also had a portable satellite dish, it would be ideal, because no doubt the local affiliate in New Zealand would be stretched to breaking point. I knew NBC would want to go live as soon as feasible. But time was excruciatingly short.

'Leave it with me,' said Zoomer. While I waited for his return call, I organised babysitters, finished packing. The clock told me four more minutes had elapsed when the phone rang.

Bingo.

'I've got a great guy. Trent Miller, out of Melbourne. He's already on a shoot, has to go home first to get gear and pack. You'll have to dance a bit with the carnet, to get all the gear through New Zealand customs.' A carnet was an international customs document that permitted duty-free and tax-free temporary importation of commercial equipment—in this case, tens of thousands of dollars of television gear. It could take hours to organise one. Hours we did not have.

'Trent's a pro. It will be tight, but he'll make it. You'll see him at the gate, if not before.'

'Zoomer, you live up to your name.'

It was time to ring New York. It had been eleven minutes, not five, but on the plus side, I could provide more than they'd asked for.

'Hey Geoff. I'm good to go. I've got a cameraman lined up, and we may have a dish. We're on a six o'clock to the North Island.'

'That's excellent. Well done.'

I felt a familiar surge of energy shoot through me. This voltage, whatever it was, flipped on circuits that had been powered down for months. I had a sudden flashback to the movie *Apollo 13*, when astronaut Jack Swigert attempts to reboot the computer of the crippled spacecraft, and everyone in the capsule and at Mission Control in Houston holds their breath, because if it won't turn on, the crew is doomed. When the panel lights up, Kevin Bacon's grin is priceless. I could feel my own switches turning on, every last one of them, and they were bright and hot and clear. I still knew how to do this. I was good to go.

'With the time difference, it'll be a late arrival,' I continued, making an effort to slow my rat-a-tat speech. 'Can you guys book us on something out of Auckland in the morning? The Christchurch airport is shut—no telling when it will reopen.'

'Leave the charter to us. But be ready for a live shot for *Today* as soon as you hit Auckland. We'll sort out the location. Call when you land.'

'There's just one more thing,' I said. I'd never been great at negotiating, which was why I'd had an agent in New York. But I couldn't do this job if I couldn't afford to cover babysitting, and actually earn money.

'Yes?'

'We need to fix the day rate, before I can get on the plane.'

If there is a time to negotiate, a time to determine your worth, it just might be when you have an airline ticket and a cameraman, and you are by far the closest foreign correspondent to a major international news story. I knew there wasn't a lot of room to bargain, but I had also learned the hard way that my value was greater before a disaster than after it. We had a quick, friendly discussion, a few calls were made, and in less than five minutes, we'd come to terms and arrived at a figure. Everyone was happy.

'Now go catch that plane. I'll talk to you in Auckland.'

I'd already called a cab, which would arrive in another fifteen minutes. I was packed—one passport, one roll-aboard suitcase, one NBC computer and my recording gear in my purse.

I looked at the clock one more time. Yes, there was time for one more thing.

With any major natural disaster, even in a first-world country, services are disrupted, often widely and deeply. It's impossible to guess when you will next be able to eat, drink or bathe. The prudent and experienced traveller plans accordingly. And so, less than two hours before an international flight, I jumped into the shower, washed my hair, dried and even styled it, grabbed my makeup kit and a few energy bars, and threw my things in the waiting cab.

As I rattled across the rickety, perilous isthmus that separated our property from the dirt road, and by extension the breadth of country Australia which lay beyond, it occurred to me that my husband might be correct when he grumbled that I was always fastest when I was getting ready for work. In the taxi, I rang home to talk to the girls, who had arrived home from school just as I was leaving.

Sophie, in particular, had questions.

'An earthquake! But will you be safe, Mum?' she asked.

'I will be super careful, darling. I promise,' I answered.

'Will you call me?'

'Every single day. More than once. You will be bored with me. And if you write an email, I'll write back.'

I arrived at the airport 59 minutes before my international flight, relieved I lived in Australia. In New York, I wouldn't have had time to clear airport security. Before I knew it, Trent and I were winging our way over the Tasman Sea, en route to New Zealand.

✳

The live shot was scheduled for 3 a.m., local time. Just an hour or so later, Trent and I were leaving the hotel to catch a chartered flight to Christchurch. It amused me to note that I had arrived in Auckland in the dark, and I had left the city in the dark. I was not to see the sun rise on the North Island.

In my rosy recollections of my former life, I always forgot how exhausting it was to be on the road. My friend Bob Woodruff, one-time anchorman for ABC News in the US, mused that ours was a profession for adults who still thought they were teenagers. But I had missed it all so much, I didn't really mind the all-nighter.

NBC and the ABC had shared the cost of the charter, and we all chatted genially. But as soon as the aircraft touched down, we immediately went our separate ways. We all had jobs to do. In our case, we needed to file both live reports and taped pieces for *Today* and *Nightly*, as well as live shots for MSNBC and the News Channel, NBC's affiliate feed service. With the time difference, this meant working virtually around the clock. But I was ready, and I knew the drill.

Trent and I picked up a hire car at the airport and drove towards the city centre. The roads were disarmingly clean and beautiful, the scenery idyllic. I remembered Christchurch from our honeymoon, its gorgeous Cathedral Square like something out of a quaint English country village. But the spire of the cathedral had toppled, and other buildings had crumbled, including the six-storey Canterbury Television (CTV) Building which had pancaked from the force of the quake. Of the 185 people who died on that February day, nearly two-thirds of the victims were in that building.

Every disaster has its jargon, its lingo. The epicentre of the cascading falls of the mighty Twin Towers in New York would come to be known as 'Ground Zero'. In the same way, the centre of beguiling Christchurch, those signature city blocks in and around the cathedral, would quickly come to be labelled 'The Red Zone'. While the epicentre of the earthquake was near Lyttelton, on the coast, ten kilometres southeast of Christchurch, the city centre and eastern suburbs were hard hit, in part because some buildings had already been weakened by an earthquake on 4 September 2010. Trent and I knew we had to get inside the Red Zone to get the best pictures and interviews.

One of the many reasons reporters race to the scene of a disaster is that all too quickly, it's simply too late to have access. The job of those in authority is to establish a perimeter. To determine who is us. And who is them. Who can and cannot cross this line. Trent and I were the first crew for an American television network to make it to Christchurch. It had been less than 24 hours since the earthquake had struck, but the barricades were already going up, as soldiers sought to prevent people from being injured by falling debris, or hurt during dangerous aftershocks.

Their job was to keep people out. Our job was to get in.

Which we did.

The contrast was stark.

'Look at those roses,' I exclaimed, as we parked our hire car near the banks of the Avon, which meandered through the city like an unspooling ribbon. I remembered this scene from my honeymoon. On any other day, I knew there would be punters, lazily stroking their way along the scenic river. The sight of those fragrant, perfect blooms, such cultivated perfection on the outskirts of unpredictable devastation, struck home. Beneath the manicured surface of this glorious city, which seemed grafted from a Tudor rose, was a land that was nothing like England.

New Zealand is part of the Ring of Fire, an arc that stretches north to Japan and the eastern edge of Asia, across to the Aleutian Islands of Alaska, then swings south again in a vast Pacific vault, to skirt the western coast of North and South America. The notoriously volatile edge to the world's vast, 'peaceful' ocean holds three-quarters of the world's active and dormant volcanos. And Earth—like Wind, Water and Fire—is yet another ancient element that can rumble and strike with little warning in this extraordinary part of the world.

I looked away from the flowers, and walked towards an attractive older couple, who appeared dazed. Something about them which I couldn't quite identify made me certain they were American. As it turned out, they were from New Jersey. The woman shook her head sadly. 'We had always wanted to come here, you know. We'd had this trip in mind for years. It's such a beautiful city, such a treasure. And now this.'

Her husband put his arm around her. 'We were very nearly inside the cathedral, when it happened,' he said, 'but my wife wanted to go across to the café, have a coffee first.'

His wife nodded, vigorously. 'We had just taken a picture of it,' she told me. 'We walked across the square, heard an enormous sound, and it was in ruins.' She shivered. 'It was only a minute later, that it fell.'

'You're very lucky to be alive,' I said.

'We know,' she said shakily.

A thought struck me. 'Do you by any chance have that photo?' I asked. 'You may very likely have taken the last photo of the cathedral while it was still standing.'

And they did. The couple dug out their camera, and Trent downloaded the photos, which showed the cathedral in all its glory, followed by several shots taken seconds later, showing a scene of chaos and confusion and ruin. Before. After.

A story idea was forming in my head. I had covered many disasters, and it struck me that there was often such randomness at play. An impulse, a whim, could be the difference between living and dying. *Go into the cathedral? No, let's have a quick coffee in the sunshine first.* A split-second decision had meant that instead of being among the casualties, this couple would be ringing their families at home to say they were all right. I thought I'd found a prism for telling this story, if I could find others who had similar experiences.

It proved remarkably easy. I talked to many people with accounts of small decisions which had major consequences, including backpackers who'd fortuitously shifted hotels at the last moment. In trying to explain a massive disaster, it is important to remember the human scale. I had long ago realised it is the Everyman dimension that moves us. The heart-thumping realisation that it could have been, nearly had been, you. The facts of reporting are crucial. But what makes us understand and remember is the story.

And that was when I knew. While television technology had changed, I possessed a skill that didn't expire, a skill that you couldn't get simply because you were an early adapter. I told stories. I'd been telling stories since I was Sophie's age. It was the sort of reporter I had always been, and would always be. I was learning the new technology, but that wasn't all there was to this profession. I wouldn't fret that I wasn't as fast as the new kids. They had their skills. And I had mine.

※

Hours later we found ourselves in the heart of the Red Zone, at Channel 3 television, which had its studios in a building bearing an uncomfortable resemblance to a famous tower in Pisa. To get to the newsroom, it was necessary to crunch across thousands of shards of broken glass from the shattered plate windows of the lobby, and walk under a chattering, wobbly chandelier. There were wide cracks in the walls and throughout the concrete floor, gaping gashes in the earth just outside the building. A handwritten permit on the wall indicated the building was condemned. Only the priority of a news organisation delivering vital information during the emergency gave these journalists any reason to be in the building. Every time an aftershock struck—and there were hundreds a day—the building shook. But there was electricity and the station was humming, reporters darting in and out, news bulletins on the air, until management could find a new TV home.

We both noted the New Zealand team's bravery and dedication, then looked at each other.

'Not ideal,' Trent said ruefully. 'But we'll be fine.'

Zoomer had been right. A good photographer, Trent was easy to work with, a whiz at technology, and calm.

Late that night, we drove to Lyttelton, the epicentre of the quake, for our live shot. It was a tortuously slow drive. Many of the roads were cut off, huge slabs of concrete missing, sudden yawning caverns opening up, big enough to swallow a car. Trent drove at a snail's pace while I peered out the open window, looking for cracks in the road, and we dog-legged, following detours.

The effects of what's known as liquefaction were already apparent. In an earthquake, soil suddenly loses its solidity, and can turn into a kind of quicksand. We passed houses, perilously leaning, or pancaked into destruction. Cars were submerged up to their axles in thick, gooey mud.

The days passed with extraordinary speed, with only a few hours of sleep between reporting for the morning and evening broadcasts. Then my colleague George Lewis arrived, with his crew, and I could go home.

As I paid my bill at the tiny caravan park where we'd stayed, the phone rang. It turned out that a hiker who'd checked in had not called home, and was among those still missing after the earthquake. The owner quickly checked the room, and returned with a sombre expression. The missing man's gear was neatly packed. It appeared likely he had been in the city centre when the quake hit. As if to add a punctuation mark, there was a quivering rumble, underfoot.

A couple from New Jersey had changed their plans to have a coffee, and been spared. A hiker had gone into the city, perhaps to wander along the Avon, or see the cathedral, and he had been in the wrong place at the wrong time. I thought of those who had lost their lives, and those whose lives had been altered, forever. The tremors showed no signs of abating, even as the good people of Christchurch struggled to rebuild. I thought of their lovely city, and of the many kind people I had met. And as I thought again of the roses, I remembered a beautiful fifteenth-century English hymn I had sung in choir, as a girl.

Lo, how a Rose e'er blooming, from tender stem hath sprung, it began. There was a later stanza, which continued, *This Flower, whose fragrance tender, with sweetness fills the air, dispels with glorious splendour, the darkness everywhere.*

I hoped that soon the darkness here would lift.

Life was precious, every minute of it. I looked forward to seeing my girls, and my guy. But this work trip had gone more smoothly. We had been in Oz longer, the girls were older, and we had a team in place. I was striking a better balance. Finding a way to tailor my old career to my new life. I smiled, as a thought struck me.

It appeared that the tyranny of distance might just be my best friend.

15

THE SUNFLOWER

It had been just one week since a massive 8.9 magnitude earthquake and subsequent tsunami had killed thousands of people in Japan, causing catastrophic failure in several nuclear reactors, which led to a dangerous radioactive release. As the world turned its attention to this unfolding crisis, New Zealand was only just beginning to assess the extent of damage from its own devastating earthquake of just a few weeks before.

I stood in a crowd of 40,000 people who had gathered in Christchurch's Hagley Park for a memorial service. It was a warm day, and many of those in the crowd wore t-shirts, shorts, bright sundresses and other casual clothing. But the crowd was hushed, even reverent in rapt attention, as a young British prince strode to the podium.

Wearing an elegant Maori cape, Prince William also wore the mantle of royalty, and wore it with confidence. I stood, scribbling notes on my pad, next to my colleague, NBC London producer, Chapman Bell, who often covered the Royals, and our cameraman, Marcus O'Brien, out of Sydney. Unlike my last trip to New Zealand, this trip had been scheduled, and we'd been vetted and approved, then issued glossy, emblazoned credentials on a lanyard to allow us entry and access. Such was the case with any trip involving the Royals.

Later, when the service ended, the three of us hurried back to our temporary quarters in a local hotel. With his reddish-blond hair and easy grin, Marcus was an Australian contradiction I'd encountered more than once. He had a laidback demeanour, wrapped around a hyper-competent core. Chapman, an engaging fellow Yank, still spoke with a hint of a drawl and had a penchant for baseball caps, but what belied his Georgia roots was a constitution entirely composed of fast-twitch fibres. Based in London, Chapman not only operated at warp speed but could survive on microscopic doses of sleep. He was a wunderkind at everything, from the formidable technological details of international live television to the complexities of the editorial side of the craft. He was constantly being parachuted into far-flung and often hostile locations, and this was the first time I'd met him.

As I hammered out a script, Chapman created a makeshift recording booth, then handed me the flash microphone to record, all the while cracking jokes with Marcus and me. He then uploaded the narration and raw vision to London for editing. Although this was the first time I'd worked with Chapman, and I'd only worked with Marcus a few times, we made a relaxed and easy trio. They were pros, and they were excellent value.

There was always a musical quality to such gigs. We might never have performed together, but our roles were as clear and defined as those in a jazz trio: we all knew who played bass, who was on keyboards singing vocals, who played the drums. With a quick riff and a flip through the score, we could be total strangers, yet belt out a polished tune which sounded as though we'd worked together for years.

It was show time. Marcus and Chapman headed out to pick a spot for the live shot and set up the satellite dish, while I got camera ready. I would be doing what was called a 'live top and tail with core'—a live shot on location in New Zealand, which wrapped around a taped news feature. I began with the Prince's opening remarks, in which he had quoted Queen

Elizabeth II: 'My grandmother says grief is the price we pay for love.'

The script went on to detail how Prince William had toured devastated coastal communities on the South Island, and had impressed those he met as an articulate, attentive and accessible young Royal. His visit was a welcome bit of fun, a chance for kids to wave flags and frolic in the street, for parents to try to forget aftershocks and plunging home prices and take a break from wondering about what would happen next. Everyone in the crowd was desperate for details about the Prince's upcoming wedding to Catherine Middleton, and he enthralled them by teasingly remarking, 'You're all invited!' I made sure to capture a bit of vision on my phone to show Sophie and Jacqui when I returned home.

We'd then followed Prince William to Brisbane, part of his tour of Queensland, which had been struck hard by Cyclone Yasi. In the sweltering tropical heat, he seemed cool and poised, and made time to pay a visit to the legendary Royal Flying Doctor Service, which clearly left him impressed. The Prince also made headlines when he met with the family of young Jordan Rice from Toowoomba. The thirteen-year-old boy had been trapped in a car during that town's terrifying flash flood. He had been hailed as a hero for telling rescuers to take his brother Blake first. Jordan and his mother Donna had perished in the raging waters.

The final segment of his tour of New Zealand and Australia had brought Prince William to my adopted home state of Victoria. Our house on a hill might be windy and fire-prone, but it was impervious to flooding. We were lucky. Much of country Victoria was under water, barely two years after it had been ablaze with bushfires. Many communities had been devastated by the deluge, including hard-hit Murrabit and Kerang.

It had been a gruelling five-day tour for the Prince, who commented to one reporter as he departed from Melbourne that the suffering he had witnessed left him 'emotionally raw'.

But he hadn't taken a wrong step, and proved himself a capable monarch-in-waiting.

I got on the final flight home, yawning. While the Prince had been ferried directly from point to point on a series of charter jets and helicopters, news reporters and crews had played a hopscotching kind of catch-up on commercial flights, many of which required connections and international customs. Mornings began in the middle of the night and ended in the wee hours of the following day, and the best and sometimes only certain place to sleep was during catnaps on flights between destinations. Working part-time was always a misnomer, but the week had flown, and I could feel my skills getting sharper story by story. I might be depleted, but I was elated, not exhausted.

It felt like the right time to expand my professional life, after consciously shrinking into a tight orbit around my family. I was grateful I'd had the financial security to do so, and would have made the same choice again. I'd wanted that time with Sophie. And I had also known I never wanted to look back and wonder if things could have turned out differently if I had done more to address Jacqui's disability.

But now the girls were older. Sophie was busy with school and friends, Jacqui settled in her new school, Andrew's business was thriving. I had experienced more frequent moments of dissonance, even panic. I remembered reading Virginia Woolf's 1929 classic *A Room of One's Own* in university: 'there is no gate, no lock, no bolt that you can set up upon the freedom of my mind.' Woolf offered a prescription to release the mind's full potential, which had been revolutionary for its time. She argued women needed freedom from financial worry as well as some measure of intellectual independence in order to write. I had been financially independent from the moment I'd graduated from university, until we'd moved to Australia. While Andrew had carried our financial burden, and never complained, I sorely missed earning a reliable income of my own.

My recent assignments not only gave me the chance to do a job I still enjoyed, but also provided a link to America. A chance to turn my thoughts outward to the big wide world. On our island of a property, far from so many and so much, I had sometimes felt restricted to a cameo of my former life. I'd felt clumsy and confined working in miniature, as if constantly bumping into the edges of too rigid and constricting a frame. Life once again was a vast mural, a sprawling canvas, to be painted in bold, colourful strokes.

I returned to find that everything looked lovely. The tall sunflowers Sophie had planted in the garden seemed to sway in greeting in these late days of summer. The house was clean and fragrant, laundry folded, the veranda swept. Nana had been at work. It was actually possible to see through the large windows, which were usually festooned with Jacqui and Sophie hand prints. Everything was perfect.

All except one thing.

'Andrew, what's up with Jacqui's hair?' I asked.

I dropped to my knees, suitcase on the ground, and inspected my six-year-old daughter closely. There was a small bald patch on the side of her head.

'I didn't want to worry you,' Andrew responded.

'Is it falling out?' I asked, wondering if Jacqui had alopecia.

'No. She's got a new habit.'

I felt a stomach-churning lurch.

'What do you mean?'

'She's actually doing it to herself. She's pulling out her own hair.'

Contentment evaporated like morning mist.

'For how long?'

'Just a few days.'

'So, since I've been gone.'

'Yeah. School's noticed. They say keep an eye on it.'

We'd weathered spitting, pushing, temper tantrums and

slamming her head into the wall. We had used various forms of correction, including time-outs, taking things away, fussing, ignoring. We had experimented with changes in diet and sleep. We had minimised, but been unable to extinguish, these behaviours. They flared and abated, waxed and waned like phases of the moon. We did not need anything else.

I put away my suitcase. Hung my aqua-coloured rain jacket in the closet of the guest room and docked the computer. I fingered the glossy collection of 'Royal Tour' media credentials, cheerful as a string of New Orleans Mardi Gras beads. '*Laissez les bon temps rouler.*'

I shoved the credentials in the back of a drawer.

✳

Over the next few days, although we constantly redirected Jacqui's hand away from her hair, the tiny bald patch increased. The spot grew to the size of a twenty-cent piece, then to a fifty-cent coin. Jacqui seemed anxious, wept for no apparent reason, repeatedly said, 'I sahwy! Sahwy!' although there was nothing to be sorry about, no reason to apologise.

More alarming still was our younger daughter's expression. She seemed to go into a snake-charmer's trance as she reached up with one little hand, grabbed a chunk of hair and pulled. We tried putting something else into her hand, holding her hands in ours, clapping and playing games, all with limited success. The moment she was left alone, she'd wander off, left hand snuggling towards her ear, to pluck a light brown curl. At night, we knew for certain she was indulging in this new habit, because tufts of her baby-fine hair lay in the bedclothes the next morning.

Although Jacqui had been known to fuss if I brushed her hair too strenuously, she showed no sign of pain when she pulled out her own hair—rather, she displayed a blissful sort of gratification. And the size of the patch grew and grew.

Yet Jacqui had had no shortage of peculiar tics and idiosyncratic behaviours in her short life, so how bad could *this* be?

We knew we'd better check. Jacqui had only been in her new school for a couple of months, and the team didn't know Jacqui well as yet. By contrast, Jacqui had attended Port Phillip Specialist School for three years, and they were expert both in her, and in her unusual problems and behaviours.

Late one night, Andrew dashed off a casual email to Jacqui's former kinder teacher, Yvonne Miller, outlining the issue. To our surprise, we heard back before school the following morning.

'Yvonne says it's trichotillomania,' Andrew said, scrolling through the response.

'Trick-a-what?'

'Here, have a look,' said Andrew, handing me his phone. 'She's talked to the psychologist at Port Phillip who apparently says call a shrink. Doesn't sound good.' Andrew shook his head. He grabbed his tie, computer, gave me a kiss and was out the door for a long day.

I checked out Yvonne's email. Then I did a computer search for the disorder. Wikipedia supplied a disturbing definition.

Trichotillomania, also known as trichotillosis, is the compulsive urge to pull out (and in some cases, eat) one's own hair leading to noticeable hair loss, distress, and social or functional impairment. It is classified as an impulse control disorder by DSM-IV and is often chronic and difficult to treat . . . it may be triggered by depression or stress.

I thought of Bette Davis's classic line in *All About Eve*. 'Fasten your seatbelts,' she said, with a grim smile. 'It's going to be a bumpy night.'

It was time to call in the experts.

'Oh, no, you take that table,' the woman said, pushing her thick mahogany hair away from her shoulder and gesturing to the red plastic seat closest to the giant indoor bouncy pillow.

'But you were here firs—'

'No, really, I insist, you have it,' she said. With a compassionate glance at Jacqui, then at me, she took the hand of a child who possessed a brown bob identical to her mother's, and they headed towards a table at the rear of the cavernous play centre.

'Well, thank you,' I said, and put down our tray. 'Jacqui, you are getting us special privileges,' I told my daughter, as I slid into a chair, offloading coffee, Jacqui's juice and a delectable looking feast of corn chips smothered in cheese, what appeared to be an entire carton of sour cream, red sauce and some wilted-looking jalapenos.

'Do you realise that nice lady actually thinks you have leukaemia?'

Jacqui looked at me quizzically. 'Leukaemia' wasn't one of the words we used in our flash cards. As in the early days, I still tried to narrate everything for Jacqui, like play-by-play commentary at a footy game. I continued conversationally, 'Yes, my darling girl, that lady thinks you have a rare form of cancer and are probably undergoing chemo because you are as bald as an eagle. A lopsided eagle, if I'm being harsh. Which I don't mean to be. Because I am not going to tell her that you are . . .'

I knew that if I said the rest of the sentence, it would act as a prompt. Jacqui would instantly reach up and pull out one of her few remaining locks and swallow it, then possibly even die as a result of ingesting hair which wound itself around her intestines. The entire reason I had brought her to an enormous warehouse with oversized padded gym equipment in primary colours was to try to distract her from that very activity.

'Slide,' said Jacqui helpfully, ignoring my monologue, pointing to a large red one next to the big bouncy pillow. Mum was speaking gobbledygook, which she did more frequently these days, and was clearly in need of redirection herself.

'Nacho?' I suggested, by way of alternative. I was eating a lot these days.

Jacqui shook her head, and repeated, 'Slide,' but woefully this time. A hand started creeping northward.

My hand shot out to catch hers as I rose to my feet, swaying.

I just wanted to sit. For a week, or perhaps forever. I craved sleep. I craved salt. And sugar. And caffeine. Something, anything, that would wake me up. Because I could never wake up, even though I seemed to go to bed earlier and earlier.

But Jacqui was impatient.

'Right you are as always, Jac. It's apparently time for the slide.'

Sophie and her friend Lucy came flying over, all smiles and giggles, breathless, speaking in a back-and-forth patter, like twins. 'That big green slide is the best! Only I think I broke my back! It's so steep! Oh, yum! Nachos! Thanks! Can we go get some drinks, too?'

I nodded, peeled a note out of my wallet, handed it over and tried to dig out a smile to go with it. My face felt rubbery, but I thought I looked normal. 'Sure, whatever you like.'

What was wrong with me? I once again found myself appreciating the buoyance, acceptance and resilience of my ten-year-old daughter and her understanding young friends. They seemed to take Jacqui's latest bizarre behaviour in stride. Yes, it was weird, there was no doubt about it, but that was just Jacqui. It was just her brain. They had known her for years, and they accepted her oddities. Lucy gave Jacqui a quick cuddle and kiss, and Jacqui smiled up at her, then tugged on my hand again.

'Okay, okay, I'm coming.' I walked her over to the base of the slide, then pointed to the netted pathway of steps and tunnels and various contraptions which had to be conquered en route to the slide. There was no way I could climb them today.

'I'll wait here at the bottom and take your picture!' I suggested. Jacqui nodded, began climbing. I snapped several action shots over the ensuing twenty minutes, then showed Jacqui, who returned to the playground equipment, now with Lucy and Sophie in tow. I reviewed the photos critically, shovelling nachos in my mouth. No one else seemed to be eating them, but the nachos were really very good.

Then my stomach did a flip. One photo clearly showed that Jacqui's hair was missing from the crown of her head, and much of the back, as well as the left side. No wonder strangers were always responding with sympathy. I had tried to explain how bad Jacqui's hair was to my parents, sisters, friends. This was the picture worth a thousand words. I quickly created a group email, attached the photo, and hit 'send'. I was too tired to write a subject. They'd know what it was about, after all.

✳

The phone rang. It was my friend Linda, from Atlanta. 'What is going on!! Are you okay? We're worried.'

The tone of her voice sounded urgent, but the text broke apart into syllables. It was hard to bend them into coherence, difficult to understand what she was saying. I groped, came up with a pronoun.

'We?'

'Yes. Not just me. Andi is concerned too. And Ginger.'

'But you all live in different places,' I said, confused. Then, 'Ginger is in Africa.'

I felt disoriented.

'That picture,' Linda said. She paused, her voice shaky. 'You sent it to all of us. We've been in touch with each other. Your poor sweet girl.'

From somewhere deep inside my brain, I accessed a piece of information. Shaky voice. Linda was sad. I couldn't think very quickly these days, found it hard to decode words, emotions. But I knew I was supposed to say something now, fill this lull.

'Jacqui,' I tried.

'Yes, Jacqui! How is her head? What's happening? Is it getting better? But most of all, how are you?!'

Another pause as I thought about this. 'We are trying medicine,' I said carefully. It felt like I was a beginner, speaking a foreign language. It took time to compose a simple sentence, subject, verb, object. I over-enunciated, a robot.

'And you?' Linda seemed very persistent. I didn't want to talk.

'I'm just tired. And I am not really very sure why I am here.'

There was silence. I enjoyed the silence because it was very quiet. I listened to the quiet sounds of an international phone line. It always sounded like water. There was so much water. Everything and everyone felt very far away.

Linda was talking again, bothering me. 'Sara, you need to go see someone.'

'I need to go now. I am okay. I am fine.'

❋

A card arrived from New York. '*Thinking of you! Love, Andi.*'

My friend Nancy wrote, and Angela, Sharon, Bridget, Lisa. I put the cards on my bedside table.

Mum and Dad called, daily. Toni rang, from Sydney. My sisters, Susan and Elizabeth, at least once a week. Afterwards, I could never remember what any of them said. But when I was on the phone, with any of them, I always felt better. And then I would hang up, and the lethargy would roll in, coil around like kudzu. It felt heavy to carry these vines, which thickened and tightened.

I walked slowly. Talked slowly. The vines constricted, a python around my lungs.

Elizabeth's husband, John, sent a care package full of chocolates and cookies. They were delicious, and the girls loved them. I thought 'thank you', but I was no longer hungry.

A parcel arrived, from Namibia. It was not my birthday. I felt confused again. I opened it, discovered a raw silk scarf in my favourite shade of green. '*I wish I was there to give you a hug,*' the card said, in Ginger's elegant handwriting. '*This will have to do.*'

I put on the scarf. It was warm. I kept trying to remember to write back.

✳

I was standing in front of a whiteboard covered in notes, in a small classroom at Sophie's school. She gave me a smile, and I smiled back. We were both excited I was teaching her class.

'Now the standard way to write a news story for print is that 'inverted pyramid' I told you about. Make sure you put your most important details at the top of your story, and the less important ones second. That way if someone doesn't have time to read the whole thing, they still get the gist of it. But you also want a snappy lead sentence.'

The group of fifth graders was nodding, ready to begin their own reports.

'Now who knows what they're going to write about?'

'The fire at the school,' one boy said.

'I'm going to write about how we did at Tournament of the Minds,' said a girl. 'We did great.'

I looked up, saw the classroom door open, someone from the front office enter. Was it time already? The bell hadn't rung. I only had one session for this tutorial, designed to teach interested students how they, too, could become reporters. But the clock said we still had another half hour.

'Is everything okay?' I asked.

'I'm sorry, but no,' the woman said. I stared.

'It's Jacqui. She's had a big seizure. Her school rang. They want you to come.'

I paused. Then immediately turned to check out Sophie's reaction. Her expression had crumpled into a worried scowl.

I turned to the whole class, which now stared attentively. 'Wow, so we have some breaking news right here at your school!'

I said, opting for a light, informative tone. Whatever was happening, it could wait one more minute for me to explain and make sure no one got anxious. 'Sophie's little sister has epilepsy, as some of you already know. It's similar to how some kids have asthma, or diabetes, or allergies to nuts.'

Nodding. So far so good.

'And that means that sometimes she has a seizure. But she will be okay. Everything is fine. I'm going to leave now, and I'm just sorry I can't stay for the rest of the class. I've had a lot of fun. But you guys finish those stories, and put them in this envelope. I'll read them, and get them back to you!'

I was scooping up my papers, coat, purse, waving and heading out the door. I gave a big smile and cheery wave to Sophie. Her face was a cipher.

When I arrived at Sunbury Macedon Ranges Specialist School, the ambulance was already there. Jacqui was on a stretcher, unconscious. Her face was white, the colour of the belly of a deceased fish. Her breathing was shallow, and her head turned to its side. Except that she was much larger, she looked as she had in that New York hospital, years before. But this time, I felt strangely calm.

'Would you like to ride inside?' one of the ambulance attendants asked.

'Sure. But tell me, what happened?'

Jo Nolan, the principal, filled me in. 'The reason we called was that she didn't come out of the seizure right away. She sat up, but then she had another one. And then one almost immediately after that. Here are the notes we took. I know you said that's not her typical pattern, which was why we rang, and called the ambulance. Also, she definitely has a high fever.' I felt very grateful to Jo. Kind and professional, she had made a stressful situation more bearable, and her report made it clear the school's response had been prompt and perfect. But what was wrong with Jac?

'You all did great. Thanks for taking care of our girl. I'll call and let you know what's what.' I climbed in, rang Andrew, who met me at the Royal Children's. It was a relief to see my husband, straight and tall as a pillar. But those on staff were as perplexed as we were.

'She's brewing something, that's for sure,' one doctor told us, patting our limp little girl. 'But it might be a few days before we will know exactly what. No reason to keep her here, though. It will be best to monitor her at home.' He filled out the discharge papers.

As it turned out, we had an answer in less than 24 hours. Jacqui developed a miserable rash which covered her head to toe, with dark patches on the tops of her knees and elbows.

'Mum, look at her tongue!' Sophie told me, fascinated. 'It's bright red!'

I took Jacqui to the local medical centre, where a doctor shook his head, then turned to his computer. 'Have a look here,' he said, after a brief search on the internet. I stared from the image on the screen to my daughter's face, then back again. Exactly the same.

'See that patch? Like a moustache and goatee? How it's bright, bright white?'

I nodded.

'I haven't seen a case in twenty years, but I can practically guarantee that your daughter has scarlet fever. You need to go back to the hospital.'

At the hospital, more tests, more doctors, more observation. 'Scarlet fever!' a nurse marvelled. 'You know, that's what Beth died of in *Little Women*.' Perhaps I looked stricken. She patted my arm. 'That was before penicillin, of course.'

On antibiotics, Jacqueline slowly improved. After two weeks, we sent her back to school. But it proved to be too soon. The following day, she took a tumble and broke the top of her arm, just under her shoulder. It was a tricky spot. There was no way to set the bone in a cast. She had to wear a sling to keep her shoulder immobilised. For a girl in constant motion, it was a tall order. Jacqueline was even more miserable than she had been with scarlet fever.

Meantime, we were still battling the trichotillomania.

Ostensibly working on the book about Port Phillip Specialist School, I found myself unable to concentrate. I instead began to write a screenplay called *Tricky Mania*. The main character, the narrator, was a ten-year-old girl. She kept insisting this was a play about her, not about her sister. Her little sister swam back and forth across the stage, behind her, wearing a swimming cap and goggles. It was revealed in time, when the girl tore off her little hat, that she wasn't a swimmer at all, but wore the cap to hide her bald head. I allowed time for the audience to gasp.

But I abandoned the play. It wasn't interesting. Neither was the book. I just looked at Jacqui's head, willing a new growth of hair.

My mum called. I was at the pharmacy. 'Hi, yeah, I'm just picking up some Prozac,' I told her.

A stranger stared at me. I realised my voice must be too loud. I suddenly had difficulty moderating myself and was conscious that my American accent cut through conversational white caps like the rudder of a sloop.

'Tutti-frutti flavoured,' I whispered. Then I began giggling, uncontrollably. 'Tutti-frutti flavoured Prozac!'

Whoops. Too loud again.

'Not for me,' I continued, although my mother wasn't laughing. I had consciously pitched my voice to be audible. 'The medicine is for Jac-que-line.'

*

'Come on, Mum, give me another one.'

Sophie stared at me, nodding eagerly.

'Okay, okay, what is a Thestral?'

'Oh, Mum, that is soooooooo easy!' Sophie grinned.

A devotee of Harry Potter, she had just reread the series for perhaps the twentieth time, and had discovered a book of quizzes for like-minded fans. 'That's the winged horse that's actually a skeleton and it leads the carriage to Hogwarts. But here's the thing that makes it special. Only Harry and Luna and other people who have lost someone they love can actually see it, so most people think the carriages just drive themselves!' she finished triumphantly.

'Too good for me!' I told her, grinning, as Sophie beamed. 'Now, time for bed.'

But the next morning, I couldn't stop thinking about Thestrals. Like Harry and Luna, those of us who had someone with a disability in their lives discovered a world others barely knew existed. An enormous world which had previously been all but invisible, a kind of parallel universe, an Atlantis of doctors and schools and specialists and experts to mine the depths of a loved one's peculiar and complicated mind.

In our Thestral world, we had a team of experts, now led by a brilliant neurologist and epileptologist, Professor Ingrid Scheffer. Dr Scheffer was a professor at the University of Melbourne, Austin Health and the Florey Institute of Neuroscience. She looked the part of a scientist and academic with her penetrating blue eyes, tousled, wavy brown hair and sheaf of papers. She possessed a warm and friendly demeanour as well as a towering intellect. As an international leader in the field of genetic epilepsy research, she was part of a tiny, luminous cadre of experts, including doctors we had consulted in New York, who were attempting to unlock the mysteries of what caused seizures like Jacqui's. We felt extraordinarily fortunate to have found her.

Our team also included Jacqui's school, assorted other doctors, a psychologist and a psychiatrist. On this day, we had an appointment with a behaviour paediatrician, Sian Hughes, who had been recommended by Dr Scheffer.

Sophie was at school. Andrew was at the office. Jacqui and I were in Broadmeadows, a neighbourhood on the western fringes of Melbourne, home to a large and varied immigrant community.

The Coolaroo Clinic was the sort of medical practice where those waiting displayed a practised, unhurried expression that indicated life had always included lengthy queues, and it was easiest to be resigned to this as a fact of life. The women, many wearing galabeyas, sat peacefully. Beside them sat clean and well-behaved children.

This was the second time I'd been to the clinic. On our first visit, Jacqui had not responded well to the waiting, and had launched into a violent temper tantrum which encompassed much of the floor. I'd dropped down beside her, and was attempting to help her control herself when the doctor came in.

Except, I hadn't realised at first it was the doctor. I'd seen a pair of briskly moving slim legs in flats and the hem of a flowered, knee-length dress. I had just craned my neck up to offer an apology, uncertain how to peel Jacqui off the floor without the 'Jaws of Life' used to extricate victims from car crashes, when there had been a gentle flop. The flowery dress had cascaded outward like a parachute, into a perfect circle, and a small face with close-cropped chestnut hair and a pair of the sparkliest brown eyes I had ever seen had peered directly at us.

'Hello, Jacqueline,' the doctor said, with an Irish lilt. She was by then lying on the floor across from us, propped up on her elbows, chin cupped in her hands. 'Thanks for coming to see me.'

Dr Hughes was a charmer, and Jacqui stopped, mid-squall.

'It's pretty fun down here on the floor! But I have lots of toys in my office, too. Would you care to see them?' Sian Hughes nodded expectantly. Jacqui nodded back. Without so much as wiping her tear-stained face, my cherub immediately sprang to her feet. I followed, too. 'By the way, I'm Dr Hughes,' the sprite told me. 'But you can call me Sian.'

A behavioural paediatrician, as I'd learned, dealt with a wide range of problems, which might include autism, aggression or self-harm. Or children who pulled out their hair and ate it.

I was glad to be back for this second visit, and delighted Jacqui was more settled. Jacqui adored people, and remembered them. If only I had better news to report.

'So the Prozac isn't going very well,' I told her.

'Oh dear,' Sian said sympathetically. 'Tell me what's happening.'

'The school called and said they had to peel her off the ceiling, and to discontinue use immediately. Apparently, instead of calming her down, it did the opposite.'

Sian nodded again. 'Not to worry. I've spoken to Dr Scheffer and we have another idea. It's called Risperdal. Now, before you go reading up on the internet and getting all worried, I want to tell you that this medicine can be used for adults with schizophrenia, but that's not what Jacqui has. This medicine can also be used for autism, and it can make people less anxious. Jacqui has a good home, people who love her. It's her brain that's doing this, and we may be able to help with medicine.'

I sat still, taking it all in. 'But the other medicines haven't worked. They always seem to do the opposite of what we expect, with our daughter.'

'There's no way to know unless you try. Each class of drugs is different.'

I shook my head. 'I feel like this is harder on Jacqui than on any of us,' I said, looking at my daughter, who at that moment was busy entertaining the two graduate students in Sian's office.

'Now there, I don't agree,' Sian replied. 'Your lovely daughter lives very much in the present. Take a look! And if we can make the present secure for her, she will be very happy indeed. The rest of us, though, we see the past, and the future, too. That's what is far more difficult.' Her look was keen and kind.

I thought about this.

'But Dr Hughes—Sian—is this, this hair thing, all because I travelled? Because I took that trip for work? Is that why Jacqui started . . .'

Sian looked at Jacqui, animatedly clowning around, then back at me.

'Possibly, in part,' she acknowledged. 'Your trip may have contributed to the anxiety. But that doesn't mean you should quit working. Far from it. Let's look at the whole picture. Remember, Jacqui has switched schools. Left a place, and people, and a routine, she knew and liked. She is on a new bus. With new people. And then there's the fact that your daughter doesn't have a very clear concept of time. That's the nature of an intellectual disability. She's not sure what is going to happen, or when or how, and that can cause tremendous anxiety. Our job is to find ways to help Jacqui feel more secure, to know what's going to happen. But don't quit your job. Jacqui needs her mum to be strong and happy, and able to go the distance. As the carer goes . . .'

'. . . so goes the family.'

Sian scrawled a script on paper, handed it to me. 'I'll send you a list of things you can do the next time you take a trip, so Jacqui understands and doesn't get anxious. Technology has wonderful tools. And let me know what happens with the Risperdal.'

✳

I did as my friends insisted, and went to see someone. She was a good listener. She probed. I talked. I wept. I returned, several times. Each time it felt like lancing a boil. But some of the poison poured out, along with the tears. And then I was done. That wasn't what I needed.

✳

There was a white lace curtain, a name in swirling letters. *Massage by Caroline.* The bell tinkled as I opened the door, and a smiling woman greeted me. 'You must be Sophie's mum.'

'That I am.'

'This may be the first time I've had a child book a massage for their mum!' she told me, as I lay down.

'She told me she saw your number when she was at her maths lesson,' I responded, 'and thought this would make a good present.'

'She tells me her sister is autistic,' the woman continued.

'Yes,' I said. I didn't speak for the next fifteen minutes, then said, 'This feels heavenly. Your hands are very strong.'

Caroline laughed. 'I get that a lot. Especially from the guys at the abattoir, where I worked for a few years.'

I lifted my head. 'A massage therapist? Who worked in an *abattoir?*'

She nodded. 'After my marriage broke up. I needed a job where I could earn money for me and the kids, and didn't have the time to think. Up until then, I'd been a massage therapist, but at that time, I don't know, I just couldn't. It was like I had nothing to give.' Caroline paused. 'Butchering meat is hard work, but believe it or not, I actually liked the job,' she told me cheerfully. 'And the blokes I worked with were great. But it's physical work, make no mistake. Next thing I knew, I was using my massage skills to work the knots out of their shoulders, and they told me I might as well start my own business and get paid for it!' she concluded with a jolly laugh. 'A lot of them are still my clients.'

'I can see why. I'd like to book another appointment. But I'll pay, this time.'

'How was it?' Sophie asked expectantly when I returned. I hugged her fiercely.

'You, my dear girl, are a love. And a mind-reader. That was exactly what I needed.'

✳

Andrew and I sat at a restaurant, moving food around our plates.

'How are you?' my husband asked. His look was as desolate as a windswept plateau.

It took effort, but I forced myself to speak. We had to talk, we had to be honest about what we needed, in order to make our way through this valley.

'I have been struggling. You?'

His sigh was deep. 'It's just sad,' Andrew said. 'She's beautiful. But her brain. It just seems unfair. Poor little tyke.'

'But I'm starting to come up,' I told him. And I was. It felt like spring, when the sap started flowing. I thought of maple trees, in melting snow. I could feel warmth and strength returning. I wasn't scared any more, I wasn't exhausted or confused. I was determined to get our family back on track.

I leaned forward. 'You know what I've realised? I simply must work. As much as I love our girls, and you, I crave it. I enjoy reporting, and it's a break from managing Jacqui's situation. It's what I need, in order to help take care of us. And I'm here to support you in whatever it is that you need—sports or racing, riding your bike, seeing your mates, working less, playing with a tractor, whatever it is. So that we have fun again. You know, we're basically a pretty happy bunch. This isn't easy stuff. But I think if we make a few tweaks, life can be better.'

Andrew nodded. And then we talked.

We talked about the fact that we had both been trying very hard and for a very long time to be strong. Like a pair of columns, we were equally determined to keep our little family aloft. It was just that even the strongest pillars are parallel. We were working independent of one another, when we needed to be more of a team. To hold one another, even though we might sometimes fail, or even fall.

My husband reached out for my hand and stroked it gently with his. His eyes were tender.

'I know,' he said. 'I know.'

We sat there for a long time.

❋

'Look, Andrew!' I said, touching the soft fuzz growing across Jacqui's head, soft as duck down. 'It's really, truly growing back!'

Jacqui batted my hand, indignant.

'Indeed,' Andrew responded with a smile.

'Guacamole?' Jacqui asked, hopefully. The new medicine seemed to make her hungrier.

'In a minute, Jacqui.'

I returned to mashing the avocado for her favourite dish. Jacqui nodded, and took my hand, prepared to wait. She understood.

The fact that she understood was nearly as significant as her peach fuzz. Jacqui had been taking Risperdal for several months, and it was obvious to us, to her school, and to everyone else that Jacqui seemed sharper and more focused. The anxiety and weeping had abated. And while she struggled with transitions, our daughter was no longer derailed by every change, no matter how small. She still had a short attention span, and the intellectual disability would always make learning slow. But those factors, like her epilepsy, we could manage.

We had always loved Jacqui, but it was impossible to love some of her behaviours. The beauty of Risperdal was that it had given us a happier, more settled and better behaved child, who was consequently more enjoyable to have around. Her quirky humour and engaging giggle were back. She was enjoying life. And we were loving our happier, healthier, more engaged and engaging little girl. Make no mistake, she could still pull some atrocious stunts. The difference was that now, she would pause to look at us and say, 'Nooo! Nevah, evah. I nah doing that evah again!'

Just like a typical kid.

And Andrew and I were making sure we did more things like a typical family. To have people over for dinner. Or go to the beach, or the farm. To play catch in the front yard after dinner. Watch Sophie play netball. Push Jacqui on her trike. Sometimes, we still had to divide and conquer. But on other occasions, we found ways to amend and alter, in order to all be together. We were determined to challenge disability, determined to make our family as normal as it could possibly be.

❉

Sophie walked in, carrying a handful of fresh sunflowers. 'I picked these for the table!' she said.

'Thanks, Sophie!'

'I'm actually going to use them for my hotel I'm doing here with Izzy. We're going to invite you to stay, and charge you and Dad. I think two dollars. Each. Would you like to see my brochure?'

'You're charging me to stay in my own house?'

'Exactly. But you get my pancakes. And maybe a chocolate on the bed at night. Do we have any chocolates? You might need to buy some.'

As I listened to Sophie tell me more about her latest money-making scheme, I thought about Risperdal and sunflowers. It occurred to me that the honeycomb of hexagons that comprised Risperdal was, for Jacqui, akin to the Fibonacci sequence at the heart of the Golden Mean. That sequence—in which each number in the pattern is the sum of the preceding two numbers—could be found in everything from the pattern of a pine cone, to the shell of a nautilus. It had been the basis for the paved flagstone patio the garden designer had included in the centre of our back garden, and the swirling spirals in the galaxy, in the glorious Australian night sky. Order created harmony, and by extension, beauty. For the first time, there was far more order and coherence in our daughter's mind, far less distraction and destruction. And like the sunflower that carries a Fibonacci spiral in the pattern of its seeds, our daughter seemed to lift her head, to reveal her beauty.

'But the hotel is tomorrow,' Sophie continued. 'Looks like I need you to take me shopping, first. By the way, what's for dinner, Mum?'

'What's this I hear about my house being used as a hotel?' Andrew asked, striding in, Jacqui already in his arms. He kissed Soph, then me. 'You'd better have awfully good service. And is that breakfast, breakfast in bed?'

I thought about the words of the British Queen Elizabeth: 'Grief is the price we pay for love.' And I thought of the American poet, Henry David Thoreau, and what he had written as he tried to recover from a broken heart: 'The only remedy for love, is to love more.'

16

GHOST GUMS

Next to my daughters, my husband Andrew says the *Titanic* is my favourite topic. Unless perhaps you count my obsession with frequent-flyer miles. It had been a career highlight to co-host the *Dateline/Discovery Channel Special* joint production, 'Raising the Titanic', a television program broadcast live from the middle of the North Atlantic, directly above an eight-kilometre debris field which was all that remained of what was then the largest ship in the world, and a supposedly unsinkable luxury liner. That show was the culmination of an assignment which had involved a flotilla of four ships, a jaunty yellow deep-sea submersible and an international team of several hundred people, including scientists, historians, conservationists, naval experts and television crews, during which we'd successfully hoisted the largest piece of the wreck ever recovered.

Interesting, yes. Recent, no.

In comparison to 2012, 1998 felt like the Jurassic Age. That era before every teenager had GPS in their phone. Fourteen years before, it had taken complicated engineering and seamless coordination to beam a signal from a heaving ship, hit a satellite in space, then hold that signal for the two hours of the live broadcast as the ship bobbed about in the middle of the ocean approximately

600 kilometres southeast of Newfoundland. 'Approximately' is not a good enough set of coordinates for a satellite transmission, and the fact that the show got on the air at all was a tribute to the engineers' technical prowess. Yet that had been just one element of the elaborate mission.

The broadcast followed on the heels of James Cameron's blockbuster *Titanic,* and interest in the doomed liner had been enormous. But the truth was that the story of the *Titanic* was something of an eternal flame, which burned most brightly at relevant mile-markers, such as the upcoming centennial anniversary of the ship's sinking. Consequently, I was writing a speech about that assignment, which had been requested by the Macedon Red Cross organisers for their annual fundraiser, to be held at the nearby Macedon View Restaurant in just a few weeks' time.

But I had writer's block.

There was no point remembering that writing and delivering speeches was something I had done literally hundreds of times over the years. I had begun my speaking 'career' as a fifteen-year-old in high school, competing in what was called the NFL. This wasn't the world-famous National Football League, but the National Forensic League, the oldest and largest speech and debate honour society in the US. Our NFL didn't have cheerleaders or stadiums full of fans. In truth, it was a huge nerd-fest. Competitors were far more interested in being chosen for Harvard Law than getting drafted by the Dallas Cowboys.

But for those of us who loved debate, oratory and extemporaneous speaking, travelling the circuit to compete against other high schools was exciting, and we relished bringing home our gaudy trophies. I'd done well enough to win the region twice, and represent Virginia; North Carolina; Washington, DC; and Maryland at the US Nationals. Where I'd promptly lost. But the skills I'd honed in all those tournaments turned out to have been the perfect training for live television. In the years since, I'd also gone on to deliver many speeches, in the US and Australia.

And on every occasion, whether it was to an audience of 30 or 40 people or a gathering in the thousands, I thought of our old high-school coach, Mona Potter. With her faux leopard-skin coat, hammer-dulcimer accent straight from the Blue Ridge Mountains and, above all, her steel-trap mind, Mrs Potter had been a powerful proponent of the philosophy that excellence was both a goal in itself and a quality that would be rewarded. She instilled in our public high school team from a middle-class suburb of Richmond, Virginia, that any kid from anywhere, with hard work and good training, could become whoever she wanted to be, could accomplish whatever she dreamed. I owed her far more than any skills I had as a public speaker.

So why did this speech have me in a tailspin?

I already knew the answer. It was in my Australian backyard. A few new friends might be there and—there was no other way to put it—I wanted to impress them. I still felt like the new kid in town. I was as nervous as a girl facing her first day at school, whose dad just gave her a bowl haircut.

I looked back out the window again, scanning the forest for inspiration, my eyes drawn as always to the pale bark of one euca-lypt that was especially beautiful. The forest, which had once seemed a dappled, grey-green sea, had long since parted to reveal it was instead a collection of interesting and distinct species. The alabaster hue and sinuous shape of this particular tree made it appear like a ghostly nude, arms outstretched. It was a *Eucalyptus papuana*, a ghost gum. An appropriate sight, it seemed, when contemplating the wraiths and spirits from a long-ago night.

The sofa was strewn with research material—books, news-paper articles, a few souvenirs from the trip, although the largest and heaviest of these had a permanent position to the right of the fireplace. It was the grey rock I hadn't bothered to move on Black Saturday, knowing it could survive anything.

That rock came from four kilometres beneath the surface of the North Atlantic, adjacent to the *Titanic*. I would never forget how the two-man crew had manipulated the tiny sub's robotic arms to hoist the rock from the ocean bed and place it in their exterior basket, which was ordinarily used to bring up artefacts retrieved from the site of the wreck. Typical loot might include an unbroken soup tureen, marked with the insignia of the White Star line, a silver teaspoon, a man's pair of boots, rivets from the ship, or perhaps a letter or a scrap of a diary.

Grateful as I was to have a souvenir of that journey, the memories had been the greatest gift. I'd never forget the moment when I peered through the sub's tiny porthole, straight through one of the ghostly portholes of that wrecked colossus. It was easy to imagine a bejewelled woman, laughing, tiara sparkling in the candlelight, pulling on a long white glove as she dressed for dinner; and just as easy to imagine a mum and dad in steerage, who'd barely been able to scrape together the funds for the voyage, awakening to find the ocean pouring in through the gash in the ship's side, aware that they and their children had been cheated of a new life in America, of any life at all.

But how to turn all of these memories and imaginings into something more? What I needed to do was to write the flanking support structure for what would be the keystone of the speech, a video excerpt of the 1998 documentary. *Dateline NBC* had just Fed-Exed a copy of the show across, and my friend Zoomer and the crew at his company RapidTV had popped the disc in their Avid editing machine and cut a clip for me to use.

Watching the doco for the first time in years, it was poignant to see footage of George Tulloch, then the head of RMS Titanic, Inc., the company which had been granted sole salvage rights to the wreck. A charming, chain-smoking, dervish of a man, full of restless vision and drive, George was the one to green-light the ultimate joyride. I'd been assigned to go down in the *Nautile* to chronicle the crew's delicate mission of attaching diesel-filled lift bags to a huge chunk of the ship, which had been standing on an angled knife edge far below us.

The idea was that the enormous bags would lift the piece to the surface. But there were lots of variables, and no one knew if it would work. I sped through the doco, checking out the vision we'd shot the following day, memories splashing over me like waves. There was George, pacing the deck, nervous as an expectant father, sucking on a cigarette cupped against the wind. Then, applause. I laughed as I watched him yell at the crew, as the unwieldy piece slammed into the side of the French salvage vessel, the *Abeilles*, during the nerve-racking operation to winch it aboard. Finally, there it was, lying on the deck like a rusted, beached whale. On the surface again, after all those years.

But fourteen years was a long time. George had died a few years before.

More ghosts.

I thought of George, thought of that assignment, when a collection of *Titanic* artefacts toured Australia, not so long before. But the Big Piece had not been one of them. Perhaps it wasn't surprising. There was a showbiz quality to American business, after all. The fifteen-ton Big Piece had been restored, and, in all its silvery splendour, was on display outside a casino in—where else?—Las Vegas.

Which brought up the question, yet again. What was it that made the *Titanic* a siren, its plunder drawing crowds in Vegas, Sydney, Melbourne and around the world? Why did people love the movie? Why did they still read the books, both new ones, and classics such as *A Night to Remember*? All of the survivors had long since died. Why did we still care?

I wandered to the kitchen for a cup of tea. Another time-honoured stalling tactic. But I was starting to gain traction. This would be the question I would try to answer: *why* the *Titanic* was still such a potent yarn, a century later, and how it was really both fact and fable. It seemed clear that *Titanic* had also been a gateway event, ushering in a new era. Then there was all sorts of intrinsic drama—the ship's unsinkability, so much hubris!—and those titans of industry who'd gone down with the ship. There were also new stories relating to passengers—chronicles of those who'd survived, and details discovered by families of those who had not. There were even links to 9/11, yet more ghosts. And the disaster had occurred in the middle of the North Atlantic. The ocean was a powerful character in this drama.

I found myself thinking about our own family's immigration to Australia, just a few years ago. Instead of a ship, we'd taken a plane—a luxury of the latter half of the twentieth century. But the greatest luxury was to be allowed entrance. While Andrew and the children were Australian, I was not. The only reason I'd been granted a visa was because I had married an Australian.

I could not help but compare my situation to the plight of desperate families who risked drowning at sea for a chance at freedom and opportunity. The catch phrase I'd heard much of recently, to 'stop the boats', disturbed me. It was in such sharp contradiction to the modern history of this nation, since most of those who called Australia home had either arrived by sea themselves, or were descendants of those who had. Managing immigration was a question for every sovereign nation, including the land of my birth. But I could not help but detect what seemed a slightly hysterical note to the debate in Australia, an anxiety about potential consequences which seemed wildly out of proportion to the number of those begging for entry.

Among the millions of people who had poured into America and Australia by sea, the majority had come by choice—willing to brave the risks, because the perceived rewards were worth the hardships and hazards of such a voyage. Or because they had little to leave behind. Or because they had been running away.

Of course, few immigrants ever travelled aboard ships anywhere near as opulent or glorious as the *Titanic*. Indonesian refugees sailing to Australia were crowding aboard dilapidated, unseaworthy vessels, rather than an ocean liner. But it was also true that *Titanic*'s disastrous end, on her maiden voyage, was proof that the ocean's perils did not discriminate. It was why the ancient maps were littered with dragons, sea monsters, terrifying creatures of every description. It must be hard-wired in us, to fear the ocean. It is a place of tempests. Pirates. Shipwrecks. And ice. And yet both the American and Australian national stories and identities were shaped in large part by the men, women and children who had defied those dangers.

Roaming far and wide must be hard-wired, too. Sophie and Jacqui were born of wandering. Andrew and I were, as well.

My thoughts bumped backward, to a diary entry: 'there was a large iceberg about a mile from us.'

This dramatic account was in a book, bound in red leather:

I shall never forget that part of the voyage . . . the grating of the ice on copper of the vessel made a terrific noise, at least as it appeared to me at the time and no doubt was very alarming to the passengers . . . The deck soon presented an appearance not easily described and impossible to forget with so many passengers, men, women and children, who had rushed on deck thinking we were about to be wrecked . . . the passengers were all ordered to their cabins and some of them had to be forced down and the latches closed over them.

And yet the man who had penned those lines had not been on the *Titanic*.

John Dill had travelled aboard the *Monarch of the Seas,* on a voyage that began in Liverpool, England, and ended on 2 November 1857, when the ship dropped anchor in Port Phillip Bay, not far from Port Phillip Specialist School. John Dill's journey took 140 days, and included a string of calamities and misadventures to boggle the mind, including sailing off course, running afoul of sheet ice south of the Cape of Good Hope, losing the main mast and rigger mast in a 'white squall', being becalmed for three weeks and very nearly running into an iceberg. Getting to Australia had been a close thing.

The red-bound volume in which I'd found Dill's harrowing account was called *The Archbold Story*, compiled by a descendant, John Oliver Archbold, of Donald, Victoria. The volume was on the bookshelf in our living room because Dill's fellow passengers had included the wife and several children of one Ralph Archbold. Ralph and his son and namesake were already waiting for them in Australia. They'd arrived in Victoria three years earlier, determined to find the family fortune in the goldfields. Tragically, Ralph's wife Mary Ann died of typhoid fever on the journey to be reunited with her husband, and was buried at sea. But the couple's children prospered in Victoria, and their descendants remained in the region.

Among the photos in the book was one showing a woman with wide-set blue eyes, a high brow and a happy smile. Her name was Sophie Archbold Butcher. She was holding a large bouquet, and the arm of the tall local cricketer and farmer she'd just married, John Richard Butcher. Everyone called him Jack. I enjoyed seeing the photo of him as a young man, taken decades before we stood alongside that fence, and silently watched his grandson play cricket. Sophie and Jack were Andrew's paternal grandparents, and our Sophie and Jacqui were their namesakes.

Ancestors. Ships. Stories. Andrew's ancestors might not have travelled aboard the *Titanic*, but there had been many a ship in his family's past, and the glint of gold as well. Jack Butcher's ancestors had caught the fever, although they travelled to Melbourne by way of what is now Tasmania, courtesy of His Majesty the King. A collection of glasses on another bookshelf was from the family reunion held in Muckleford in 1981. In gold lettering, they proclaimed:

THE BUTCHER FAMILY REUNION:
MUCKLEFORD 15/11/1981
Celebrating the 150th anniversary of the arrival in Australia
of James Butcher on board the 'Strathsfieldsay'.

263

James landed in Van Diemen's Land on 15 November 1831. He married Margaret Clarke in 1840 (sentenced for seven years in 1834). The family settled in Port Phillip Colony in 1848 and took up land at Muckleford in 1857.

The Archbolds, and the Butchers, then, both arrived in Victoria the same year—1857—but it would be several generations before Sophie met Jack.

Ghost gums. Family trees. My husband's history. By extension, the history of our daughters.

The wine glasses and the red leather book were just some of the souvenirs of two families who had wandered far from home, all the way across the globe, to wind up close to one another, near Castlemaine.

There were no riches of the goldrush on display in Muckleford, where Andrew had grown up, as there were in Bendigo or Ballarat. But the scrub forests adjacent to the Butcher family farm were pockmarked with shafts and deep holes. The remnants of these old mines were traps for young children off in pursuit of a rabbit, or out for a wander. It was easy to imagine the prospectors panning for gold in Muckleford Creek.

Andrew tried to explain to our Sophie that sleepy Muckleford had been a boom town back then. Everyone was trying to strike it rich. Some had. Others, including some of his ancestors, had not.

'They would have had a tiny house, Sophie. Like that.'

'But Dad, that's a bus shelter!'

'You're right. Their house would have been a lot smaller. Maybe not a house at all.'

It was hard for Sophie—and for me—to imagine that this tiny hamlet, population 70, which included the family farm, Trevor and Helen's home, a pet cemetery, a B&B, a cricket oval and hundreds of sheep, had, in 1857, been a bustling town with as many as 3000 tents. In a book about the quaint tourist town of Maldon, just up the road, I'd found a map of Muckleford from those bygone days. The town had been set out in a grid layout, with Bank Street, Store Street and High Street marked 'East' or 'West', as Cross Street neatly marked the divide. The book also included a line drawing of what I had always assumed was an old miner's cottage along the main road. It was, it turned out, part of what had once been the bustling Orville Hotel, which included pleasure gardens and a post office.

It was easier to see ghosts in some places than others. Nana's ancestors could be spotted in the thick black hair and dark skin, but in the red hair, too, of some in the family. The story went that this combination could be traced to sailors aboard a ship from the Spanish Armada, which had made landfall on the coast of Ireland. The story of that long-ago love, or conquest, was told in the colour of Andrew's sister's hair, his brother's skin, the red flecks in Andrew's beard. It was in the genes.

Ships from Spain. From England. From Ireland.

And ships to the Antipodes.

All those miles. All those hazards. But they had survived. Ultimately, they had thrived.

I thought of my own family history. One reason I would always love *Titanic* was that my sisters and I were the later products of a shipboard romance. Like Jack and Rose in James Cameron's movie, Robison Brown James had met Anne Sutherland Marple in the middle of the North Atlantic, travelling from Southampton, England, to New York City. My father had been returning from a Rotary scholarship in Edinburgh; my mother, from her junior year abroad in Paris. My father was from Alabama; my mother from Connecticut. They lived 1790 kilometres apart. Their chance intersection, at a dance on the last night of the voyage, was at least as unlikely as my serendipitous meeting with Andrew all those years later in New York. But had it not been for those few days aboard the *Liberte*, they would never have met, and my sisters and I would never have existed.

The various routes my parents' ancestors had taken to America were the stuff of photographs, oil paintings and oral history. Some had arrived all the way back in the 1600s. Some descendants fought in the Revolutionary War, others in later conflicts. On my father's side, there was a framed portrait of his great-great-grandfather wearing a Confederate uniform, sabre at his side. That ancestor would have been the sworn enemy of my mother's people, who fought for the Union during the Civil War.

And yet, although my parents were from two such different regions of the United States before they ultimately settled in the middle of the East Coast, in Virginia, it was interesting to trace back both branches. As with the Archbolds and Butchers in Victoria, there were missed opportunities for earlier intersections decades, even centuries, before. Intersections that had never occurred because so many in our families just kept moving.

Consider my maternal great-grandmother, by all accounts a charmer, unless you were a child. She infamously loathed all children, including her own. But the enormous oil painting in its gold-leaf frame that hung in my grandparents' home depicted an appealing young woman with golden ringlets, wearing a silk dress with a wide striped sash, holding her pet mockingbird. This portrait of Josephine was painted in New York's Central Park. Over my mother's sideboard hangs the portrait of Josephine's father, a whiskered mining magnate originally from Bristol, England, whose once considerable fortune was swindled by his business partner, family lore has it, when he took a ship back to the Mother Country.

The family were forced to leave New York City for Upstate to economise. But as it happened, pretty Josephine subsequently married a wealthy husband of her own. I could only imagine her relief—she had a taste for fine things—until disaster struck again. During World War I, her husband, like her father, lost *his* fortune. A divorce, scandalous for the day, was made worse as she was Catholic. She moved west to Chicago. There Josephine lived with her two daughters in an interesting household that included her unmarried sisters and a handsome divorced man called 'Uncle

Jim', who was a family friend and loved by all. I had a question or two about Uncle Jim, but there were no further details to be had.

The Depression struck. Hard times got harder. But Josephine's daughter Jean met a nice man working at the bank. Though some considered her an antique bride at the age of 31, Jean Sutherland escaped her mother, and married William Marple. Back East they went, aboard what was then dubbed 'The Most Famous Train in the World', the Twentieth Century Limited. This express train from Chicago to Grand Central Terminal in New York could make the trip in an astonishing sixteen hours. But that December day of 1935 was so bitterly cold that the switches kept freezing, and the engineers had to use blow torches to unlock them, to keep the mighty engine moving. Apparently, my grandmother's sister, who for an unrecorded reason accompanied the newly-weds, sobbed the entire way.

Jean and Bill loved New York and lived in Greenwich Village 'above a speakeasy', my grandmother told me, when I was later living in the city. My mother had been born there, before the expanding family moved to Connecticut. Although my ancestors on both sides seemed to have scattered in all directions, Chicago had been a temporary home for both the northern and southern branches of my American family tree.

My father's people had passed through the region when Chicago was little more than a small town on the banks of Lake Michigan, the terminus of their journey along the newly built Erie Canal, which began in Buffalo, New York. In a family with many a tale of lost riches, there was an amusing anecdote about these European ancestors, who apparently lost their fortune before it had ever been received.

My father is a professor. Turns out, teaching may be in the genes. My father's maternal ancestors included the last in a heredi-tary line of tutors to the children of the Duke of Saxony. On the promise of his future income from the royals, this ancestor lived very well indeed—and presumably racked up quite a few debts with various creditors—until the prince decided the tutor was too liberal, and hired someone else to teach his children.

The tutor and his wife fled to America—a common enough dodge in the day for scallywags of all sorts—where they wound their way across to Chicago and, later, down to Kentucky. His descendants ventured further south, from the bluegrass into the pine barrens of Alabama. In the US, Friedrich von Riedel's last name became 'Seed', and his descendants by that name were successful in politics, which also ran in the line. But the open question was whether his name had been changed because of a mistake on a customs form, or because he feared being returned to Saxony, in chains, as a debtor.

I found myself ruminating on boat people again. Boat people of the present, and those of long ago. Musing on the human drive to do whatever it takes to escape poverty, including setting sail to make a new life for your family, in a new land.

I have one early ancestor who did not travel to America aboard a ship. One of the great-great-great-great-grandmothers on my father's side was a Choctaw squaw. As a child, I often wished I'd inherited her dark skin, long straight hair and aquiline nose, instead of being fair with curly hair and freckles. And perhaps she would have traded her features for mine, for her people were herded to a reservation in Oklahoma by the US Army. But as is the case with the colouring in Andrew's family, which can be traced back to the Spanish Armada, there are still those in the family who are judged to have the Choctaw ancestor's glossy hair, her straight nose.

Diving into the wreck, into memories, into the past. I made a note to tell the girls about a glancing encounter with the most famous of French generals. It seemed Riedel was married to the daughter of the Mayor of Cologne. She told her American children about the day she scampered into her father's study, where he had been conducting business with a group of soldiers. A gentleman wearing the fanciest uniform asked her if she intended to marry a man in a red coat. Her answer is unrecorded, but the oral history tells us that the gentleman who posed that question was Napoleon.

Any family has its share of intriguing, unfinished stories. Bits and pieces, fragments from long ago. Dalliances with danger. Brushes with greatness. Tales of fame and fortune, desperation and despair. Some traits and professions seem to course through the centuries; I think of all the teachers in my family, the farmers in Andrew's.

But descendants can change, too, try new careers, new lands. So many factors can redirect the current, alter the trajectory of a life. To look into the past is to see a glittering clutch of stories; but, like a riverbed picked clean of gold, many never pan out. Branches of a family tree disappear abruptly, or end in a confusing tangle of loose threads, in part because there has been so much moving. There have been many towns, cities, states, even countries, and not everyone has been a diarist. There would have been many stories forgotten, as well as others consciously left unrecorded.

And now, as an American wife and mother in Oz, I was figuratively writing the next chapter, in a family history that would be continued by our girls. There was much to consider, and history suggests there was no way to guess. I blew on my tea, looked back out at the ghost gum. The idle moments spent avoiding a speech and remembering ancestors had been oddly comforting. It occurred to me that Andrew and I had settled well. Perhaps that was also part of our birthright. Many, in both of our family trees, had transplanted, and done so successfully. Perhaps Andrew and I had just followed in the family tradition. After more than four years in Australia, this was starting to feel like home. I had a huge advantage over those in the past. My family might be far away, but we were in constant touch, saw each other as frequently as I could manage. And here, I had Andrew's family and a growing number of friends.

Many of whom would be coming to this speech. I began to squirm. The speech I still had not written.

I opened the laptop. In telling the story of the *Titanic* that night, I would not only discuss those who had been famous but also include stories of passengers who were not well known. Passengers whose names might just as easily have been Archbold. Or von Riedel. Or Sutherland. Or Dill.

Time to write.

✳

'Do you think it will hurt?'

'Probably a little.'

'A little, or a lot?'

But Sophie didn't wait for the answer to that rhetorical question about her impending braces, because she had launched into another. 'Why are you stopping here?'

'Because I—'

'I thought you said we should not eat fast food. It's not good for you.'

'As a rule, it's not a good idea, but I didn't get a chance to have breakfast or lunch and I'm starving and if I don't have a coffee there's a strong chance I am going to hyperventilate.'

'Dad says you are a coffee addict.'

'That is ridiculous.'

'Then can I have chicken nuggets and fries?'

'Didn't you have lunch at school, before I picked you up?' I pulled into the drive-through, pressed the button to roll down the window, as a cheery female voice welcomed me and asked to take my order.

'May I have a skinny latte and a grilled chicken sandwich please?' I asked.

Sophie gave me a pleading look. 'And an order of chicken nuggets and a small fries?' I continued.

'Sundae?' Sophie whispered, pressing her advantage.

'You're going to the orthodontist!'

'Did you say you'd like a sundae?' the voice asked helpfully.

The slippery slope called parenting. 'No thanks, we're fine.'

I handed Sophie her snack, took a swig of coffee, which was quite delicious, and a bite of my chicken sandwich, which was not. They could have cooked it a bit longer.

'Lukk!' I said, channelling Jacqui.

Sophie grinned. These days we were always quoting her little sister, who had an increasing number of amusing expressions. Jacqui was doing so much better. She was both fun and funny, cracking jokes and showing lots of personality. Her brain did so much better on Risperdal, a medicine that revealed who she was. I looked at the clock on the dash. She would be finishing school soon, and our new babysitter Holly would be picking her up.

But the clock also told me we needed to hustle. I took another bite of the sandwich. I'd forgotten how unsatisfying fast food was. I should have just ordered the nuggets like Sophie, abandoned any pretence of healthy eating. But I was hungry and I wolfed down the sandwich.

Sophie's orthodontist appointment in Melbourne was at 3 p.m. I needed to be at the Macedon Views Restaurant for the *Titanic* speech at 6.30. The two locations were an hour and fifteen minutes apart, and in between I had to go home, shower, dress and get ready. I hadn't noticed how close these two appointments were on my calendar until it had been too late to reschedule. I would really need to hurry. But the speech was ready, my outfit laid out. Just relax, I reminded myself. This will be easy.

✳

I pulled into the car park of the Macedon Views Restaurant but remained in the car.

'Are you going to be okay?' Sophie said with a faint lisp, thanks to the new metal in her mouth. She looked very pretty in her long dress, if anxious.

'I am not sure.'

'But Mum, couldn't it be a virus?'

Unbidden, an old Monty Python sketch ran through my mind. 'Not the salmon mousse!'

'I think it was the chicken.'

'But can you do your speech?'

I slid out, wonky on my heels. I didn't say anything.

'But you have to!'

As we slowly walked towards the restaurant, we saw Nana and Pa, who'd come down from Muckleford, the pair of them looking fit and happy. Beside them stood my sister-in-law Kate and her husband Andrew. They'd driven all the way from their farm near Bells Swamp to be here for the speech, and I was surprised and touched.

Nana saw my face and suddenly looked stricken. 'Sara, what is wrong?'

'She ate a chicken sandwich at—' Sophie began.

'Bad chicken,' I interrupted. Surely we didn't have to confess the whole fast-food debacle.

'Not nerves, then?' asked Nana.

'No, I'm pretty sure it is food poisoning.'

Kate sighed, shook her head. And then she giggled. 'You are kidding, right?'

But I was already sprinting for the ladies' bathroom.

A couple of minutes later, Kate came in. I was still bent over, mildly amused that I'd had enough self-control to keep my blue silk suit clean.

'I brought towels,' said a sympathetic voice from outside the stall. 'And I found a bucket.'

'Oh, Kate,' I wailed, as I emerged. 'What am I going to do?'

'I don't know,' she answered. 'Do you think you're finished?'

The double entendre was troubling.

'I think I'm going to be sick again, if that is what you mean.'

'But how are you going to do this?' Kate asked. 'Everyone's

already starting to arrive! It looks like they're set up for more than 100 people out there.'

Sophie popped into the bathroom. 'I've called Dad. He says you were a duffer to eat that sandwich. He also says he'll be here from work in just a few minutes. Also, the Red Cross lady is worried about you.'

'Thanks, honey.' I leaned against the counter.

'What should I tell her?'

It occurred to me that Sophie was very grown up. Perhaps it was her long dress, or her long hair. Or maybe it was the fact that she was taking charge, and taking care of me. I smiled at my big girl. I figured I had ten good minutes before I was sick again. Ten minutes to figure out how to cancel a speech for which the audience had already assembled. Maybe Sophie could give it.

'Tell her I will come out to talk in a moment.'

I wiped my face, put on fresh lipstick with a shaky hand.

I walked out into the hallway, where Marion, who had organised the speech, was waiting. She looked nervous, as any person might be after spending months planning an event only to learn the guest might barf all over the audience.

'Any better?' she asked solicitously.

'I'm sorry, but not really.'

'Well, I have an idea,' she took my arm. 'This is the Red Cross, and that means we always have a doctor at the event.'

I marvelled. That was indeed good planning. I felt a faint stirring of hope.

She continued. 'We've sent him off to get some medicine for you. Oh, look, there he is now!'

'But where will she get the shot?' asked Katie.

'Not the bathroom!' I said. The very thought made me ill.

'I know,' said Kate, confidently. She propelled me by the elbow, opened a door off the entry foyer. 'This is the perfect place!' Her humour was the only thing helping at that point. In front of us was a tiny laundry cupboard with a vacuum cleaner, brooms, dust pans and shelves laden with folded napkins and tablecloths.

I could feel another spasm tightening across my stomach, and stepped inside with my sister-in-law and the doctor, who was carrying a bag. We closed the door behind us. The quarters weren't quite as small as the *Nautile* sub, but certainly qualified as intimate.

The pair of them began speaking, over and around me. 'She's got food poisoning.'

'Right, this shot will fix it.'

'Where do you give it?' I was briefly alarmed.

'I need her arm.'

'Sara, he needs your arm. I think you're going to have to unzip your top.'

The scoop-necked, cobalt-blue silk Carla Zampatti jacket was fitted, with a gold zipper up the front. I wasn't wearing a blouse underneath. Oh, better and better. I hoped no one opened the door, thinking this was the loo, or they would get far more than they bargained for. There was nervous laughter among the three of us as I peeled open the jacket, and the doctor quickly jabbed the needle into my upper arm. The combination of the next wave of nausea and the pain from the shot caused me to sit down, close my eyes and put my head on a tablecloth. Outside I heard the cheery hubbub as the crowd walked past, headed for their tables. This would never work.

'I think she's fainted,' I heard Katie say, concerned.

I lifted my head, wiped away the drool. 'I am fine.' I struggled to sit up, zip the jacket, as Kate helped me to my feet.

'How fast will the shot work?' Kate asked the doctor.

'Just a few minutes. You'll get through the speech.'

'Well, this is a first,' I said, trying to sound light-hearted. I had never felt sick before a live shot or speech, not once in my entire career. I fervently hoped I never would again.

I took a few deep breaths, and the three of us attempted a

casual departure from the broom closet. There were a few startled glances. I darted back to my hiding spot in the bathroom, so I didn't have to make small talk with arriving guests, and was dismayed to see that I looked pretty much exactly the way I felt.

Marion came in. 'Are you any better?' she asked, concerned.

'Much!' I lied. 'Good as gold.'

When she left I was close to tears. I'd worked hard on the speech, and had been so anxious to do a good job. Now, because of a bloody piece of raw chicken, I would be lucky to make it through without embarrassing myself.

'Buck up, you fast food–eating idiot,' I told myself as I headed for the podium.

I looked out at the crowd. It was larger than I'd imagined, about 150 people, with Andrew and Sophie in the front row. Andrew gave me the sort of encouraging smile the co-pilot gives the pilot when three of four engines have blown up 600 kilometres from land.

I was grateful to have a podium, something to hold on to so I didn't sway. My shoulder throbbed, and a wave of fatigue crashed over me. I felt an overwhelming urge to go to sleep, standing up, like a horse. The sensation was nearly as disconcerting as the nausea had been. The doctor sat in the front row, next to my family. He gave an encouraging nod. I nodded back.

I could not, I would not, I must not sink while giving a speech on the *Titanic*.

'Good evening,' I began, those two little words getting me two words closer to the end. I figured I had an 80 per cent chance of getting through this with my clothes still clean. Odds which had improved approximately 79 per cent since the shot.

Perhaps it's not surprising that I don't remember much about the speech. I was drugged, after all. I do remember that my mouth was constantly dry, and that I struggled to summon up the energy that gives any oration pace and punch. My high school coach Mona

Potter would have scolded me mercilessly, curls bobbing, for not extemporising, but I read that speech word for word, like a last will and testament. When I got to the point where the doco clip ran, it was a chance to sit down. I kept my eyes averted from vision of the heaving ship, and pinched each arm in turn, again and again, until I had an attractive tattoo of half-moon prints along my forearms, to keep from falling asleep. Only ten minutes to go.

I told the audience about a young musician named Jock Hume who had been a violinist on board, part of the illustrious band that continued to play, even as the ship sank. Today, such extraordinary courage would have turned Hume and his fellow band members into instant international heroes. No doubt Bono and the Boss, Beyonce and Lady Gaga would have sung at the telethon to raise money for their widows and orphans.

But not in 1912. In the book *And the Band Played On*, I learned that Hume's pay had been stopped the moment the ship sank—a devastating blow to his pregnant fiancée. To add insult to injury, a few weeks later, his father received a bill for the brass buttons and epaulettes on his son's band uniform.

There were many legacies of *Titanic*, and one was that the ship's sinking had set the stage for the destruction of a rigid class structure. I'd also been struck to find a link between that long ago tragedy, and one I remembered all too well. In a book about the aftermath of 9/11 entitled *Ghosts of Vesuvius*, author Charles Pellegrino had written:

I found a new hope today in the most unexpected of all places—in the cemetery at Halifax at the grave of a man named Jock Law Hume. The Jock Humes of this world were immediately apparent (on 9/11 at the World Trade Center) helping to keep the crowds calm and prevent panic . . . asking nothing for themselves. Hume—to me he came to represent all of them. They will come out again, if they are needed. And it's enough for me to know that they are near us, though we don't always see them there. They are hope. They are the future.

I had closed the speech this way:

And that is the final reason we remember Titanic. *Because while* Titanic *is a tragedy, it is also a deeply uplifting tale. It is a reminder of the power of honour, of courage, of character, in the most desperate circumstances. Qualities which make a young and struggling violinist every bit the equal of an American tycoon. The 'Big Piece' is but a tiny chunk of history. The enormity of valour and self-sacrifice are enduring, and why we remember* Titanic *one century later, and will remember* Titanic, *forever.*

I looked up from the paper. I fervently wished I could have done better. At least I was still standing. The faces in the crowd looked like they were underwater, but I could hear the sound of clapping. That meant it was really over. Thank the Lord.

Although faces blurred and merged into the shadows in a disturbing fashion, the bobbing sea included many I knew. My Australian family. The ladies from the Red Cross. Sandie. Emma and Bernard, and Kirsty and Alex. Jacqui and Keith were there, and new friends I was just getting to know, including Jane, several Fionas, and Valerie. And giving my arm a squeeze was Pete, with a troupe of gorgeous women from the mountain. I saw Prue and Fiona and Rhonda, whom we had met when they helped Jacqui during early intervention. Brigid, an old friend of Andrew's who had recently moved to the area with her family. Corrina, the teacher who had been our first nanny for the girls. Jenny from tennis, and her good friend, Gill, married to Zoomer, who'd helped me cut the video clip for tonight's event. Wheels within wheels, the circuits of a small town.

I felt sure there were others I knew, perhaps even had seen, if the crowd would only stop expanding and contracting like an image in a fun-house mirror. But one thing was clear. Four and a half years ago, with the exception of Andrew's family, I had known none of these people. Now they were friends. It was hard to remember that Andrew and I had done the equivalent of throwing a dart at the map—we'd chosen this region simply because it was halfway between Melbourne and the Butcher homestead. What a lucky throw.

I stepped away from the podium, and into Andrew's arms.

'Well done,' he whispered, propping me up.

'Was it okay?' I asked.

He hesitated a beat too long. 'I can't say that I really listened. I was too busy hoping you'd make it through.'

'Wow. That bad.'

'Don't worry, Boof. You got out alive. Now let's get you out of here.'

The following day, when I was vertical, it occurred to me that the evening had held overtones of another joyride, years before. Immediately after Gulf War I, I foolishly hopped aboard a US Air Force F-15E Strike Eagle with a fly boy. He showed off his laser-quick reflexes with an impressive series of loops and turns, during which my G-suit contracted and expanded mercilessly like a series of Heimlich manoeuvres to force blood out of my legs and stomach and into my brain so I didn't pass out. At last we landed, and I dizzily fell out of the jet. I refrained from kissing the ground only because there was an audience. The pilot grinned, and said, 'Thanks for leaving the jet clean.'

As a speaker, my performance had deserved a C–. But I hadn't capsized. And I'd made a clean getaway.

17

THE PUGGLE

'This is my favourite,' Bindi said, stroking the quills of the Aussie monotreme. 'The baby is called a puggle. Isn't he cute?'

'He sure is.'

'Would you like to try something fun?'

How could anyone possibly say 'no' to Bindi Irwin?

'Sure. I think.'

'Take your shoes off.'

I looked behind me. Chapman gave a shrug. Marcus kept rolling. I could see the corner of his mouth twitch upwards. This could be interesting. I complied, and Bindi scooped up a disgusting mash—squished insects, she informed me matter-of-factly—and carefully placed it on my bare toes, like glops of wet sand at the beach. The baby echidna immediately uncurled and waddled over for a visit, giving me an up close and personal encounter with one of the most unusual creatures in Australia. The echidna looked nothing like a platypus, but I knew that both species laid eggs, yet suckled their young. It still stunned me, after five years, what wacky and intriguing creatures lived in Oz.

'Ooooggh,' I said involuntarily, as a long, pink tongue uncoiled from the spiny anteater's thin, tapered snout. I watched in fascination as it slurped up the dead bugs, and couldn't help but smile. I should have known from prior experience that the unexpected and extraordinary were always on order when you hung out with the Irwins.

'Isn't it fun?' Bindi said, with a sweet look in her large brown eyes. I realised that exotic experiences with wild animals were just a part of daily life for her. She was keen to help me, as I was clearly a novice, and nodded encouragingly. 'It's kind of like an echidna foot massage!'

I looked up at Terri, who was standing with Robert nearby. The zoo held all manner of surprises.

'Ready to see the crocs?' Terri asked, since the puggle had finished lunch—on me. I was handed a baby wipe to clean off my feet.

'Yeah, let's go!' Robert nodded vigorously.

After having my toes licked by an echidna, what could possibly lie in store at the crocodile tank?

'Sounds good,' I said, getting up. 'I can't believe how your zoo has grown,' I continued, surveying the immaculate grounds. When I first visited the Australia Zoo many years before, it had looked more like the beloved but slightly ramshackle animal park which had been the ultimate impulse purchase in the movie *We Bought a Zoo*. 'It's hard to believe it's been fifteen years since we chased snakes and crocs in the Outback.'

Terri gave her open, friendly smile and pushed aside a curtain of long hair. She appeared not to have aged, save for a few fine lines which hinted at sorrow as well as sun. She remained the attractive, warm and enthusiastic woman I remembered, in spite of losing her larger than life partner—the love of her life, as she'd said many times—who was the father of her children. I liked Terri, and I also admired her, very much.

'I was just thinking about that trip,' she answered cheerfully. 'I remember how we went out looking for fierce snakes, and I teased Steve because he said we would find one by 7.30. And

I said, "It's 7.31, and we haven't seen one!" and, of course, one minute later he spotted one.'

'I remember,' I said.

I could still picture Steve, crouched low, moving towards the Inland Taipan, which possessed the deadliest venom in the world, with the practised assurance of the wildlife expert. I was on tiptoe, trailing a bit too far behind, attempting to lean backwards while walking forwards. When the snake predictably coiled and struck, I made a complete goose of myself by screaming.

'I'm still not real great with snakes,' I confessed.

'Have you seen many where you live now?' Terri asked with interest.

Like Steve, she could handle any reptile.

'Unfortunately, yes.'

Not only had there been that first memorable occasion just weeks after we'd moved in, but a subsequent far more terrifying event. Mystifyingly, a Red-bellied Black slithered its way up to our front door like a demented Avon lady and repeatedly beat its head against one of the glass panes. I am not making this up—a deadly snake knocked on our front door.

At the time, Andrew surmised that the snake had seen its reflection and was attacking the 'other' snake. But it turned out the snake also had been injured, which might have made it behave in such an uncharacteristic fashion. Andrew, who was at home with Jacqui at the time, scooped up our younger daughter and deposited her in the room farthest away from the snake with an entire box of Oreos. Jacqui didn't understand the dangers posed by snakes. He then sprinted back up the hall, morphing into one of the Avengers en route. Rather than recount that entire saga I summarised, 'I wish Steve had been there to capture them!'

Terri nodded, her expression wistful.

The truth was, I kept expecting to see Steve. To hear his voice, to see him come around the corner. More than six years after Steve Irwin's death, it still felt impossible. 'I am very sorry about Steve,' I said. 'I can't imagine. You must miss him so much.'

'Every. Single. Day.'

We walked for a while in silence. Then we talked more about Steve, about how she missed him, about raising children as a single parent. And then I found myself telling Terri about our girls, and about Jacqui's situation. It wasn't the same, of course. Terri's husband had died in an unpredictable accident involving the wildlife he loved. I'd had a child born with a significant disability. And yet there is a sort of Esperanto of grief, a shared vocabulary of loss and heartache. You are in the club, or outside it. Those in the club don't play silly games like compare and contrast, whose is better, whose is worse. They commiserate. They understand.

Terri and I followed Bindi and Robert towards the zoo's hospital, to visit a koala who was recuperating from being hit by a car. The koala, who had a broken back, was on the mend, and almost impossibly cute. He was sitting in a high chair to have his lunch. I wondered how many people who came to the zoo wanted to adopt an animal by the time they left.

Terri explained more about the hospital, and the zoo. 'Just before he died, Steve and I wrote up a plan for what we wanted to do here, at the zoo,' Terri told me. 'It's uncanny. It's almost as if he knew. He'd say "I don't think I'll have much time", and I'd cover my ears and say "La, la, la!" But it was good that we had that plan, because I keep it going. I keep his vision alive,' she continued.

'You're an incredibly positive person.'

'I have my days. I miss Steve like crazy, but the kids and all their projects keep me happy and busy,' she continued.

The family had just returned from being on location to shoot Bindi's latest movie, *Return to Nim's Island*.

Terri's kids are busier than most, and they are famous. But I found myself impressed by how relaxed and happy the children seemed and how natural all three of the Irwins were when they talked about Steve. Bindi is the kind of gorgeous, cheerful fourteen-year-old any mother would be proud of, in addition to being a natural on camera; Robert is energetic and happy, scampering up trees when he isn't darting after lizards. More importantly, both children are kind, well-mannered and good listeners, as well as skilled performers. It is obvious Terri is an excellent mum.

It is also evident that the Australia Zoo provides something of an extended family. The makeup artist who accompanied us had been with the Irwins for years. Terri's personal assistant, a professional young woman who had greeted us at the front gate, walkie-talkie in hand, golf carts ready for our gear, turned out to be none other than Hannah, a young girl I remembered well from fifteen years ago. She came with her parents, friends of Terri and Steve, on that long-ago camping trip in Far North Queensland. We'd pitched tents on the banks of a billabong infested with crocs, including a wily and notorious fellow nicknamed Old Faithful. It seemed inevitable and right that Hannah would grow up to work at the zoo.

Those relationships, that stability, clearly serve the Irwin family well. The trio are united in their passion for wildlife, lighting up when they talk about the 135,000-hectare Irwin reserve in Far North Queensland, the conservation work as Wildlife Warriors and the zoo.

'Got one!' Robert squealed, interrupting our conversation.

He darted over, his smile like a sunbeam beneath a nose dusted with freckles, and held out a lizard for us to inspect. 'He's like a mini-me of Steve,' Terri confided, shaking her head, with a rueful smile.

'Cool lizard,' I responded, although I declined his offer to hold it.

We had arrived at the crocodile enclosure.

NBC producer Chapman Bell, photographer Marcus O'Brien and I had come to Australia Zoo on the heels of our two-week assignment for the *Today Show* and *NBC Nightly News*, following the most famous newlyweds in the world. 'Will and Kate' had tied the knot some months before, and the Prince and his bride had officially become the Duke and Duchess of Cambridge. This tour of the South Pacific was part of the Queen's Diamond Jubilee, but also marked Catherine's first major overseas assignment, and her first public speech, at a hospice in Kuala Lumpur.

It had been hectic but entertaining to be part of the press corps as the couple threaded through Singapore, Malaysia and the Solomon Islands. The carefully choreographed trip had begun brilliantly; the Duchess, ever elegant in her signature combination of couture and High Street, hadn't put an L.K. Bennett-clad foot wrong. And when paparazzi photos briefly stole the spotlight, the couple responded with grace and dignity.

But while Catherine might be a young and modern royal, the world seemed desperate for her to step into the most traditional role of all. The 'is she or isn't she?' gossip was all-consuming. Senior royal watchers analysed the significance of the Duchess drinking water rather than wine at a state dinner; then, huddled over snaps taken on their own mobile phones, discussed whether perhaps the Duchess's cheeks were a trifle plumper? Might it be possible to detect the tiniest bump? The Duchess was clearly sick to death of the rumours, the speculation, the endless hopeful headlines, and was as stick thin as she was gracious when we had had the opportunity to meet her in person. But surely, it couldn't be long. The entire world seemed to wait, expectantly.

And now we were back in Queensland, to check in on an eight-year-old boy who had been making international headlines since he was a baby—back when his dad tucked little Robert into the crook of his arm while feeding a croc. There had been a great deal of tsk-tsking over Steve's decision, which had made big news on the *Today Show* in the States, prompting this follow-up. But as I watched the young son of the Crocodile Hunter, flanked by several adult wranglers, stride confidently into the enclosure, it was easy to see the future. Like the House of Windsor, this was a family business. This was Robert's birthright, in the same way that Will and Kate's baby would be raised to inherit a throne.

As we headed to the gate to say goodbye, Terri and I exchanged numbers, and a hug.

'Let's not wait fifteen years next time, okay?' she said.

'That is a promise.'

✳

Annemarie Rolls, publisher at ACER, leaned over to squeeze my hand. I squeezed hers back. It was hard to believe we were finally here, at the launch for *An Extraordinary School*, listening to the Minister of Education for Victoria, Martin Dixon, give the keynote address. The project I imagined would take a few months had taken a few years, but it had been worth it.

Even before publication, I'd been invited to speak about the school's revolutionary approach in my former hometown, at the national convention of the National Arts Education Association. It had felt like six degrees of separation to stand in front of a thousand people in the ballroom of the Hilton Hotel in midtown Manhattan, around the corner from NBC, to talk about our daughter's school in Melbourne. It had been in that very ballroom, on a wintry night in 1994, that I had met the dark-haired wit who would become Sophie and Jacqui's father.

After a year and a half at the special school near our home, we'd re-enrolled Jacqui at Port Phillip. Our daughter was older, and handled the drive better. And with her complex needs, the size and diversity of the staff, as well as the school's teaching approach, made it the right place for her. As I looked out into the audience, at the unabashedly partisan crowd of families, teachers, disability advocates and political leaders, I hoped one day all children with disabilities would have similar opportunities.

Bella Irlicht, whom I'd met on Jacqui's very first day, and whose vision and leadership had created the school, had retired as principal some years before. Bella rose to thank those who had helped her, and the school, a list which included the Pratt Foundation.

I looked at the little book in my lap. It seemed very small. But perhaps, just perhaps, it might serve as a blueprint for some other schools, in Australia and overseas; if it could help other kids like our Jacqui, every minute had been worth it. I knew what a school like Port Phillip could mean for an entire family, which was why my favourite speech of the night was delivered by an eleven-year-old girl who was the sibling of a child with a disability:

I didn't even know there was anything wrong with my sister until I got older. At school I often felt embarrassed seeing her kissing strangers while waiting for me to come out of my classroom—and especially so at one particularly interesting assembly where she bit the principal. Yet I have always loved her, and that is one of the things I like best about Port Phillip—they are forever nurturing our love as a family.

I know that there are many other people in our situation, but sometimes the knowledge my sister will never get better knocks me over, takes me by surprise. But then there are moments of joy—like in the last Port Phillip School Production, where Jacqui stole the show with her glittery costume—it's moments like that when I swear I couldn't live without her or my family. Thank you, Port Phillip—without you, without Jacqui's bright smiles, without seeing her talk excitedly about her classes and friends—yes, without you I think my life would be much harder.

Soph hates it when I cry; she won't even cut me a break for tears of joy. I nodded emphatically when she sat down. Her smile was beautiful.

❋

When we arrived in Australia, we'd been too consumed by Jacqui's condition and our international move to think about much beyond ourselves and our two little girls. But we had lived in the country for more than five years.

Our family was stronger now than we had been then. The

girls remained the centre of our family constellation, but there was greater balance and harmony. We were now supported not only by Andrew's family but also by an intricate network of friends, which had expanded and become increasingly interconnected. When we got together for dinner at someone's home, or on the deck of the Mount Macedon Hotel, Sophie never knew if we were getting together to see her friends, or ours.

Andrew enjoyed being his own boss, and business was booming. But if my husband had a work obsession, it was making sure he kept the hours civilised, in order to have plenty of time for the girls. I loved watching Andrew and Sophie, heads bent over a calculator, working on her maths homework. Or out feeding the chooks and putting fresh straw in their cages, or perfecting her treehouse.

Andrew had bid farewell to his days as a fast bowler, but enjoyed an occasional game of Super Rules footy with his mates. He relaxed most evenings reading car magazines, the better to regale us with vehicle trivia. Because you really never knew when someone was going to give you a pop quiz, and you would ace it because you knew that the gold bulldog on a Mack truck indicated the entire truck was built of genuine Mack parts, including its Maxidyne engine.

I had cobbled together what one friend called 'a portfolio career'. It was an elegant way of saying I juggled, like many mums I knew. We had solved the geographical complications of having our children in two schools, an hour apart, by hiring a full-time nanny called Holly, whom Jacqui adored. The result was that I was once again able to do work I loved: writing, speaking and reporting, especially for NBC. As a Yank, I was pleased the network now had a de facto Australia bureau. Sure, the Brits might have one of their own, but it certainly didn't come with a commanding view of the Wombat State Forest.

Sophie had graduated from primary school, and attended a secondary school she adored. She had been elected class captain, and tried out for virtually every school activity. It was hard to believe the long-haired pre-teen with braces, who was nearly as tall as me, was the gumnut-collecting six-year-old I remembered, though I caught glimpses of that younger Soph when she chased Nanci Drew around the back garden. Our elder daughter was busy lobbying for more animals. Her menagerie didn't need to be quite as large as Australia Zoo, it seemed, but she was desperate to own a horse.

Jacqui was thriving too. The child who hadn't been able to talk, to walk, to sing, could now crack a joke.

'What's a baby mug called?' she'd quiz us, pottering about the kitchen, an espresso cup perilously dangling from her pinky. 'A muggling!!' she would answer her own question, then giggle uproariously. Getting a laugh, by fair means or foul, was one of her favourite pastimes.

I continued to investigate ideas and strategies that might help our daughter. She could not yet read a book or write her name or tie her shoes. But I played the long game. I was no longer troubled that she skipped thirteen when she counted to twenty, or that she sometimes fell apart. Well, so did I.

And the list of what she *could* do grew longer every day, including the recent development of latching onto the first letter in words.

'T! T is for tiger! And tummy! And *toilet*!' More paroxysms of laughter.

We appreciated things other families might take for granted, like the fact that we could now hang out with Jacqui watching TV. That we could snuggle and read a book. Do yoga, even if it might be speed yoga. I sent photos to Elizabeth and Susan. And Jacqui's sumo-wrestler squeezes—'Best mummy/daddy/Sophie in the whole wide world!'—had been worth the wait.

I wasn't worrying as much, and Andrew was lighter, more relaxed. I was able to let go when Jacqui couldn't master a skill, or when she derailed and had a tantrum. I'd never stop looking for tools to help her learn—I was the daughter of educators, after all—but I no longer expected miracles.

It was uncomfortable to recognise that I might have been something of a drill sergeant, with an unspoken motto straight out of a US Army recruitment poster: 'Be All That You Can Be!' Uncomfortable, because it had taken me too long to realise that our younger daughter was being just that. I had been on a quixotic quest to defeat disability. It hadn't worked. In being determined to make sure I tried every relevant therapy, and every possible strategy, I hadn't always been able to realise how much our daughter *had* accomplished. She would continue to progress, at her own pace, in her own way.

I had also given up on trying to discover whatever it was that had caused her disability. It simply didn't matter. She was our wonderful little girl, and we loved her. I could let go of trying to find a diagnosis. I could let a lot of things go. Both of us were happiest when I reminded myself to sit back, relax and enjoy the flight.

But while I might be more sanguine about Jacqui, Andrew and I believed there was plenty of room for improvement when it came to how the world dealt with those who had disabilities, and when it came to helping siblings. I had opportunities through writing and speaking; Andrew followed a different trajectory, serving on the board for the 2014 Special Olympics National Games.

One day, a mate emailed Andrew about a frightening experience. A young boy standing next to him on a street corner had suddenly stepped off the curb and into the path of a taxi. Reflexively, the mate pulled the boy to safety. It turned out the child had autism. He'd wandered away from his parents, who had only lost sight of him for a moment. It was a situation Andrew and I had no trouble imagining. I could still picture Jacqui at the picnic table, with strangers, in the Castlemaine Gardens.

The friend was David Penberthy, the former editor-in-chief of the Sydney *Telegraph,* who was editor-in-chief of a News Limited news site, and of an opinion website, *The Punch.* Andrew replied to David at length. David wound up writing a column entitled *Don't Mess with the NDIS*, regarding support for the National Disability Insurance Scheme, and quoted from the email Andrew had written him:

What you experienced, as shocking as it is—and it is shocking—was just another day for those parents, and the parents of tens of thousands of other kids with autism or any intellectual disability in Australia. A mother's tears that you witnessed are so often a daily release valve to get through the stress of just another normal day, where packing a car can become a life-threatening experience for a child. The whole family is under constant pressure, with the siblings often the forgotten victims of the stress . . . I can guarantee that when the parents of that little boy get into bed each night, the last thing they talk about is how he went at school today, what the speech therapist said, how he seemed a bit aggressive or sleepy. They'll wonder if the medicine doses are right, they'll talk about the babysitter coming to look after him for a few hours this weekend so they can take his big sister off to netball together, they'll plan what has to happen tomorrow with the visit to his psychiatrist, and they'll fall asleep exhausted thinking about him . . . And always, lurking in the back of their minds not far from their thoughts, is the fear of what happens when they're gone.

The response to that column had been tremendous. It occurred to me that Andrew and I were accidental advocates. We hadn't set out to find a cause. A cause had found us.

✳

I was at home cooking dinner, scraping carrot and potato peelings into the chook bucket when the phone rang.

'Good evening, Sara. It's Ingrid,' Dr Scheffer said, in her pleasant way. 'I'm calling because I'm doing some research. I don't want to get your hopes up, but I wanted to let you know that it may be possible to discover what is wrong with Jacqueline.'

I sat down. The call was utterly unexpected.

'What exactly do you mean?'

'We are working in cooperation with scientists in Belgium and in Seattle, Washington, and have identified a gene which causes seizures in some children. It may tell us what is causing Jacqueline's seizures.'

I looked idly at my hand, still clutching the peeler.

'But we've had so many tests. Have we missed something?'

'No. This is new research. Cutting edge.'

I felt myself click over a track, to the familiar and more comfortable line of being a reporter.

'Can you tell me what you think it is?'

I could almost hear her smile, through the phone line. 'I would rather not say. I could be wrong.' Then she continued matter-of-factly, 'But there is a good chance I'm correct. Now, we already have a sample of Jacqui's blood, which has been analysed. The only way to know for certain is to take blood samples from you and Andrew. Are you both willing to do that?'

We had lived with not knowing for years. Was it wise to learn now? What if the answer were troubling, or something scary? I thought of Pandora and her box.

But I've never met a reporter who blamed Pandora. She was the Mother of all Wikileaks. And I've always wanted answers, if there were answers to be had.

'I'll speak to Andrew to be sure, but I'm confident he will be willing, and I am. But I do have a couple of questions first.'

'I'll certainly answer if I can.'

'If Jacqui turns out to have this, whatever it is, could Sophie's children inherit it?'

She paused. 'I think that is highly unlikely. But the blood work will tell us for certain.'

But even as I exhaled one fear, I braced for the next answer.

'One more thing. Is there a chance that what you are looking at is something degenerative? Will Jacqui get worse, or, God forbid . . . Anyway, before we test, I just need to be prepared.'

I squeezed the phone very tightly.

'That I can answer. If she has this, she will be exactly the same girl that you know and love.'

I rang off, mind racing. Dr Scheffer was an international expert in the genetics of epilepsy. And she was the woman who might have the answer to a question we'd wondered about for more than eight years.

✳

As everyone knows, if you are seeking a heart, or a home, or some courage, or a brain, you had best find the Wizard of Oz.

Or perhaps she will find you.

'I have an answer for you,' there was a note of elation in Dr Scheffer's voice. 'We have a match.'

This was like genetic bingo, I thought.

'Yes?'

'Jacqui has something called KCNQ2,' she said.

I asked her to repeat it and wrote it down.

'What does it mean, exactly?' I was calmer than I had imagined.

'It means that her kind of epilepsy is genetic. It is a change in the DNA code of one gene. It is a form of epilepsy that presents in newborns. And all of the problems that Jacqui has—her seizures, the intellectual disability, the behaviour problems—stem from this one genetic mutation. It is not inherited, by the way. It's *de novo*. Neither you nor Andrew have it.'

'Then why does Jacqui . . .?'

'Bad luck. This is simply a case of bad luck.'

I nodded, thinking of all the children I knew, with all kinds of syndromes and conditions, where a random split, a tiny deletion, an extra chromosome, had major consequences, sometimes catastrophic.

Bad luck. That was something I could live with, and I knew Andrew could too.

But Dr Scheffer hadn't finished. 'There is something else I must tell you,' she continued brightly. 'Jacqui will be in my paper.'

I laughed, but even as I did so, I thought about what a wizard she must be, to leave me cheerful and chuckling, actually happy, after telling me that Jacqui had a genetic defect. But we already had accepted Jacqui's disability, had known something was wrong. Now that something had a name. 'And why is that?'

'Because she is doing well, all things considered. You see, many children with KCNQ2 can't walk or talk. They can't even sit up. And they have a very severe intellectual disability. Jacqui is making progress.'

The sweet with the bitter. And a healthy dose of perspective.

The next night, Andrew and I went out to dinner, talked it through, both of us clearly feeling good, to judge from our big appetites.

'I like having an answer,' Andrew said, munching on a piece of roti bread, 'because it tells us what it wasn't, as well as what it is. I'm glad it wasn't anything that went wrong at the hospital. And we also know she's not going to grow out of it, because that's not how genetics works. She's still our Jac,' he smiled.

'That she is! I just hope they'll change the name to Scheffer's syndrome, or something easy to remember,' I said, 'because I am never going to be able to remember the letters and numbers.'

Andrew snorted. 'It's easy! Just use a mnemonic. Look, think KC, like KC and the Sunshine Band. And NQ, for North Queensland. And 2? Just because. KCNQ2.'

We were both laughing. Our daughter had had every test under the sun. Until a wizard in Oz had come up with one more, and given us an answer.

I thought about wizards, especially the one from that famous old book, and the movie. The truth was, you never got everything you wanted. Dorothy had killed the Wicked Witch of the

West, and then the wizard took off in the balloon without her. Okay, he hadn't meant to, but the result had been the same.

But Dorothy found a way home, with a click and a sparkle of red. All by herself.

This diagnosis wouldn't take us all the way home, either. It was an answer, but not a solution. Knowing what Jacqui had wouldn't cure our daughter, or even make her better.

So why did we care? In part, because like the Scarecrow being awarded his diploma, the Lion his medal, and the Tin Man his heart, names and symbols are important. And so is what you believe. And there was also science to consider. As more children are diagnosed with KCNQ2, the pool will grow broader and deeper. We might meet other families, with children like Jacqui. We would gain more insights into this condition, into the best drugs to treat our daughter's seizures. They might help us, and we might help them. And perhaps, down a winding yellow road, our children might get better. Perhaps, one day, there might even be a cure.

Regardless, we could get ourselves the rest of the way home.

18

CHOOKS

Sophie and I sat side by side as the Acela train thundered up the northeast corridor from Union Station in Washington, DC, towards New York's Penn Station. We were midway through a whirlwind post-Thanksgiving trip in the States, which would include visits to see family and friends in LA, as well as Virginia, Washington, DC, and New York. Sophie was exhausted. I had bought her a hot chocolate and a bagel, but it wasn't enough to make up for seeing so many people we loved, only to leave them so soon. I knew the feeling.

'We still have New York, Soph,' I reminded her.

'Mum, I miss everyone here. I've known my friends Mary Ben and Phoebe since I was six months old! I don't want to leave.'

I hugged her. 'Leaving is hard. You'll feel better when we get home.'

I paused for a moment, pondering that word, 'home'.

Sophie shook her head, fiercely, a dog shaking off water. 'You don't understand, Mum, this affects me a lot more than it affects you.'

I shook my own head back at her. 'Soph, there are a lot of things you can say to me. That's just not one of them.'

I thought for a moment, tried again. 'Honey, no one is making you choose. Our family is both Australian and American. Two pretty amazing places. Believe me, I wish our trip was longer. And it would be very convenient if everyone lived in one country, I grant you. But Aunty Bethy is coming over next year. And Granne and Opa. And Aunty Susan and Uncle Danny and the cousins, for their very first visit!

'We have a wonderful life, Sophie. Remember, back when you were three, you always told me you couldn't live in New York, because you needed to stretch your long legs? Think of all the legroom you have in Oz.'

But neither logic nor humour worked. I watched the emotions that roiled inside of me spill down my daughter's cheeks. To be an American in Oz meant that sometimes, you missed where you were from, desperately. Missed seeing people so frequently, you never saw them change.

But I had meant what I said. We had a fortunate life.

'Think of it this way, Sophie,' I said. 'We are very lucky to have a lot of people we love, all over the world, who love us back.'

I shook my head. I was sounding more and more like Pollyanna. The truth is, nobody actually likes Pollyanna.

And then I had a flash of inspiration. 'Hey, Sophie, I have an email from Dad I think you should read. It just might make you feel better.'

Sophie perked up, wiped her eyes with an elbow, and commandeered my phone. Andrew emailed daily updates from home. The day before, I'd received word that an elderly, ailing kangaroo had wandered into the front yard and promptly expired. This was a first. So was what happened next. In order to get rid of the carcass, my practical, farm-raised husband had taken matters into his own hands, so to speak. The details were relayed in the most recent missive, in his succinct, matter-of-fact style:

All good and uneventful down here. Took Jacqui for a motorbike ride and she settled down. Ate an enormous Nana dinner of steak and veg.

I cut the legs and tail off the dead roo for Nanci. She found a foot I had discarded and decided that was better to chew on instead. She's buried the leg I gave her somewhere. I've put another leg and the tail in the granny-flat fridge.

I'm heading to bed. Love you both.

My farming-in-her-DNA daughter immediately brightened, her smile like shafts of sunlight through rain. I thought of Melbourne and its famed four seasons in one day.

'Mum, you're right! That makes me feel much better! Funny old Nanci eating that leg. She sure loves a good kangaroo bone. But I wonder what happened to that kangaroo? What made it get sick? I can't wait to show Dad's email to my friends!'

'Sophie, I'm not sure that kangaroo bone story is going to translate well in New York,' I cautioned. We Americans idolise kangaroos, and tend not to think of them as dog chow. I wasn't sure it would make any difference to know that this particular kangaroo had died of natural causes, and that Australian retrievers fetch old marsupial bones, the way their American counterparts might drag home the remnants of a deer or a rabbit. Some things about life in the bush needed a little context.

'Don't worry, Mum,' Sophie said, nodding conspiratorially, 'I get it.'

We got off the train in a cheery mood, chattering about the cold air, the honking taxis, the glorious, neon cacophony that was New York. We would always adore it, both of us. It would always feel like home. And so would a ridge in the Macedon Ranges. In the same way that a parent can love more than one child, a person can love more than one country.

✳

'I always forget how beautiful the view is,' I said, panting.

'It is dazzling,' Kirsty agreed. Kirsty, Pete and I had climbed through Kirsty's chestnut grove and up a steep and thickly wooded slope to stand at the summit of Camel's Hump, on Mount Macedon. We took time to catch our breath and survey the pastoral scene spread below us. At its centre rose Hanging Rock, the mysterious volcanic eruption where I'd had many a picnic in recent years, and never without a moment devoted to discussing the vanishing of Miranda. Peter Weir had turned an Australian literary classic about disappearing schoolgirls into a hauntingly beautiful arthouse film, which I'd seen years before I ever met Andrew. Shrouded in mist, the rock could appear eerie. There were even stories of visitors who had stolen small chunks as souvenirs, only to send them back by post, with tales of bizarre misfortunes linked to their theft.

Major Mitchell gave Hanging Rock the name by which we knew it, but I had read that its indigenous name was uncertain. Various clans had links to the area, including the Woi Wurrung, the Djadja Wurrung and the Ediboligitoorong. It is interesting to note that Aboriginal experts agreed this site would have been as important to the indigenous people of Victoria as world-famous Uluru is to those in the Northern Territory. The Rock is an elemental place, with an aura of magic and power, and, on this day, a gobsmackingly glorious sight.

'Aren't we lucky to live here,' Pete said with an appreciative sigh, and we all agreed.

As we traipsed further up along the ridgeline, I thought of those first Australians, who had lived here for thousands of years. And of what we knew about the first encounters between Aborigines and Europeans from the journals of Marine Lieutenant Watkin Tench, who arrived with the First Fleet in 1788, in Botany Bay. I wondered if the indigenous communities here in Victoria had used the cry he had been taught, the one that carried across forest and mountain, the cry we had taught our daughters—'cooee'.

My thoughts turned to the early Europeans who had made Victoria their home. There was the famous Australian triptych, *The Pioneer*, which I'd pondered during visits to the Ian Potter

Centre at the National Gallery of Victoria, a short walk from Andrew's office. Artist Frederick McCubbin was born in West Melbourne, in 1855, during that tidal wave of goldrush immigration that also brought Andrew's ancestors to Victorian shores. Along with Tom Roberts, Arthur Streeton and Charles Conder, McCubbin created the Heidelberg School, an impressionistic style of painting of distinctly Australian themes. McCubbin painted this masterpiece shortly after Federation in 1901, in clear homage to the country's birth as a modern nation.

While Hanging Rock is ancient, and *The Pioneer* modern by comparison, both are beautiful, mysterious and open to interpretation. The woman in McCubbin's first panel looks downcast; perhaps missing her homeland, or uncertain about life in such rustic surroundings. In the middle panel, she holds a baby on her hip, and is in conversation with her husband. It makes me smile to think of what they might be talking about. The third panel is the most ambiguous. A new city shimmers on the horizon, like the first glimpse of the Emerald City in Oz. But who is the young man? At whose grave does he kneel? The questions add to the painting's allure.

But there is another feature to this series that moves me. McCubbin went to great trouble to paint this masterwork outside, in the bush. He organised trenches to be dug along a forested slope, into which he carefully lowered the enormous canvases. And he actually painted *The Pioneer* right here, on Mount Macedon. In fact, not far from where we stood.

It delighted me that Frederick McCubbin had lived on Mount Macedon, in a home he called Fontainebleau. The beauty of Mount Macedon acted like a magnet, for all of us. But it was scenery we knew so well, we sometimes almost didn't see it, until we reminded ourselves to take walks like this. The vaulting eucalypts in *The Pioneer* could be the very ones in front of us.

I remembered how charmed I had been by my first sight of this mountain. But it no longer reminded me quite as much of

Virginia or Upstate New York. This wasn't North America, any more than it was England. Those of us from overseas might call our homes by European names. We might plant rhododendrons or dogwoods or azaleas, and I appreciated their colourful addition. But they would not change the fundamental character of this place. This could only be Australia.

As giddy infatuation fades when the faults of another are discovered, only to deepen and strengthen as the soundness of the core is recognised, I had come to love this mountain, with all its moods and caprices. I had overcome the paralysing fear I'd felt in the aftermath of Black Saturday. Andrew had been right that this was a land of seasons and cycles. The risk of fire was the price to be paid for living anywhere in the vast enchantment that was the Australian bush. It would be the same in America.

This was a good place to settle, to call home.

*

I was back from Western Australia and had nearly finished my script. Sophie was in the office with me, sitting at the old zinc-topped table that we'd turned into her desk.

'Mum, I write lots of stories, but I can never come up with an ending,' Sophie said, frowning.

'What do you mean?'

'It's easy to start a story. I've started lots of them! But then I just don't know how to finish them. Where to stop.'

'It's tricky,' I commiserated. 'There's got to be an arc, things that happen. Maybe there's some kind of quest, or dramatic events. Interesting characters along the way. But the protagonist needs to change, or learn something. Maybe discover something, or resolve something. Has that happened for your characters yet?'

Sophie looked at her computer.

'Not yet. I'm kind of stuck.'

'Don't worry.' I sat back in my chair. 'I had an old friend named Ann, back in Virginia. She was 70 when I met her. Ann had been one of the first flight attendants, and then she was a mum, and later she became a photographer, and then ran a museum. She did all kinds of things. Ann was also a great cook. She's the person who taught me how to make oysters Rockefeller and paella, in her beautiful kitchen, when there were otters playing in the stream just outside.'

Sophie loved any story and was intrigued. But her expression indicated she was well aware I'd wandered off on a digression. It was time to scamper back to the path.

'Soph, Ann was the first person who told me that life happens in chapters. That you can do lots of things, but it's best to take them one at a time, not try to do everything at once. Well, this is our Australian chapter. And like we were talking about on the train to New York, it's a very different life from the one we had in the US. That's a lot of material to work with. Maybe you can write about a girl who has moved from the US to Australia.'

Sophie was nodding. 'She's going to be ten. Or twelve. Maybe she gets caught in a fire! Her parents die! She's all alone! I think she has a dog. And a horse. Definitely a horse.'

'The parents in your books are always dying, you know. Just saying.'

Sophie nodded. 'Don't get hurt feelings, Mum. It makes for a better story.'

'I understand. I killed off plenty of mums and dads too, back when I was your age and writing stories. Now I tend to appreciate them more.'

Sophie chewed on her pencil, looking thoughtfully out the window. The sky had darkened. The days were growing short.

I printed off my script, read it through.

It concerned a deeply moving saga, and one which had ties, coincidentally, to Upstate New York. The tale began with a mysterious box, left to languish in a corner of a museum. But not so long ago, someone at Colgate University had stumbled across that forgotten box, and opened it, to discover a bequest from a graduate who had been a wealthy art collector. A stunning collection of landscapes of Australia.

But as curators looked into the gift more carefully, an even more astonishing fact emerged. It turned out these accomplished artists had been children. Aboriginal children, who had been forcibly removed from their families, to be raised in an institution. Their story was but one sad example of a terrible policy under which the government had attempted to extinguish Aboriginal culture—indeed wipe out the Aborigines as a distinct race—and create an all-white Australia. These indigenous child artists were part of the Stolen Generation. Colgate University decided that all of the artwork should be returned to Australia, and was donating the entire collection to Curtin University in Western Australia.

As far back as 1997, I had filed reports on the Stolen Generation, and was instantly interested. I'd flown to Perth to meet a dynamic pair, Colgate University Provost and Dean of Faculty Doug Hicks, and Professor Ellen Kraly, who was hand-carrying the first of the 119 paintings in the collection. With Ellen and Doug in the lead, we drove out of Perth, through a landscape studded with grasstrees, healthy specimens which reminded me guiltily of the spunky tree we'd inadvertently killed in our first year of living in Australia.

The Noongar children had been taken to what was then called the Carrolup River Native Settlement. As we walked around the desolate, abandoned camp, relic not only of a time, but of a way of thinking, Noongar Elder and community leader Ezzard Flowers acted as our tour guide. He told us about those who had attended the school here, and how one teacher had taught them to paint. Between 1945 and 1951, the youngsters had painted these loving tributes to a land they knew so well—sometimes working by candlelight. They had dreams; hopes of a bright future. But just as their artwork began to gain international acclaim, the institution was closed, the children dispersed. By and large, their lives had not been happy or easy ones. Returning the paintings had been the right thing to do.

As we left the camp, I fell into conversation with Simon Forrest, the head of the Aboriginal Studies Centre at Curtin University. Simon had grown up in WA and was a natural teacher. He regaled us with stories of indigenous peoples and Australian animals, stories of lives lived on the land and of the traditions of his people. I was fascinated by his story of hunting for emu eggs, how the emu was crafty enough to make his tracks disappear.

I thought back to the first emu I had seen in Australia, just a few weeks after we'd moved. The enormous bird had raced our car down the dirt road, as Jacqui screamed a new word. That emu had been my accidental introduction to our Macedonian neighbour, Penny. It all seemed a long time ago. Now Penny was 'retiring'—by which she meant she would simply run an international farm-stay program. Penny told me she'd sold her remaining emus. With a smile she informed me they had gone to a very posh new home called Burnham Beeches. The 1930s mansion in the Dandenongs, east of Melbourne, had been bought by chef and restaurateur Shannon Bennett, of Vue de Monde fame, and developer Adam Garrison. The emus would provide eggs for the property, which was being turned into a luxury boutique hotel.

Back when I met Penny, I hadn't been able to tell a kangaroo from a wallaby. Back then, I couldn't pick an Aussie accent from a Kiwi one. And back then, I had regarded the emu as a large, ungainly and uninteresting creature, little more than Australia's answer to the ostrich. But the more I learned about old man emu, the more he fascinated me.

'How does the emu do that? Surely he can't erase his tracks. And he can't fly,' I asked Forrest.

Simon shrugged his shoulders. 'Maybe he does know how to fly, after all, and just doesn't let us see him. Or perhaps he can jump,' he answered. 'But however he does it, when you are tracking an emu, and the tracks disappear, *that* is when you know to look for the nest. And we know when it is the right season to find eggs, by looking up.'

'What do you mean?' I asked, perplexed.

'We've shown astronomers, and they can scarcely credit it,' Simon told Doug and Ellen and me. 'But when we look into the night sky, we don't look for constellations. It's not the shape made by stars we seek, but the patterns formed by their *absence*. The emu in the sky can be found in the space *between* the stars. And when we see it, that is when we go hunting for eggs.'

I had been in Australia for more than five years, and I was only just beginning to learn its many mysteries. There was so much more to learn, to see, to do.

It would be several months later, in September of 2013, that Andrew and I attended another museum, closer to home. Andrew's appointment to the board of Museum Victoria gave us the opportunity to be on hand for the opening of the First Peoples exhibition at Melbourne Museum. There, in the heart of the city, the city only imagined in McCubbin's *The Pioneer,* was a tribute to the country's indigenous culture.

The museum had collaborated with the First Peoples Yulendj Group of Elders and community representatives. They had shared their knowledge and stories; their beautiful artefacts, both ancient and purpose-made for the exhibition; and, most of all, their passion. As Andrew and I walked through the exhibits, it was abundantly clear that the program of assimilation that resulted in the Stolen Generation had failed, utterly and absolutely. As singer Archie Roach told the crowd, the Aborigines were part of Australia's history, but also very much a part of its present. This was a varied and vibrant culture; a key to Australia's past, a vital part of its future.

But on that early evening, in my office with Sophie, I was musing about children, and art, and emus. I was mulling over an impromptu lesson. And I was wondering how we might have fared, had our lives depended on understanding this land.

'Hey, Soph,' I asked. 'Have you collected the chicken eggs?'

She looked up with a start. 'I'll do it now. By the way Mum, when can I go see Penny's peacock babies? Did you know someone gave her another peacock, to replace the one that disappeared? Anyway, she has a pair, and they've had eggs, and they just hatched! When can we go see them?'

'Soon, Soph. We'll go soon.'

'And my horse?'

I put up a hand. 'Stop! We'll talk about a horse later. Right now, chooks. And I've got to go track this script, or you'll need to make my excuses to New York. I don't like your chances.'

As Sophie pulled on her boots, Jacqui burst through the door, fresh from swimming, holding her arms over her head. 'Put your paws up!' Jacqui shouted.

'Jac's back!' Sophie reported with a smile, and was off. She knew what came next. We all did.

But Holly and I stayed, to give Jacqui the audience she deserved, as she belted out her abridged version of the Lady Gaga song that had become her personal anthem. 'Mumuh taw me wha ah wa young—we all supa stahz!' Jacqui sang, in her own fashion. Then she kicked it up a notch. 'I on the wight twak baby, I wah bohn this way. I bohn this way! Baby, baby, I bohn this way!'

'She's certainly in a good mood.'

'Great swim lesson,' said our nanny Holly with a big smile. A British woman who had years of experience working with children with disabilities, Holly adored Jacqui, and the feeling was mutual. 'I'll start dinner.'

'Thanks. I'll be back in fifteen.'

I picked up the script, and my DAT recorder and microphone. But I no longer had to go to my bedroom closet. I no longer needed to pull a blanket over my head.

I walked across the gravel drive to wrench open the heavy door of Andrew's big shed, which gave a complaining screech. There, in the corner, next to the Mustang, and not far from the chook house, was a large rectangular box. It looked like an enormous refrigerator.

But it was far more precious. This was my own recording booth, personally constructed to my specifications by Andrew and his dad. Inside was foam-egg crating for soundproofing. A linoleum counter to hold a mike stand and microphone. A battered kitchen chair. A lightbulb overhead. No need to bring a torch.

It was beautiful.

I touched the box gently. I was a long way from my old life, but I still had a red carpet. As additional soundproofing, the exterior of the booth had been covered in the tattered crimson carpet from the floor of the church on the family farm. The very carpet Andrew and I had stood on when we said our vows. It had faded with age. And sheep had been known to wander into the church when the door was left open. But I figured that time and stories gave something character. I gave the carpet a pat, and a cloud of dust made me sneeze.

That's what you got for reminiscing. I sat down on the rickety chair, turned on the DAT recorder, and pulled the door closed behind me, as I addressed the mike.

'Hi, New York. This is Sara, in Oz. And this will be the Stolen Generation Art Story, coming to you in three, two, one.'

I had just filed the latest bulletin from the Wombat State Forest Bureau of NBC News.

And the sound engineers back in New York said the sound was pitch perfect.

ACKNOWLEDGEMENTS

A very special thanks to my dear friend and editor, the ever so talented Foong Ling Kong. It was Foong Ling who imagined this book into being. After reading an article by reporter Charles Happell in *Good Weekend* about our move to Australia entitled, 'I Live in a Place that Doesn't Exist', she wrote to ask if I might have 'a story or two' to tell. Turns out, I did. Foong Ling's literary flair, belief in the project, and our shared experiences as transplants made her the perfect editor. And a big thank you as well to Charlie, for writing such a lovely newspaper story that it inadvertently launched a book.

I would also like to thank my literary agent and good friend Mary Cunnane. A fellow New Yorker who now calls Australia home, Mary is yet another Yank who adores Oz. An editor herself, Mary's keen insights as a former denizen of The Big Apple, and her appreciation of the beauties and complexities of both countries, were invaluable.

I cannot say thank you enough to my Australian family, especially my mother- and father-in-law, Bev and Bert Butcher. You have treated me as a daughter, always. Your devotion to our little family has been extraordinary. I love you. And the same holds true for the entire glorious Butcher Family. I'm very glad to have made the team. Thanks for making our transition here go so very well.

I would especially like to thank my darling mom for driving me to those writing classes when I was twelve, and for always believing I would be a writer. You are my role model with our girls. And I would like to thank my dad for never letting me feel like I made a mistake I couldn't fix, and for always believing that everything will turn out well. Your optimism is matched by your sweetness. Most of all, thank you both for supporting a move that resulted in two of your beloved grandchildren living quite far away.

And thanks to my gorgeous and wonderful sisters, Elizabeth and Susan, and their families. I love and admire you both. Thanks to the entire James gang for racking up all those Qantas miles coming to visit us, not to mention the phone bills. What would I do without you! (For the record, Sophie and Jacqui, it's a really good idea to live really near Dad and me.)

Thank you to Sue Hines and her team at Allen & Unwin, for your support; Sue, your attention to detail with an individual book and author are just exceptional. I am blessed. And to Sarah Baker, thank you for shepherding this book through the in-house editing process.

And most of all, thanks to my adorable girls, Sophie and Jacqui, and to my dear husband. I love you, infinity. How lucky was I to meet you, Andrew, in New York. It has been a remarkable journey. Here's to many more adventures for our little family down the track . . . be it dirt, or paved.

ABOUT THE AUTHOR

Sara James is an Emmy award-winning foreign correspondent, author and commentator. Born and raised in the United States, she covers Australasia for the American *Today Show* and other broadcasts on *NBC News*.

Until she moved to Australia with her family in 2008, Sara was based in New York, where she covered some of the most significant international stories of our era, including 9/11, the Bosnian War Crimes Tribunal, and war and famine in Somalia. She was also the first network reporter to travel to the wreck of the *Titanic* for the *Dateline/Discovery Channel Special*, 'Raising the Titanic'. Sara frequently served as substitute anchor and news-reader on NBC's *Today Show*, anchored on MSNBC, and was the first host of *NBC Nightside*.

In Australia, James is a regular guest commentator for the ABC on *ABC News Breakfast*, *Planet America* and *Evenings with Lindy Burns* on 774 ABC Melbourne. She has also appeared on Channel 7's *Sunrise*, and Network Ten's *Meet the Press* and *The Project*.

Sara is the author of *An Extraordinary School*, about Port Phillip Specialist School in Melbourne, and *The Best of Friends*, co-authored with *National Geographic* wildlife film-maker Ginger Mauney.

She lives in the Macedon Ranges near Melbourne with her Australian husband, Andrew Butcher, their daughters, Sophie and Jacqueline, a Golden Retriever called Nanci Drew, and a henhouse full of chooks.